DAY of
RECKONING

Also by Patrick J. Buchanan

State of Emergency

Where the Right Went Wrong

The Death of the West

A Republic, Not an Empire

The Greatest Betrayal

Right from the Beginning

Conservative Voices, Liberal Victories

The New Majority

Churchill, Hitler, and "The Unnecessary War"

DAY of RECKONING

How Hubris, Ideology, and Greed
Are Tearing America Apart

✮ ✮ ✮ ✮ ✮

Patrick J. Buchanan

Thomas Dunne Books
St. Martin's Griffin
New York

THOMAS DUNNE BOOKS.
An imprint of St. Martin's Press.

www.thomasdunnebooks.com
www.stmartins.com

The Library of Congress has catalogued the hardcover edition as follows:

Buchanan, Patrick J. (Patrick Joseph), 1938–
   Day of reckoning : how hubris, ideology, and greed are tearing America apart / Patrick J. Buchanan.—1st ed.
      Includes bibliographical references.
      ISBN-13: 978-0-312-37696-3
      ISBN-10: 0-312-37696-0
      1. United States—Politics and government—2001– 2. United States—Foreign relations—2001– 3. Elite (social sciences)—United States—Political activity. 4. Pride and vanity—Political aspects—United States. 5. Ideology—Political aspects—United States. 6. Avarice—Political aspects—United States. 7. United States—Emigration and immigration—Government policy. 8. Pluralism (Social sciences)—United States. 9. Social conflict—United Sates. 10. United States—Social policy—1993– I. Title.
   E902.B633 2008
   973.93—dc22

                                                                    2007042724

ISBN-13: 978-0-312-53938-2 (pbk.)
ISBN-10: 0-312-53938-X (pbk.)

First St. Martin's Griffin Edition: January 2009

10 9 8 7 6 5 4 3 2 1

To Russell Kirk (1918–1994)
Friend and Teacher

A day of reckoning is approaching. It is my hope that the price in blood, treasure, and humiliation America will eventually be forced to pay for the hubris, arrogance, and folly of our reigning foreign policy elites is not, God forbid, war, defeat, and the diminution of the Republic—the fate of every other great nation or empire that set out on the same course.

—PATRICK J. BUCHANAN, *A Republic, Not an Empire,* 1999

Contents

Introduction: How Nations Perish   1

1. The End of Pax Americana   13

2. End of a Unipolar World   27

3. The Gospel of George Bush   55

4. Imperial Overstretch   109

5. Who Shall Inherit the Earth?   137

6. Deconstructing America   169

7. Colony of the World   191

8. Day of Reckoning   235

Acknowledgments   265

Notes   267

Index   283

Introduction

How Nations Perish

Things fall apart; the centre cannot hold;
Mere anarchy is loosed upon the world. . . .
—W. B. YEATS, "THE SECOND COMING"

Nations pay a severe price for lost wars. So the last century taught us.

The Russian, Austro-Hungarian, and German empires went down to defeat in the Great War. The Romanovs were overthrown and murdered and the czarist empire was torn apart at Brest-Litovsk. The Austro-Hungarian Empire was dismantled and Vienna reduced to the capital of a landlocked nation of 6.5 million. The Hapsburgs were sent packing. Germany lost her colonies and navy and an eighth of her territory. The kaiser fled to Holland. Germans and Hungarians in the millions were put under the rule of Belgians, French, Italians, Serbs, Czechs, Poles, Romanians, and Lithuanians.

The fall of France in 1940 led to the collapse of the Third Republic and the end of the French Empire in Indochina, the Maghreb and Middle East, and sub-Saharan Africa. Britain's exhaustion and bankruptcy after 1945 led to the rout of the Tories, the ouster of Winston Churchill, socialism, and the decline and fall of the empire on which the sun was never to set. Defeat in

Afghanistan brought the collapse of the Soviet Empire, over-throw of the Communist Party, and the death and decomposition of the Soviet Union.

These were epochal events. But soon after these empires passed into history, which progressives celebrated, the cheering stopped. For something unanticipated began to happen. The once-subject peoples, discontented with life in their liberated homelands, began the greatest mass migration in human history. Northward, they came, in the millions, to the First World countries that had held their ancestors in colonial captivity. And the nations of Europe, no longer imperial, no longer great, began to disintegrate.

Ireland had shown the way early in the century, breaking free of the United Kingdom in 1921, as these Catholic Celts considered themselves a persecuted minority of Protestant England. Every Irish child knew of the icy British indifference to the famine of '45 and the execution of the martyrs of the Easter Rising, when, in Yeats's words, all was "changed, changed utterly," and a "terrible beauty" was born. And with the lifting of the nuclear sword of Damocles that had hung over Europe in the Cold War, the disintegration accelerated. The fault lines upon which the states began to break apart were ethnicity, religion, language, and history.

In 1991, the Soviet Union shattered into fifteen nations. Most had never before existed, or existed only in centuries past. Ukrainians knew from their culture of the Ukraine of history. The Baltic republics had not forgotten czarist rule or the horrors of the 1940 annexations by Stalin. The Armenians, Azeris, and Georgians of the Caucasus are not Russian. The Turkomans, Tajiks, Uzbeks, Kirgyz, Kazakhs, all of whom now have their own nations, are Muslims and do not cherish memories of rule by Christian czars and Soviet commissars.

In the Velvet Divorce of January 1, 1993, Czechs and Slovaks went their separate ways. Yugoslavia disintegrated into six nations: Slovenia, Croatia, Bosnia, Serbia, Macedonia, Montenegro. A seventh, Kosovo, is about to be born. Ethnicity, religion, and history were the reefs on which Yugoslavia was battered and broke apart. Slovenes had belonged to the Hapsburg Empire, not the Ottoman. Muslims are dominant in Bosnia. Orthodox Serbs and Catholic Croats have horrible memories of mutual slaughter in World War II. Kosovo is to Serbs what Jerusalem is to Jews, but the province is now 90 percent Albanian and Muslim. The Orthodox churches and convents of Kosovo have been vandalized and destroyed.

Yugoslavia and Czechoslovakia, it is said, were artificial nations created by the treaties of Versailles and St. Germain in 1919. And the Soviet Union was but the Russian Empire reconstituted by the Red Army, the KGB, the Communist Party, and Leninist ideology, not a nation at all. The breakup of the USSR, Czechoslovakia, and Yugoslavia did not come, however, until after they embraced democracy. Communist rule kept them together. Indeed, it seems a truism. To hold together a multiethnic or multilingual state, either an authoritarian regime or a dominant ethnocultural core is essential.

The sudden disintegration of these three nations into twenty-six seemed to substantiate Strobe Talbott's prediction in his 1992 *Time* essay, "The Birth of the Global Nation."

All countries are basically social arrangements, accommodations to changing circumstances. No matter how permanent and even sacred they may seem at any one time, in fact they are all artificial and temporary. . . .

[W]ithin the next hundred years . . . nationhood as we

know it will be obsolete; all states will recognize a single, global authority. A phrase briefly fashionable in the mid-20th century—"citizen of the world"—will have assumed real meaning by the end of the 21st century.[1]

Is the time of nations over? Is the nation-state passing away? Are the bonds that hold them together so flimsy? Since Talbott's essay, events have not contradicted him.

In 2007, the Scottish National Party, which seeks to dissolve the Acts of Union of 1707 and break free of England, displaced Labour as first party in the Scottish Parliament. Scots whose grandfathers were proud to be the fighting sons of the British Empire are less desirous of being ruled by Little England. Welsh separatists made gains in the same election. Like the Irish, the other Celts wish to be free of the English, who are themselves setting aside the Union Jack of the United Kingdom for the red Cross of St. George.

Londonistan is not the London of Victoria or Edward VII. With the empire gone, people are less proud to be Britons. In America, one sees a trend of British journalists quietly applying for U.S. citizenship for themselves and their children.

Catalans and Basques seek independence from Spain. Corsicans and Bretons want out of France. Belgium, in the fall of 2007, was on the verge of breakup into a Dutch-speaking Flanders in the north and a Francophone Wallonia in the south. The Lega Nord hopes to secede from Italy. Turks and Greeks have divided Cyprus. Only immigrants who prefer rule by Ottawa prevent the Québécois from breaking free of Canada. Russia is bedeviled by new secessionist movements in Dagestan and Chechnya.

Beyond the West, disintegration has not ceased since the old empires fell. Pakistan broke from India in 1947 over religion, and East Pakistan (Bangladesh) seceded in 1971. A secessionist movement has arisen in the Baluchistan region of Pakistan and Iran. Azeris, Kurds, and Arabs, too, chafe at domination by Persians, who are but half of Iran's population. Iraq is breaking apart into a Kurdish north, a Sunni west, and a Shia south. Two-thirds of all Christians have fled. Eritrea has broken away from Ethiopia. Lebanon is disintegrating.

Wherever Islam rubs up against other civilizations, there is violence—from the Philippines to Indonesia, Thailand, Kashmir, Chechnya, Palestine, Sudan, Nigeria—and the *banlieues* of Paris. Be they Filipino Catholics, Thai Buddhists, Hindu Indians, Israeli Jews, Orthodox Russians, Nigerian Christians, African animists, or French secularists, sons of Islam are at war with them all. And as we see from the election battles in Peru, Bolivia, Venezuela, Ecuador, and Mexico, race and ethnicity are not receding as issues that divide peoples and nations; they are rising again.

In Milton's *Paradise Lost,* Pandaemonium is the capital of Hell, the "high capital of Satan" where the first council of demons was held after the expulsion from Heaven. Sen. Pat Moynihan took *Pandaemonium* as the title of his 1993 book on the ethnic conflict he saw coming. After Los Angeles exploded in racial violence and a Europe liberated from Communism was rudely shaken by a return of ethnic savagery to the Balkans, Moynihan feared a coming dystopia where nations would break apart in tribal hatreds inexplicable to the modern mind. He was not wrong.

What has this to do with us? Everything. For few nations are as multiracial, multiethnic, multilingual, and multicultural as the United States. And as Talbott wrote, "The big question these days is which political forces will prevail, those stitching nations together or those tearing them apart?"[2] This is the existential question facing America. Will what separates us—race, ethnicity, culture, morality, and faith—prove stronger than what unites us?

On a visit to Japan, after the Los Angeles riot in which whites were dragged from their vehicles in South Central and beaten and stomped, and the Korean community was subjected to a pogrom, Vice President Dan Quayle was politely asked if perhaps America did not suffer from an excess of "ethnic diversity."

"I begged to differ with my hosts," Quayle told the Commonwealth Club of California, "I explained that our diversity is our strength."[3]

But our national motto is "E pluribus unum"—"Out of many, one." It is in our unity that our strength resides.

In 2007, the Harvard political scientist Robert Putnam, author of the bestseller *Bowling Alone,* reported that his five-year study of 30,000 residents in forty-one American cities found that racial and ethnic diversity go hand in hand with Balkanization, a breakdown of community, and a general retreat into social isolation.

When the Irish came to America, they were separated from their new countrymen by their Catholic faith, nationality, brogue, and history of having been despised and persecuted by the English from the time of Cromwell's massacre at Drogheda forward. *The Gangs of New York* depicted the hatreds of nativist Protestants for the immigrant Irish. When the Italians, Jews, and peoples from Eastern Europe came, they, too, were separated from the national majority, and chose, as do today's immigrants, to dwell apart.

Like the fingers of a hand that closes to form the fist, it was when we came together in unity that we became strong, for America was greater than the sum of her parts.

What formed us into one nation and people?

For generations, we worked side by side. Our fathers fought together in the Civil War, Spanish-American War, and the world wars. We went through the Depression together. Though separated by race in the 1950s, there was, as I wrote in *State of Emergency*, a definable American nationality:

> In 1960, 18 million black Americans, 10 percent of the nation, were not fully integrated into society, but they had been assimilated into our culture. They worshipped the same God, spoke the same language, had endured the same depression and war, watched the same TV shows on the same four channels, laughed at the same comedians, went to the same movies, ate the same foods, read the same newspapers, and went to schools where, even when segregated, we learned the same history and literature and shared the same holidays: Christmas, New Year's, Washington's Birthday, Easter, Memorial Day, Fourth of July, Labor Day, Columbus Day. Segregation existed, but black folks were as American as apple pie, having lived in this land longer than almost every other group save the Native Americans.
>
> That cultural unity, that sense we were one people, is gone.[4]

Truly, America faces an existential crisis. Are the racial, political, social, and cultural forces pulling us apart overwhelming the forces holding us together?

It is the belief of the author and premise of this book that

America *is* indeed coming apart, decomposing, and that the likelihood of her survival as one nation through midcentury is improbable—and impossible if America continues on her current course. For we are on a path to national suicide.

"At what point then is the approach of danger to be expected?" said Lincoln in his rhetorical question to the Young Men's Lyceum in Springfield: "I answer, if it ever reach us, it must spring up amongst us. It cannot come from abroad. If destruction be our lot, we must ourselves be its author and finisher. As a nation of freemen, we must live through all time, or die by suicide."[5]

How is America committing suicide? Every way a nation can.

The American majority is not reproducing itself. Its birthrate has been below replacement level for decades. Forty-five million of its young have been destroyed in the womb since *Roe v. Wade*, as Asian, African, and Latin American children come to inherit the estate the lost generation of American children never got to see.

According to the U.S. Census Bureau, from 2005 to 2006, our minority population rose 2.4 million to exceed 100 million. Hispanics, 1 percent of the U.S. population in 1950, are now 14.4 percent. Since 2000, their numbers have soared 25 percent to 45 million. The U.S. Asian population grew by 24 percent since 2000, as the number of white kids of school age fell 4 percent. Half the children five and younger today are minority children.[6]

In the 1990s, for the first time since the Spanish came to California, whites fled the Golden Land. Two million left. From July 1, 2005, to July 1, 2006, 100,000 more packed and headed back over the mountains, whence their fathers came. The Anglo population of California is down to 43 percent and falling fast.

White folks are now a minority in Texas and New Mexico. In Arizona, Hispanics account for more than half the population under twenty. The American Southwest is returning to Mexico.

Unlike the Ellis Island generations, all of whom came from Europe, those pouring in today come from countries, continents, and cultures whose peoples have never before been assimilated by a First World nation. And they are coming in far greater numbers than any nation has ever absorbed. History has never seen an invasion like this. For there are more illegal aliens in the United States today than all the Irish, Jews, and English who ever came, and the total number of immigrants here now almost equals the total number who came in the 350 years from the birth of Jamestown to the inauguration of JFK.

Yet the great melting pot of yesterday that turned us into one people is cracked and broken—reviled by our elites as an instrument of cultural genocide. Immigrants are encouraged to keep their culture, customs, traditions—and not let their children be immersed in the English language. In Chicago's schools, children are taught in two hundred languages. Five million of the 9 million people in Los Angeles County speak a language other than English in their homes.

This writer stood on the steps of Lincoln Memorial, a few feet away from Dr. King in 1963, when he declared, "I have a dream that my four little children will one day live in a nation where they will not be judged by the color of their skin but by the content of their character."

But segregation did not give way to the color-blind society. Rather, its demise ushered in identity politics and a bewildering array of ethnic and racial entitlements. Talk radio and cable TV now nationalize racial conflicts, as students resegregate themselves in dorms and at graduation ceremonies, while armies of bureaucrats try to impose diversity in the workplace. America's obsession—for an unattainable equality of all races and ethnic groups—has led to a loss of liberty, which is what America was all about.

In 1915, Theodore Roosevelt warned in a speech to the Knights of Columbus, "The one absolutely certain way of bringing this nation to ruin, of preventing all possibility of its continuing to be a nation at all, would be to permit it to become a tangle of squabbling nationalities. . . ."[7]

But that is the destination for which America is on course. Before us lies the prospect of two, three, many nations, separate and unequal.

Almost as many African-American males are in jail or prison as are in colleges or universities. Half of all African-American and Hispanic students drop out of high school. The other half graduates with the math and reading skills of seventh-, eighth-, and ninth-graders. Yet by 2050 the number of African Americans and Hispanics will have almost doubled from today's 85 million, to 160 million. The future seems more ominous than it did in the hopeful days of civil rights. For these burgeoning scores of millions will not long accept second-class accommodations in the affluent society, where they are the emerging majority. The long hot summers of yesterday may be returning.

As critical, the greatest cohort of immigrants here today, legal and illegal, is from Mexico. One in five Mexicans is already here. But unlike the immigrants of old, Mexicans bear an ancient grudge against us as the country that robbed Mexico of half her land when both nations were young. By one survey, 72 percent of Mexicans look on Americans as "racists."[8] By another, 58 percent of Mexicans believe the American Southwest belongs to them.[9]

At the Guadalajara soccer game where Mexico played the United States for the right to compete in the 2004 Olympics, each Mexican score was greeted with chants of "Osama! Osama!"[10] During the Miss World contest in Mexico City in 2007, Miss USA's every appearance was hooted and jeered.

By 2050, more than 100 million Hispanics will be in the United States, concentrated in a Southwest that borders on Mexico. As the Serbs are losing Kosovo, so we may have lost the Southwest.

Why did America not secure her borders, enforce her laws, repel the invasion, expel the intruders? Because our leaders are terrified of charges of racism and lack moral courage, and because the United States has ceased to be a democratic republic. The will of the majority is no longer reflected in public policy. State and local referenda to deal with the illegal alien crisis are routinely invalidated by federal judges, as immigration laws go unenforced by federal officials.

Perhaps the greatest threat to the survival of this nation as a sovereign and independent republic comes from transnational elites who seek to erase our borders and merge America, Mexico, and Canada into a North American Union—the penultimate step toward a World Federation of Nations and Peoples. There, as Talbott rhapsodized, "nationhood as we know it will be obsolete; all states will recognize a single, global authority, and the phrase 'citizen of the world' will have assumed real meaning." This is the nonviolent path to national suicide America is now on.

But for the New World Order to be born, the old republic must die. Loyalty to transnationalism is thus treason to the republic.

There is another force for disunion—the social revolution

America has passed through since the 1960s. This revolution created a chasm between Americans on those matters—history, heroes, holidays, religion, morality, customs, culture—that once united us. We are no longer one people. And we no longer have a great danger or great cause to unite us, as in the world war or the Cold War. "Without the cold war," asks Harry "Rabbit" Angstrom, in the fourth and final book of John Updike's series of "Rabbit" novels, "what's the point of being an American?"

President George W. Bush declared the "world democratic revolution" to be our great cause, and "ending tyranny in our world" to be America's national goal. But the people yawned and Bush lost the country long ago. Moreover, America may be headed for a disaster in the Middle East that will eclipse Vietnam in its awful consequences.

The defeats in war suffered by the European nations led to the collapse of their empires, falling birthrates, a plunge into self-indulgence, indifference to immigrant invasions, and their unraveling in a return to tribal roots. Are we about to follow Europe on the path to national suicide?

Is our day of reckoning just ahead?

1

The End of Pax Americana

Never glad confident morning again!

—ROBERT BROWNING, "THE LOST LEADER"

The American Century is over.

Pax Americana has come to a close. Gone now is all the hubristic chatter of an American Empire. Gone is the "unipolar world" where the United States was the undisputed hegemonic power.

"The US has had its unipolar moment for about fifteen years but is beginning to realize that it isn't getting the things done it wants," says Paul Kennedy, author of *The Rise and Fall of the Great Powers*. The essay that carried his verdict was titled "Imperial Sunset."[1] Kennedy now believes that America's task is "managing relative decline."[2]

Yet after the startlingly swift U.S. triumph in the Afghan war, the rout of the Taliban and fall of Kabul, Kennedy himself had succumbed to hubris, declaring of George W. Bush's America:

Nothing has ever existed like this disparity of power, nothing. . . . No other nation comes close. . . . Charlemagne's empire was merely western European in its reach.

The Roman empire stretched farther afield, but there was another great empire in Persia, and a larger one in China. There is, therefore, no comparison.[3]

Now we can see clearly that the American tide has begun to recede. We have entered a new world—a world of a multiplicity of powers like the world of a century ago, when the British Empire, following the Boer War, found itself divided at home and challenged abroad by rising powers in Asia, Europe, and North America.

The signs of decline abound. From the Davos Conference of 2007, *Newsweek* foreign editor Fareed Zakaria reported: "[F]or the first time I can remember, America was somewhat peripheral. . . . In this small but significant global cocoon, people seemed to be moving beyond America."[4]

Wrote Zakaria: "[W]e might also be getting a glimpse of what a world without America would look like. It would be free of American domination but perhaps also free of American leadership—a world in which problems fester and the buck is passed endlessly until situations explode."[5]

Zakaria titled his report "After America's Eclipse."

From a Doha conference on U.S.–Middle East relations, columnist David Ignatius reported a similar phenomenon:

We are in the ditch in the Middle East. As bad as you think it is watching TV, it's worse. It's not just Iraq, but the whole pattern of American dealings with the Arab world. People are not just angry at Americans . . . they're giving up on us—on our ability to make good decisions, to solve problems, to play the role of honest broker.[6]

"Giving up on us" puts it precisely. After King Abdullah of Saudi Arabia brought Hamas and Fatah together in a unity government and revived the Saudi plan for Palestinian peace and Arab recognition of Israel, Secretary of State Condoleezza Rice refused to speak to any member of Hamas. At the Arab summit in March 2007, Abdullah denounced the United States: "In beloved Iraq, blood is flowing between brothers, in the shadow of an illegitimate foreign occupation."[7]

Not since Franklin D. Roosevelt met King Abdul Aziz ibn Saud aboard the cruiser *Quincy* in the Suez Canal in 1945, where the U.S.-Saudi friendship was cemented, had a Saudi king so insulted the United States.

Ignatius cited a Zogby poll of six friendly Arab countries— Egypt, Jordan, Lebanon, Morocco, Saudi Arabia, and the United Arab Emirates. Only 12 percent of the people in the six nations had a favorable view of the United States; 38 percent named President George W. Bush as the foreign leader they most despised. Ranked behind Bush were Ariel Sharon at 11 percent and Ehud Olmert, who had launched the summer war on Lebanon, at 7 percent.[8]

"The American era in the region has ended," writes Richard Haas, president of the Council on Foreign Relations, who served on President Bush's National Security Council:

> The American era was one in which, after the Soviet Union's demise, the US enjoyed unprecedented influence and freedom to act. What brought it to an end after less than two decades? Topping the list is the Bush administration's decision to attack Iraq and its conduct of the operation and resulting occupation.[9]

Zakaria, Ignatius, and Haas were echoed by *Washington Post* columnist Robert Samuelson.

With hindsight we may see 2006 as the end of Pax Americana. Ever since World War II, the United States has used its military and economic superiority to promote a stable world order that has, on the whole, kept the peace and spread prosperity. But the United States increasingly lacks both the power and the will to play this role.[10]

But if Pax Americana is at an end, what will replace it?

Several years ago, British historian Niall Ferguson described a dystopian vision in "A World Without Power."

Anyone who dislikes U.S. hegemony should bear in mind that, rather than a multipolar world of competing great powers, a world with no hegemon at all may be the real alternative to U.S. primacy. Apolarity could turn out to mean an anarchic new Dark Age: an age of waning empire and religious fanaticism; of endemic plunder and pillage of the world's forgotten regions; of economic stagnation and civilization's retreat into a few fortified enclaves.[11]

"Be careful what you wish for," Ferguson warned.[12]

For America and President Bush, 2006 was, in Victor Hugo's phrase about 1870–71, that year of defeat in the Franco-Prussian war, "L'Année Terrible." For in 2006 it became clear the United States was failing in Iraq.

In December, former secretary of state Colin Powell described the situation as "grave and deteriorating." America is "losing" the war, he said.[13] Powell echoed the Iraq Study Group of former secretary of state James Baker, which concluded, "A slide toward chaos could trigger the collapse of Iraq's government and a humanitarian catastrophe. . . . The global standing of the United States could be diminished."[14]

Chief of Staff Gen. Peter Schoomaker informed Congress that the U.S. Army of 500,000 was stretched to the breaking point by the insurgencies in Afghanistan and Iraq.[15] Yet those two wars had not cost as many casualties as the Philippine insurrection of 1899–1902, which is not regarded as a major U.S. war.

Early in the New Year, Tony Blair, his premiership a casualty of Iraq, announced a withdrawal of 1,600 of the 7,100 British troops. The South Koreans, Danes, and Lithuanians were to follow the Brits out. The Spanish, Italians, Ukrainians, and Japanese had already gone.[16]

Two thousand and six was the year North Korea's Kim Jong-Il defied the Bush Doctrine—the world's worst regimes would not be allowed to acquire the world's worst weapons—by exploding a North Korean nuclear device in America's face. It was the year Mahmoud Ahmadinejad of Iran defied a Bush ultimatum and continued to enrich uranium for nuclear power—or nuclear weapons. It was the year Tehran's Shia allies took power in Baghdad, while its Hezbollah allies stood off the Israeli army in a five-week war in Lebanon.

As Iraq ends its fifth year of fighting, Tehran appears the true victor of the U.S. wars to oust the Taliban and overthrow Saddam that had cost 4,000 American dead and 27,000 wounded, over half a trillion dollars, and the unity of the nation.

In 2006, the elections Bush had demanded of the Middle East were held and produced victories for the Muslim Brotherhood in Egypt, Hamas in Palestine, Hezbollah in Lebanon, Moqtada al-Sadr in Iraq. Bush's vision of a peaceful and democratic Middle East had vanished as completely as Wilson's vision of a peaceful and democratic Europe by 1938. Indeed, the Israelis seemed to see 2006 as a year like that of Munich, as former prime minister Benjamin Netanyahu told CNN, "Iran is Germany and it's 1938. Except that this Nazi regime that is in Iran . . . wants to dominate the world, annihilate the Jews, but also annihilate America."[17]

In 2006, Pakistan pulled its troops out of the tribal areas on the Afghan border and created a sanctuary from which the Taliban could attack U.S. and NATO forces. France and Italy contemplated pulling out. Germany refused to send its units south to the fighting. Early in 2007, *The New York Times* reported that

American intelligence and counterterrorism officials believe that Al Qaeda has rebuilt its notorious training camps, this time in Pakistan's loosely governed tribal regions near the Afghan border. Camp graduates are fighting in Afghanistan and Iraq—and may well be plotting new terrorist strikes in the West.[18]

By midyear, said the CIA, Al Qaeda had reconstituted itself.

Two thousand and six was the year Hugo Chavez, ideological heir to Fidel Castro who had mocked Bush as El Diablo from the rostrum of the United Nations, coasted to a reelection victory and saw radical allies Evo Morales in Bolivia, Daniel Ortega in Nicaragua, and Rafael Correa in Ecuador carried to power on a populist wave. Radical leftist Andrés Manuel López Obrador came within a point of winning the presidency of Mexico. In Brazil, said Roberto Abdenur, the former ambassador to the United States, the ascendant ideology is "anti-capitalistic, anti-globalization, anti-American."[19]

The year 2006 saw U.S.-Russian relations deteriorate and Chinese-Russian relations deepen. At the Munich security conference in February 2007, President Vladimir Putin denounced America's alleged attempt to create a "unipolar" world of "one centre of authority, one centre of force, one centre of decision-making."[20] By August, Russian and Chinese forces were holding joint maneuvers, and Russian bombers were making practice runs toward U.S. territory.

In Ukraine, the Orange Revolution that had brought pro-American Victor Yushchenko to power collapsed. And Georgia, home of the Rose Revolution, whose President Mikheil Saakashvili had sought to join the European Union and NATO, was under an economic blockade by Moscow, with only the feeblest of protests from NATO capitals.[21]

From Latin America to Russia, from Old Europe to the Middle East, we had entered an era marked by anti-Americanism of a depth and breadth Americans had never known. In the Middle East, Osama bin Laden was more highly regarded than President Bush. In Europe, China was seen as less a threat to peace than the United States. U.S. hard power was being defied and U.S. soft power—its political, diplomatic, and cultural influence—dissipated all over the world.

The military forces Ronald Reagan had left to George H. W. Bush had shrunk. Instead of the 15 carriers in a fleet of 574 ships in 1990, America had 12 carriers in a fleet of 284 ships. The army of 18 divisions was down to 10. The 24 fighter wings of the air force had been cut to 13.[22]

As America stumbled toward the worst defeat in her history, nations great and small rejoiced in the impending humiliation.

Sen. John Kerry's wail at Davos that America had become an "international pariah" was excessive.[23] Yet never before had the country seemed so isolated. Like the Brits of the Boer War era, America, in the fifth year of the Iraq war and sixth year of the Afghan war, seemed almost friendless.

In 2006, too, the ideology undergirding the global economy was exposed as another god that failed, as Middle America arose in rage at news that a Dubai company would be taking over operation of half a dozen U.S. ports. America's elite was stunned.

"This Dubai port deal has unleashed a kind of collective mania we haven't seen in decades . . . a xenophobia tsunami . . . a nativist, isolationist mass hysteria. . . . God must love Hamas and Moqtada al-Sadr. He has given them the America First brigades of Capitol Hill," wailed David Brooks of *The New York Times*.[24]

Times colleague Thomas Friedman awoke to the realization the world just might not be flat after all. This is "borderline racist," Friedman ranted of America's reaction to news Arab sheiks might be running her ports in a war on terror.[25] "There's a poison loose. . . . If we go Dark Ages, if we go down the road of pitchfork-wielding xenophobes, then the whole world will go Dark Ages."[26]

In 2006, the Doha Round of trade negotiations foundered over a First World refusal to slash subsidies to their diminishing numbers of farmers to appease Third World regimes. In November, economic nationalists of the Democratic Party rolled to victory. In December, Treasury Secretary Hank Paulson led a delegation including the chairman of the Federal Reserve and half a dozen cabinet officers to Beijing to persuade the People's Republic to reduce the $233 billion trade deficit America had run with China in 2006.[27] Paulson & Co. were sent home with a bag of stale fortune cookies.

In 2006, Ford Motor Company posted the largest loss of any company in history, $12.7 billion, breaking the General Motors record of $10.6 billion set in 2005. After four decades of free trade, America had ceased to be the self-sufficient republic she had been at the dawn of the twentieth century. U.S. industry was being hollowed out. One in six U.S. manufacturing jobs, 3 million in all, had been lost in the Bush years. The job falloff was heaviest in computers and electronics. The proportion of U.S. jobs in manufacturing was down to 10 percent, a figure unseen since before the Civil War, as the U.S. trade deficit in goods reached $836 billion and the current account deficit $857 billion—all-time records for the fifth consecutive year.[28] No world power has long survived the levels of debt and dependency America is incurring. As in colonial times, Americans rely again on foreigners for the necessities of our national life and the borrowed money to pay for them.

In 2006, China's trade surplus with the United States became the largest ever between two nations. Where U.S. gross domestic product had grown by 3.3 percent, China's had grown 10 percent, accelerating to near 12 percent by mid-2007, when China's hard currency reserves exceeded $1.3 trillion and Americans were borrowing $2 billion a day to cover imports. The dollar was in free fall, sinking toward its lowest level against the British pound since the Carter era and lowest level ever against the euro. For the first time since before World War I, U.S. stock market capitalization had fallen behind Europe's.[29] And retired Fed chairman Alan Greenspan was talking of the euro replacing the dollar as the world's reserve currency.

The 2006 rout of the Republicans brought the curtain down

on a political era. Nixon and Reagan had won forty-nine states in reelection landslides. Bush won thirty-one states in 2004 and, in 2006, lost both houses of Congress. The Reagan Revolution was over, the Reagan Democrats had gone home, the New Majority had gone the way of FDR's New Deal coalition. America was a nation with no governing party and no prevailing political philosophy. Independents could make as strong a claim to being "America's Party" as Republicans or Democrats.

By mid-2007, America was no longer the united, confident nation she had been from September 11 to "Mission Accomplished," but a sour and polarized country. The president's approval rating had plunged from 80 percent to 30 percent, and his reputation for competence had been ruined beyond repair by Katrina and Iraq. The country had stopped listening to him.

According to a Yankelovich poll sponsored by the Council on Foreign Relations, eight of ten Americans thought Bush's unilateralism had caused the world to see America as arrogant and 90 percent saw this as a threat to the national security. Writing in *National Journal,* Paul Starobin reported that a poll of eighteen- to twenty-four-year-olds found that 72 percent did not think the United States should take the lead in solving the world's problems.[30]

A BBC survey of twenty-seven nations found only Israel and Iran viewed less favorably than America.[31]

The sudden and shocking end to Pax Americana is an epochal event. Since 1945, it has been the United States that helped to rebuild Europe, held back the tide of Asian Communism, insured the security of the Free World, and led mankind into the most prosperous era it had ever known.

At the end of the Cold War, it was America that chaperoned the liberated nations of Eastern Europe and the former Soviet

Union and China into the world community and global economy, established the rules of trade, threw open her markets, and enabled developed and developing nations alike to prosper as never before. From the Balkans to the Gulf, when crises erupted, it was America that answered the call.

That era is over. We built this world, but the world has turned its back on the master builder. Militarily, America remains the strongest nation on earth. No other nation is close. But she is no longer able to translate strength into power, which, as Machiavelli said, is the ability to get others to do what you want and to prevent them from doing what you don't want them to do.

At home, confidence in the president and Congress alike had, by mid-2007, plummeted to near-record lows, with Bush's support at 29 percent and not one in five Americans approving of Congress.[32]

By August 2007, U.S. Comptroller General David Walker described the U.S. government as on a "burning platform" and laid out "chilling long-term simulations" for the nation's future.[33] Risks included the possible need for "dramatic" tax hikes, slashed government services, and a sudden foreign dumping of U.S. debt. Comparing his country to Rome, Walker bewailed the "declining moral values and political civility at home, an over-confident and over-extended military in foreign lands, and fiscal irresponsibility by the central government."[34] Said Walker, "Simply stated, America is on a path toward an explosion of debt."[35]

What Happened?

At the end of the Reagan decade, America found herself the last superpower. The United States had no peer rival or great antagonist anywhere. The phrase "Not since Rome" began to appear in usage among our elites. Almost all were in agreement: The twenty-first century would be the Second American Century.

What happened? How did the baby boomers squander the patrimony of the Greatest Generation? What happened in the fifteen years between that June day in 1991 when President George H. W. Bush stood in a reviewing stand on Constitution Avenue to take the salute of the victorious army of Desert Storm as it paraded past—and that November of 2006 when President George W. Bush was forced to fire his war minister Donald Rumsfeld, the morning after his country had repudiated him and his war policy by removing his party from power in both houses of Congress?

As President Bush moves toward the end of his term of office, his country is alienated from much of the world and headed toward the worst debacle in its history. How did he preside over so sudden an end to the promise of a Second American Century?

What America lost between 1992 and 2008 calls to mind what Britain lost between her victory over France in 1763 and her defeat at Yorktown in 1781. At the end of the Seven Years' War, Britain ruled North America from the Atlantic to the Mississippi and from Spanish Florida to the pole. Fifteen years later, 3 million colonial subjects had cut their ties to the mother country, formed an alliance with the former enemy, France, and effected the expulsion of British power from the thirteen seaboard colonies that were the crown jewels of the empire.

What happened to America between 1992 and 2008 is a tragedy of historic proportions. And, like the tragedies of literature, it came of a character flaw, a failure of vision that cost the country its legacy from the Greatest Generation: the leadership of the world.

How did America lose the world? Through an ignorance of history, an embrace of ideology, and an arrogance of power—hubris. And George W. Bush came to personify all three. Great empires and small minds go ill together, said Burke. Small minds, wedded to great egos, may have cost us the Second American Century.

"Great Britain has lost an Empire and has not yet found a role," said Dean Acheson in 1962.[36] Wounding, but true. Half a century later, so may it be said of America. What does the future hold? Who inherits the earth if Pax Americana is at an end?

2

End of a Unipolar World

Emphatically our only alternative to isolationism is not to undertake to
police the whole world nor to impose democratic institutions on all mankind
including the Dalai Lama and the good shepherds of Tibet.

—HENRY LUCE, 1941, "THE AMERICAN CENTURY"[1]

When people speak to you about a preventive war, you tell them to go
and fight it. After my experience, I have come to hate war.

—PRESIDENT DWIGHT D. EISENHOWER[2]

Only months after Ronald Reagan returned to California the Soviet Empire began to fall apart. Solidarity came to power in free
elections in Poland. Czechs, Slovaks, and Hungarians overthrew
decrepit Communist regimes. On November 9–10, 1989, the
Berlin Wall was torn down by German patriots as the Pankow
regime sat paralyzed. Russia's tanks did not roll.

It was V-E Day over Stalin's empire, a bloodless victory in
a Cold War some believed would not end in our lifetimes.
We were on top of the world. Francis Fukuyama declared the
end of history. Democratic capitalism had won the struggle
for the world—and the world must soon come to embrace its
destiny.

In August 1990, however, Saddam Hussein, led to believe the

United States would not interfere, invaded Kuwait and declared the oil-rich emirate Iraq's lost nineteenth province.

"This will not stand!" thundered George H. W. Bush.

The New World Order

The forty-first president had found his mission. With skillful diplomacy, Bush and Secretary of State James Baker cobbled together a worldwide coalition. With financial support from Germany, Japan, and the Gulf Arabs, the unanimous backing of the U.N. Security Council, the acquiescence of Russia and China, approval of Congress, and British, French, Egyptian, Syrian, and Saudi troops deployed alongside Americans, Bush launched Desert Storm. After five weeks of air strikes, Gen. Norman Schwartzkopf needed but one hundred hours of ground warfare to drive the Iraqi army out of Kuwait and back up the Highway of Death to Basra and Baghdad.

Bush's approval hit 90 percent. In June 1991, the victorious army of Desert Storm paraded up Constitution Avenue before a presidential reviewing stand. In October, Bush went before the United Nations to declare America's global mission—the establishment of a New World Order.

In the last days of December 1991 the Soviet Union disintegrated. Our Cold War adversary had collapsed and was dead of a massive stroke. The great cause Americans had sacrificed for, prayed for, fought for, had triumphed. The Red Army was going home; the Soviet Empire was no more; Lithuania, Latvia, Estonia were free; the USSR was breaking up into fifteen nations. Ukraine was free. Never had so vast an empire vanished so swiftly. The Russia over which President Boris Yeltsin presided extended no farther west, save for the tiny enclave of Kaliningrad, than at the time of Peter the Great.

All America ever sought had come to pass. But rather than seize the opportunity to shed our Cold War commitments, pull up the trip wires for war planted around the world by Dean Acheson and John Foster Dulles, recapture our freedom of action, and restore a traditional foreign policy, Republicans began colluding with Democrats to tie us down in a New World Order in which U.S. wealth and power would be conscripted for causes having nothing to do with the vital interests of the United States. America, after a half century on stormy and violent seas, had reached safe harbor—only to have her captain lift anchor and set sail for destinations unknown, without consulting the crew.

But America was the last superpower, and she had proclaimed her new mission: Punish aggressors, preserve the peace, police the planet, in service to mankind. Pax Americana had been declared. But the American people, who would have to contribute the blood and treasure to sustain the New World Order, had yet to be consulted on their new imperial role. Nor had the world.

Nevertheless, from the day George H. W. Bush took office to the day his son took the oath, the United States would invade Panama; smash Iraq; drive its army out of Kuwait; intervene in Somalia; occupy Haiti; move NATO to the border of Russia; establish a protectorate over Bosnia; bomb Serbia for seventy-eight days; occupy Kosovo; adopt "dual containment" of Iraq and Iran; challenge China in the Taiwan Strait; and deploy thousands of U.S. troops on Saudi soil sacred to all Muslims. No one resisted. No one could.

All these military adventures had one thing in common.

None was in response to an imminent threat to U.S. vital interests. The United States had become the policeman of the world.

The Wolfowitz Memorandum

Having won the Cold War and smashed in six weeks an Iraqi military that had fought eight years against an Iran three times its size, America was at the apogee of her power and prestige. The United States had no rival. President Bush had no peer. America was dominant in Europe, the Middle East, the Near East, the Far East.

Then appeared the first and unmistakable signs of imperial hubris.

A secret Pentagon memorandum was leaked to *The New York Times*. Prepared under the direction of Under Secretary of Defense Paul Wolfowitz and his deputy, I. Lewis "Scooter" Libby, the forty-six-page memo was described by *The Washington Post* as a "classified blueprint intended to help 'set the nation's direction for the next century.' "[3]

The Wolfowitz memorandum, wrote the *Post*'s Barton Gellman, "casts Russia as the gravest potential threat to U.S. vital interests and presumes the United States would spearhead a NATO counterattack if Russia launched an invasion of Lithuania." Annexed by Stalin in 1940, as agreed to in a secret protocol of his pact with Hitler, Lithuania had been free for only a year. Yet Lithuanian independence had now become, in the Wolfowitz memo, a "U.S. vital interest."[4]

But how could the United States save Lithuania, should Russia move back in, when Eisenhower, with armed forces larger than those George H. W. Bush commanded, had been impotent to save Hungary? Wolfowitz's plan, wrote Gellman, contemplates a major war by land, sea and air in which 24 NATO divisions, 70 fighter squadrons and six aircraft carrier battle groups would keep the Russian Navy "bottled up in the eastern Baltic," bomb supply lines in Russia and use armored formations to expel Russian forces from Lithuania. The authors state that Russia is unlikely to respond with nuclear weapons, but they provide no basis for that assessment.[5]

The memo appeared to be the work of a madman. For America to commit to a war on a Russia that still possessed thousands of nuclear weapons, over Lithuania, seemed convincing proof of a suicidal insanity. What made the scenario astonishing was that a year earlier President Bush barely protested when Mikhail Gorbachev ordered Spesnatz units into its capital, Vilnius. Three weeks before the leak, Bush and President Yeltsin had issued a joint declaration that "Russia and the United States do not regard each other as potential adversaries."[6]

The Wolfowitz memo also called for U.S war guarantees to Eastern Europe and permanent U.S. involvement on every continent. America's dominance was to remain so overwhelming as to deter "potential competitors from even aspiring to a larger regional or global role."[7] America was to become Rome. Preventing the emergence of any rival superpower was a

dominant consideration underlying the new regional defense strategy and requires that we endeavor to prevent any hostile power from dominating a region whose resources would, under consolidated control, be sufficient to generate global power. These regions include Western

Europe, East Asia, the territory of the former Soviet Union, and Southwest Asia.[8]

The Pentagon strategists had decided the United States should never again allow another nation—Russia, Germany, Japan, China, India—to rise to the status of a dominant regional power. To maintain world hegemony, the Pentagon anticipated military intervention for ends far beyond protecting vital U.S. interests. The memo declared:

> While the U.S. cannot become the world's "policeman," by assuming responsibility for righting every wrong, we will retain the preeminent responsibility for addressing selectively those wrongs which threaten not only our interests, but those of our allies or friends, or which could seriously unsettle international relations.[9]

Containment had given way to a breathtakingly ambitious offensive strategy—to "establish and protect a new order."[10]

Reaction was sharp. Former secretary of defense Harold Brown warned that extending war guarantees to Eastern Europe would provoke Russian nationalism, risking the "same grave danger of nuclear war" that prevented intervention there for forty-five years.[11] Sen. Joe Biden mocked the memo as a formula for "a Pax Americana."[12] Edward Kennedy said the Pentagon plans "appear to be aimed primarily at finding new ways to justify Cold War levels of military spending."[13]

The Wolfowitz plan appeared to have been hooted down. But by 1998 the Clinton administration, with Biden and Kennedy's backing, had brought Poland, Hungary, and the Czech Republic into NATO, and was offering membership to the Baltic states.

Having opposed the Gulf War, the permanent stationing of U.S. troops on Saudi soil, and the extension of NATO war guarantees to Eastern Europe, this writer warned in *A Republic, Not an Empire*, published in 1999, of the certainty of blowback from America's imperial overreach.

> The United States has unthinkingly embarked upon a neo-imperial policy that must involve us in virtually every great war of the coming century—and wars are the death of republics. . . . [I]f we continue on this course of reflexive interventions, enemies will one day answer our power with the weapon of the weak—terror, and eventually cataclysmic terrorism on U.S. soil . . . then liberty, the cause of the republic, will itself be in peril.[14]

As a presidential candidate, I repeated the warning:

> How can all our meddling not fail to spark some horrible retribution? . . . Have we not suffered enough—from Pan Am 103 to the World Trade Center [bombing of 1993] to the embassy bombings in Nairobi and Dar es Salaam—not to know that interventionism is the incubator of terrorism? Or will it take some cataclysmic atrocity on U.S. soil to awaken our global gamesmen to the going price of empire? America today faces a choice of destinies. We can choose to be a peacemaker of the world, or its policeman who goes about night-sticking troublemakers until we, too, find ourselves in some bloody brawl we cannot handle.[15]

America is today embroiled in that "bloody brawl we cannot handle." And, on September 11, 2001, the "cataclysmic atrocity on U.S. soil" was carried out? Almost three thousand dead in one day. The "cataclysmic terrorism" of 9/11 was an unpardonable atrocity. But it was not unpredictable. For terrorism *is* the price of empire. They were over here because we were over there.

We Are All Americans

After 9/11, America demanded retribution and President Bush delivered. Nine days after the World Trade Center towers fell, Bush went before Congress and, in the most powerful address of his presidency, laid down the principles and policy America would pursue:

> Our war on terror begins with Al Qaeda, but it does not end there. It will not end until every terrorist group of global reach has been found, stopped and defeated. . . . Every nation, in every region, now has a decision to make. Either you are with us, or you are with the terrorists. *From this day forward, any nation that continues to harbor or support terrorism will be regarded by the United States as a hostile regime.* [emphasis added][16]

These words were pointed and precise. What Bush seemed to be offering was a chance for nations that had used terror tactics in the past—Libya, Syria, Iran, Iraq, North Korea—to come in from the cold by supporting the United States in running down and killing Al Qaeda and "every terrorist group of global reach."

America was enraged, America was resolute on retribution, Bush was saying, but even old enemies were welcome to join us—as Hafez al-Assad's Syria had joined Bush's father in the Gulf War. Secretary Rumsfeld, too, seemed to be saying this was the time for rogue states to get out of the penalty box by joining us in a war on Al Qaeda. "What we are looking at today is how are these states going to behave going forward."[17] President Bush and Rumsfeld were talking about the future, not the past.

Iran responded. Though it is forgotten now, Tehran supported the United States in the Afghan war. The Iranians had themselves almost gone to war against the Taliban and had sustained the Northern Alliance Bush would use as his ground forces to take Kabul. When the World Trade Center towers fell, France, too, rallied to us. "We Are All Americans," ran the banner in *Le Monde*. So long as we were fighting the terrorists of 9/11, the world was with us and the president had a united nation behind him.

As effectively as his father, George W. Bush pulled together a coalition to oust the Taliban enablers of Osama bin Laden. He won President Vladimir Putin's approval to base U.S. forces in former Soviet republics. He won Pakistani President Pervez Musharraf's complete cooperation. He won the passive support of Iran and China and the active support of NATO, which invoked Article 5, whereby an attack on one NATO ally was to be considered an attack on all. And after U.S. special forces enlisted the Northern Alliance, Bush ordered the Taliban overthrown and Al Qaeda destroyed. In three months, the war was over.

Hubris Comes to the West Wing

But September 11 had changed George W. Bush.

At the Reagan Library in November 1999, candidate Bush had rejected the triumphalism of the Clinton administration, with all its braying about America being the world's "indispensable nation."

"[L]et us have an American foreign policy that reflects American character," Bush had said. "The modesty of true strength. The humility of real greatness. This is the strong heart of America. And this will be the spirit of my administration."[18]

In a debate with Vice President Al Gore, Governor Bush added,

[O]ne way for us to end up being viewed as the ugly American is for us to go around the world saying, we do it this way, so should you. . . . The United States must be humble . . . humble in how we treat nations that are figuring out how to chart their own course.[19]

This was the candidate the nation elected. But as his father found his mission when Iraq invaded Kuwait, George W. Bush seemed to have found his destiny standing on the rubble of the Twin Towers in lower Manhattan. That destiny: To lead America in a worldwide war on terror to continue through his presidency and for the rest of our lives—the Long War.

Even as Americans were uniting behind his resolve to find and finish Al Qaeda, its enablers, and accomplices, Bush began to see retribution for 9/11 as only the first battle of a climactic struggle between good and evil for the future of mankind, a struggle in which neutrality meant hostility. In November 2001, at Fort Campbell, home of the 101st Airborne, Bush began to expand his definition of America's enemies.

America has a message to the nations of the world: If you harbor terrorists, you are a terrorist. If you train or arm a terrorist, you are a terrorist; if you feed a terrorist or fund a terrorist, you're a terrorist, and you will be held accountable by the United States.[20]

Saudi Arabia had given sanctuary to Idi Amin and Zimbabwe to Colonel Mengistu, the deposed dictator of Ethiopia. Did this include them?

Bush was no longer talking about destroying "every terrorist group of global reach." He had put on America's enemies list all "state sponsors of terror" designated by the Department of State, a list that included Libya, Sudan, and Iran, though all three had passively supported us in the war in Afghanistan, and Tehran had been far less tolerant of the Taliban than Washington before 9/11. And "terrorists" would include the Basque ETA, the IRA, Chechen rebels, Maoists in Nepal, Tamil Tigers in Sri Lanka, the FARC in Colombia, Hezbollah in Lebanon, and the Uighur separatists of western China.

The Axis of Evil

But it was in his State of the Union in 2002 that the American Caesar crossed his Rubicon. Identifying Iran, Iraq, and North Korea as an "axis of evil," President Bush delivered virtual ultimata to all three nations:

> We'll be deliberate, yet time is not on our side. I will not wait on events, while dangers gather. I will not stand by, as peril draws closer and closer. The United States of America will not permit the world's most dangerous regimes to threaten us with the world's most destructive weapons.[21]

By threatening preemptive strikes and preventive wars on nations that had not attacked us, Bush began to lose many who had supported the U.S. war in Afghanistan. Why, before Al Qaeda and its collaborators had been eradicated, was he considering war on Iraq, Iran, or North Korea? Or all three? When had any of them threatened the United States with "the world's most destructive weapons"?

By declaring the three an "axis of evil," Bush consciously called to mind Reagan's designation of the Soviet Union as an evil empire, and the Axis powers of Nazi Germany and fascist Italy. Their fate will be your fate, the president seemed to be saying.

Bush's threat of preventive war was unprecedented. Harry Truman never proposed war on Russia to stop Stalin from building atom bombs after the initial Russian test in 1949. Lyndon Johnson did not threaten war on China when Mao exploded a nuclear device in 1964. While it was U.S. policy to discourage the proliferation of nuclear weapons, Russia, Britain, France, China, Israel, South Africa, India, and Pakistan had all acquired them without U.S. military retribution.

Yet Bush had put Iran, Iraq, and North Korea on notice: Should any of the three seek to possess nuclear weapons, or biological or chemical weapons, some of which dated to World War I, America reserved the right to attack and disarm them, and effect "regime change" inside their nations.

Though Bush may not have known it when he issued his ultimata, North Korea and Iran had secret nuclear programs already under way. He would now have to abort these programs, or attack these nations, or his own and his country's credibility would be permanently impaired.

The axis-of-evil speech was the most rash and reckless ever delivered by an American president. It led inexorably to the worst strategic blunder in the history of the United States—the invasion and occupation of Iraq—and the ruin of the Bush presidency.

What impelled President Bush, with the nation and world behind him in America's war on Al Qaeda and its collaborators, to threaten war with three nations that had nothing to do with 9/11, two of which, far from being part of any axis, had fought the longest, bloodiest war of the 1980s against each other? Not only did President Bush have no forces in place to launch these wars, he had no authority to carry out his threats. The Constitution does not empower presidents to wage war against nations that have not attacked us. Seeking to reach Churchillian heights, Bush's speechwriters had taken him over the top. Yet, as events would reveal, Bush fully intended to go where his speechwriters, intoxicated by ideology, were taking him.

The West Point Manifesto

After President Bush had widened the war on terror to include axis-of-evil nations that had nothing to do with 9/11, the domestic and foreign coalitions that had come together behind his leadership began to crumble. Bush was unmoved. At West Point, on June 2, 2002, he spoke of a new and expanded mission for the armed forces of the United States:

Our nation's cause has always been larger than our nation's defense. We fight, as we always fight, for a just peace—a peace that favors human liberty. We will defend the peace against threats from terrorists and tyrants. We will preserve the peace by building good relations among the great powers. And we will extend the peace by encouraging free and open societies on every continent.[22]

With these words the president was opening the door to a global mission no president had dared to proclaim. And the Wilsonian rhetoric aside, the United States had never gone to war for any such gauzy goal as a "just peace . . . that favors human liberty."

America's wars were fought for national ends. We fought the Revolution to be rid of British rule and the War of 1812 because the Royal Navy refused to respect the rights of our seamen and war hawks saw a chance to grab Canada. We fought Mexico to hold all of Texas and take California. Lincoln fought the Civil War to restore the Union. We fought Spain because we wanted her off our doorstep. The Spanish-American War may also have been fought to liberate Cubans, but it ended as an imperial war to subjugate Filipinos and establish an American Empire on the far side of the Pacific.

Wilson's rhetoric notwithstanding, we entered World War I because Kaiser Wilhelm II refused to respect our right to supply the Allies and his U-boats began to torpedo our merchant ships. We entered World War II only after we were attacked at Pearl Harbor and Hitler declared war on us. We intervened in Korea and Vietnam to prevent those nations from falling to a Communist empire whose ultimate ambition was the defeat of our country and an end to our way of life. We fought the Gulf War to evict Iraq from Kuwait and keep Kuwaiti and Saudi oil in friendly hands. We fought the Cold War to defend our freedom and our allies, and because we were given no other choice after the Communists declared the United States to be the main enemy in their drive to world conquest.

At West Point, President Bush rejected as obsolete and irrelevant the policies of containment and deterrence that had won the Cold War.

Containment is not possible when unbalanced dictators with weapons of mass destruction can deliver those weapons on missiles or secretly provide them to terrorist allies. . . . If we wait for threats to fully materialize, we will have waited too long. . . .

[T]he war on terror will not be won on the defensive. We must take the battle to the enemy, disrupt his plans and confront the worst threats before they emerge. In this world we have entered, the only path to safety is the path of action. And this nation will act.[23]

In dealing with terrorists like Al Qaeda, Bush was right. No threat will deter a suicide bomber determined to die a glorious death flying an airliner into a skyscraper. But in dealing with dictators, deterrence has never failed us. We contained and deterred Stalin and Mao, though both had nuclear weapons. But with the "unbalanced dictators" of today, Kim Jong-Il, the Ayatollah, and Saddam, Bush was saying, deterrence could not be relied upon. Why not? After all, not one of these dictators had ever attacked the United States.

President Bush then made another great leap. He asserted a right to prevent any other nation from ever again acquiring sufficient power to challenge U.S. supremacy. Bush had adopted and internalized the tenets of the Wolfowitz memorandum his own father's White House had repudiated.

Competition between great nations is inevitable, but armed conflict in our world is not. . . . America has, and intends to keep, military strengths beyond challenge—thereby making the destabilizing arms races of other eras pointless, and limiting rivalries to trade and other pursuits of peace.[24]

This was breathtaking. Bush was saying to Beijing, Moscow, New Delhi: Henceforth, you may compete with us in "trade and other pursuits of peace"—the Olympics, for example—but we will not permit you to increase your power to where it might challenge America's power.

This Bush declaration—we will brook no peer rival ever again; for we are the new Rome, and mankind's future is one where the benevolent global hegemony of the United States is eternal—was a gauntlet thrown down to every aspiring world power and an incentive to lesser powers to unite against us. Had Britain adopted this policy in the nineteenth century, Parliament would have asserted a right to go to war to prevent any American president from ever enlarging U.S. battle fleets to rival the Royal Navy.

This was hubris of a high order. But the president was not done.

"All nations that decide for aggression and terror will pay a price. We will not leave . . . the peace of the planet at the mercy of a few mad terrorists and tyrants. We will lift this dark threat from our country and the world."

Upon what meat had this our Caesar fed?

Consider what the president is saying here. Every act of aggression, anywhere, can expect U.S. retaliation. Every act of terror, anywhere, will bring a U.S. reprisal. For we are responsible for "the peace of the planet" and we "will lift this dark threat" of tyranny and terror from the world.

When in all of history has any nation been able to do this?

Israel has been unable to lift the "dark threat" of terror from the West Bank. Not only do Hamas, Hezbollah, and Islamic Jihad employ terror, so, too, do resistance fighters all over the world.

Are the graduates of West Point to fight them all?

Prudence is the mark of the statesman. Where was the prudence in the president's address at West Point? Yet Bush was not done.

"[W]e will defend the peace that makes all progress possible," Bush told the cadets. "You will help establish a peace that allows millions around the world to live in liberty and to grow in prosperity."

But the U.S. armed forces do not take an oath to "defend the peace." They take an oath to defend the Constitution. Throughout our history, the United States has wisely stayed out as other nations went to war. This was true of the Crimean War, the Franco-Prussian War, the Boer War, the Russo-Japanese War, the Balkan wars of 1912 and 1913, World War I from 1914 to 1917, the Sino-Japanese War, the Chinese Civil War, and France's wars in Indochina and Algeria.

Before the North Atlantic Treaty Organization was formed in 1949, an impassioned debate took place. Should the United States, for the first time in 170 years, enter an alliance that would require us to go to war to defend ten nations of Western Europe extending from West Germany to Iceland. Was it prudent? Was it wise to abandon the great tradition and disregard the counsel of Washington and Jefferson, who had warned against "permanent alliances" and "entangling alliances"? Was it necessary?

By the time of Bush's address at West Point, America had treaty or moral commitments to go to war to defend all Western and Central Europe against the Soviet Union, to keep the peace in the Balkans, to defend Israel and the Gulf states from Iran and Iraq, to defend Taiwan and Japan from China, to defend South Korea from North Korea.

Yet President Bush was now unilaterally declaring a new worldwide mission. The U.S. Army of 500,000 men and women was now responsible for ending all terrorism, opposing all tyrants, defending the "peace of the planet," permitting no rival nation ever to build up its power to where it might challenge U.S. supremacy in any region—and waging preventive war against any and all rogue nations seeking weapons of mass destruction.

Imperial pride strutted in the capital city in those days.

The National Security Strategy

On September 21, 2002, the White House issued the *National Security Strategy of the United States,* a thirty-three-page codification of the principles and policies laid down at West Point. Ambiguity was not its dominant feature.

> In the new world we have entered, the only path to peace and security is the path of action . . . we will not hesitate to act alone, if necessary, to exercise our right of self-defense by *acting preemptively.* [emphasis added][25]

Why could not Cuba, Libya, Syria, Iraq, Iran, and North Korea be deterred, as Stalin's Russia and Mao's China had been deterred, by a threat of U.S. retaliation? The *NSS* explained:

Deterrence . . . is less likely to work against leaders of rogue states more willing to take risks, gambling with the lives of their people, and the wealth of their nations. . . .

[O]ur enemies see weapons of mass destruction as weapons of choice. For rogue states these weapons are tools of intimidation and military aggression against their neighbors. These weapons may allow these states to attempt to blackmail the United States . . . to prevent us from deterring or repelling the aggressive behavior of rogue states.[26]

History contradicts this declaration.

Did Stalin's possession of atomic weapons "blackmail" the United States into not coming to the defense of South Korea? Did Mao's bombs prevent our sending half a million troops to Vietnam, or challenging China in the Taiwan Strait? Deterrence worked.

With the exception of Korea in 1950, where Stalin and Kim Il-Sung miscalculated, believing the United States would not fight, deterrence never failed us. Since Pearl Harbor, no nation had ever directly attacked America. Every rogue regime engaged in a terror attack against us—Libya with Pan Am 103, Iran at Khobar Towers—covered its tracks.

How can 9/11, a single terrorist attack in which no state has yet been found complicit, invalidate a doctrine of deterrence that has worked with every hostile state America has faced for sixty years?

From the passage above, the White House appeared to fear that if nations like Iran should acquire nuclear weapons, they would curtail our freedom of action and end our dominance of their region, as Moscow's nuclear arsenal deterred U.S. intervention in Eastern Europe in the Cold War.

The *NSS* stated anew Bush's warning that any nation that seeks to acquire power to rival America's power is risking war with us.

> Our forces will be strong enough to dissuade potential adversaries from pursuing a military buildup in hopes of surpassing or equaling the power of the United States.[27]

The *National Security Strategy* of 2002 was the imperial edict of a superpower out to exploit its temporary supremacy to declare itself Lord Protector of the Universe. Against whom was this threat directed? China and Russia, the only rivals to U.S. global hegemony. Reviewing the *National Security Strategy*, Andrew Bacevich, a foreign policy scholar at Boston University, marveled at "its fusion of breathtaking utopianism with barely disguised *machtpolitik*. It reads as if it were the product not of sober, ostensibly conservative Republicans but of an unlikely collaboration between Woodrow Wilson and the elder Field Marshal von Moltke."[28]

Monroe to Bush

With the address at West Point and the *National Security Strategy*, President Bush was consciously crafting a Bush Doctrine that he and his advisers believed would mark him as a great president who had seen further than others and had laid down a policy America would forever pursue and that would bear his name.

In 1823, President Monroe had issued the first and most famous doctrine, the Monroe Doctrine, which closed the western hemisphere to further European colonization.

On March 12, 1947, President Truman introduced containment in a speech to Congress that closed with the historic statement: "I believe it must be the policy of the United States to support free peoples who are resisting attempted subjugation by armed minorities or outside pressures."

This was the Truman Doctrine—to contain Communism by assisting with arms beleaguered nations on the frontiers of the Soviet bloc. Truman applied it by sending military aid to Greece and Turkey.

The Eisenhower Doctrine (1957) extended the Truman Doctrine to the Middle East. It was invoked in Lebanon in 1958, when U.S. Marines went ashore to secure the Beirut government after the monarchy in Baghdad was overthrown in a bloody coup and revolution seemed to threaten all the pro-Western Arab states.

The Nixon Doctrine (1969) assured allies that the United States would continue to aid nations fighting Communist subversion and aggression, but, henceforth, they would have to provide the troops. It was a message to the nation and world: No more Vietnams.

The Carter Doctrine (1980) committed the United States to war to prevent a Soviet takeover in the Persian Gulf. It was issued after the 1979 coup in Kabul and Red Army occupation of Afghanistan.

The Reagan Doctrine was never formally declared. The term is used to describe the political and economic pressure Reagan applied to the Soviet Empire and the aid he gave freedom fighters in Afghanistan, Angola, and Nicaragua. The Reagan policy was "containment-plus"—to contain Soviet expansionism, force Moscow into fatal competition with the United States, impose on the Soviets costs in blood and treasure like those they had imposed on us in Korea and Vietnam, and weaken and roll back the Soviet Empire.

Of the Truman, Eisenhower, Nixon, Carter, and Reagan doctrines, it needs be said: All dealt with threats or acts of aggression by the Soviet bloc against nations friendly to the United States. None threatened the USSR or its vital interests. They were redlines drawn around independent nations warning the Communist bloc it faced resistance, and possible war with the United States, should it cross those lines. None entailed preemptive strikes. None endorsed preventive wars. All were defensive in character, with the exception of the Reagan Doctrine, which amounted to U.S. rejection of the Brezhnev Doctrine of 1968, which held that, once a nation became Communist, it would never be allowed to recant or rebel.

Conservatives credit the Reagan Doctrine with expediting the West's victory in the Cold War. But Reagan never asserted a U.S. right to launch preemptive strikes or preventive wars. Grenada was no exception. The island was being converted into a Soviet and Cuban base of subversion in the Caribbean, its Marxist ruler had been overthrown and murdered, and U.S. medical students appeared in imminent peril of being taken hostage.

Morality and Preemptive Strikes

Bush's strategists believe the right to launch preemptive attacks or preventive wars is inherent in the national right of self-defense. JFK, they rightly contend, was prepared to attack the missile sites in Cuba rather than let them become operational. But that threat was grave and imminent. Those missiles were armed with nuclear warheads that could strike Washington in fifteen minutes.

Yet to declare a national policy of preventive war seems alien to American character and tradition. Polk waited for the Mexican army to shed "American blood on American soil" before asking Congress to declare war. Lincoln waited for Fort Sumter to be fired upon before issuing his call for volunteers. We did not declare war on Germany until 1917, when U-boats began to sink our ships. We did not declare war on Japan until Pearl Harbor. We did not go to war in Korea or Vietnam until those nations were under attack.

Preemptive strikes have been the war option exercised by aggressor nations like Japan at Port Arthur in 1904 and Pearl Harbor in 1941 and Nazi Germany against Poland in 1939. Or small nations in imminent peril that believe they cannot afford to lose a battle, like Israel in the Six-Day War. Preemptive strikes have never been America's way.

What, then, are the edicts of the Bush Doctrine as enunciated in the presidential speeches and statements in the year following 9/11?

- The War on Terror is not just between America and Al Qaeda, but between good and evil for the future of mankind.
- This is a "long war" that will not end until all terror networks of a global reach are eradicated.
- "Either you are with us, or you are with the terrorists."
- No axis-of-evil nation—Iran, Iraq, or North Korea— will be allowed to acquire weapons of mass destruction.

- America has the right to launch preemptive strikes and preventive wars to stop nations from acquiring weapons we have had in our arsenal for sixty years.
- No nation will ever again be permitted to rise to a position of power in any region of the world to challenge American power.
- America intends to maintain global hegemony—forever.

Truly, here is a formula for "perpetual war for perpetual peace."

In addition to the new commitments, unilaterally declared by George W. Bush, the United States retains these commitments from the Cold War and Bush I-Clinton era, and from 9/11 to the release of the *NSS*:

- A commitment to victory in Afghanistan and a democratic peace, insuring the country is anti-Taliban and pro-West.
- A commitment to go to war if necessary against a nuclear-armed Russia to defend Europe all the way to the Baltic republics.
- A commitment, reinforced by a new U.S. base in Kosovo, to maintain the peace of the bloodstained Balkan peninsula.
- A commitment to defend Israel against all enemies.
- A commitment to the "dual containment" of Iran and Iraq in the Persian Gulf.
- A presidential guarantee to do "whatever it takes" to defend Taiwan from China, though we consider Taiwan "a part of China."

- A permanent commitment, backed by 30,000 U.S. troops, to defend South Korea from a North Korea with a million-man army.
- A commitment to go to war for Japan, should she be attacked by China or North Korea.

To meet these extraordinary commitments, the United States possesses air, land, and sea forces dramatically shrunken from what Ronald Reagan left us in 1989. The 1.4 million men and women in the armed forces, who would have to carry out these commitments, are half the forces Eisenhower had in the peacetime 1950s, and little more than one-tenth of the forces America had at the end of World War II.

To call America's condition in 2002—as Bush was issuing his edicts, warnings, and threats to the world and preparing a new war—imperial overstretch is understatement.

The Cakewalk War

In the summer of 2002, this writer and several friends launched *The American Conservative,* a magazine dedicated to opposing the U.S. invasion of Iraq, for which the war drums were loudly beating. In my first column in the first edition of that magazine, I wrote:

> If Providence does not intrude, we will soon launch an imperial war on Iraq with all the "On-to-Berlin!" bravado with which French poilus and British Tommies marched in August 1914.... But what comes after the celebratory gunfire when wicked Saddam is dead? ...

With our MacArthur Regency in Baghdad, Pax Americana will reach apogee. But then the tide recedes, for the one endeavor at which Islamic peoples excel is expelling imperial powers by terror and guerrilla war. They drove the Brits out of Palestine and Aden, the French out of Algeria, the Russians out of Afghanistan, the Americans out of Somalia and Beirut, the Israelis out of Lebanon. . . .

We have started up the road to empire and over the next hill we shall meet those who went before.[29]

"The only lesson we learn from history is that we do not learn from history," I concluded. This was written six months before Bush invaded Iraq.

But the president's mind had been made up. Having named Iraq an axis-of-evil nation possessing weapons of mass destruction, having laid out his doctrine of preventive war, Bush, in March 2003, ordered the invasion. In three weeks, it was over. Yet the United States has never been able to find any evidence Iraq was plotting to attack us or its neighbors, has never found any solid tie between Saddam and Al Qaeda or the perpetrators of 9/11, has never found an Iraqi nuclear program, has never found any weapons of mass destruction. We attacked, invaded, and occupied a nation that had never attacked us or threatened us—to strip it of weapons it did not have.

As U.S. troops occupied Baghdad, America celebrated and President Bush soared to the 90 percent approval his father had received. All of America seemed to share in the hubris of George Bush. The victory of U.S. arms seemed even more impressive than the triumph of Desert Storm. But on the fall of Baghdad in early April 2003, I began my column thus:

No one knows how America's occupation of Iraq will play out.

Optimists say this will be like Germany and Japan after World War II, which were converted into democratic allies for the Cold War. Pessimists point to Lebanon and Israel's invasion of 1982.

Put me down among the pessimists.

I think B'rer Rabbit just hit the tar baby.[30]

Hubris, the arrogance of power, led Bush to attack Iraq. But behind the arrogance lay an ideology, a fixed set of ideas about the world and the providential role of the United States. To this ideology, Bush had been wholly converted in the days after 9/11, just as he had been converted to evangelical Christianity. What is that ideology? What are the ideas that steered the greatest nation in history into the greatest blunder in its history?

3

The Gospel of George Bush

To be ignorant of what occurred before you were
born is to remain always a child.
—CICERO[1]

Pity the nation that is full of beliefs and empty of religion.
—KHALIL GIBRAN[2]

The conservative mind and the ideological mind
stand at opposite poles.
—RUSSELL KIRK[3]

When people cease to believe in God, they do not then believe
in nothing, they believe in anything, said Chesterton.

For generations, many among our Western intellectual and
cultural elites have disbelieved in a God who is Creator and
Judge of mankind. And like the Israelites at the foot of Sinai
who, impatiently awaiting the return of Moses, created a
golden calf to worship, modern man creates his own golden
calves.

Ideology is modernity's golden calf. Ideology is our substitute for religious faith. Ideology, wrote Russell Kirk, is "a

dogmatic political theory which is an endeavor to substitute secular goals and doctrines for religious goals and doctrines."[4]

The term has come to mean a set of cohesive beliefs about man, society, and the world that gives meaning and purpose to men's lives, directing their actions in the public realm. "Ideology is a guiding vision of future social action," said scholar Michael Novak, for whom the vision was of the worldwide triumph of "democratic capitalism."[5]

Ideologies are created by men of words to explain the world to come, in which their vision will guide society and they will carry the lamps, lead the way, and enjoy the prestige and power of the priestly class to be displaced. For deracinated intellectuals, ideology holds an irresistible attraction, for it both offers a coherent and compelling explanation of how the world works—and satisfies the lust for power. As Raymond Aron wrote in "Opium of the Intellectuals," "When the intellectual feels no longer attached either to the community or the religion of his forbears, he looks to progressive ideology to fill the vacuum."[6]

Dr. Kirk spent his career as a man of letters fighting "the curse of ideological infatuation." In "The Drug of Ideology," he defined what ideology was, and what it was not:

> "Ideology" does not mean political theory or principle, even though many journalists and some professors commonly employ the term in that sense. Ideology really means political fanaticism—and, more precisely, the belief that this world of ours can be converted into a Terrestrial Paradise through the operation of positive law and positive planning.[7]

Kirk deplored "democratism," the ideology of the neoconservatives who had attached themselves to the party of Reagan. He considered them "often clever . . . never wise."

An instance of this lack of wisdom is the Neoconservatives' infatuation with ideology. Ideology . . . is political fanaticism: at best, it is the substitution of slogans for real political thought. Ideology animates, in George Orwell's phrase, "the streamlined men who think in slogans and talk in bullets."[8]

The neoconservatives' ambition to create "an American ideology" was to Kirk a "puerile infatuation." Yet it was not unsuccessful. For it was the conversion of George W. Bush to neoconservative ideology that took America into the war that destroyed his presidency and brought an end to the American Century.

Characteristics of Ideology

As ideologues believe themselves possessed of a true faith that has been denied to others, and see a golden future others cannot see, they are impatient with and intolerant of dissent. Like many sects, ideologues tend to be exclusionary, to rely on one another, to promote their own, to punish all defectors and heretics, to form cliques and cabals—to realize the vision. And as their vision is of a world that has never before existed, or existed only in the mythical past, they are prone to utopianism. The brave new world is on the way—if only we keep the faith!

Ideology has one foot grounded in reality, but the other is ever on quicksand. For no one can know the future. Yet the True

Believer has moral certitude, for his ideology foretells a future certain to come if the sacrifices are sufficient and the anointed leaders are faithfully followed.

Ideologues ignore or sweep aside evidence that contradicts the dogma. They stay steadfast in the faith even when failure is apparent. Indeed, it is the mark of an ideologue that he will "stay the course" when others have fallen away, like the Communists who stayed true to the cause, when news of the Hitler-Stalin pact broke. There are faculty Marxists in our universities who yet insist it was not Marxism that failed in Cuba, Russia, or Eastern Europe, but leaders who did not truly understand what Marxism was.

Ideologues cherry-pick history, to make it conform to the ideology. A prime example is *Dangerous Nation* by Frederick Kagan, which crams U.S. history into a neoconservative mold, as though America has always been a crusader state, going abroad and using its power to strike down dictators and totalitarians to advance democracy. Ideology is ever at war with truth. Not all ideologies are totalitarian. Yet all tend toward authoritarianism. When the people vote the wrong way, they are considered to have made a mistake, and their decision must be ignored or bypassed. Rejection of the constitution of the European Union by the voters of Holland and France brought demands that the voters be bypassed, by letting parliaments decide, or that the constitution be resubmitted until the voters got it right.

To Karl Marx, writes Kirk, ideology was "a cloak for class interests, an outwardly rational instrument of propaganda, a veil of argument produced to disguise and defend an established social order."

Marx attacked the social theories of his own time and of earlier ages as ideologies meant to maintain capitalism, feudalism, imperialism, and other systems. Marxism itself, however, rapidly developed into an ideology, or dogmatic system of politics professing to found its structure upon a "reality" ascertained by sensory perception alone.[9]

Exactly. Marx regarded ideology as a body of ideas invented to rationalize and defend a political order. To Marx, organized religion was both an opiate of the masses and an ideology to preserve the power, exalted position in society, and possessions of popes, bishops, and priests. Leninism, Stalinism, and Maoism fit Marx's definition perfectly.

In Russia, Communist ideology dictated that the party hold an absolute monopoly of power and privilege that the Romanovs never knew. Why, in a worker's paradise, ought workers be unfree? Because the party, in Leninist ideology, was the protector of the state and vanguard of the revolution to build paradise on earth. Communist ideology was the cover story of a minority addicted to power—to convince the majority to let them keep it.

Napoleon and the pigs who led the revolution in *Animal Farm* soon seized absolute power over the other animals and moved into the farmer's house to enjoy the comforts of the sheltered home. The slogans they invented to justify the new order expose what Communism was all about: absolute power for the Communist dictatorship. As Fidel showed the world, the Communist does not make the revolution to abolish the dictatorship. He makes the revolution to establish the dictatorship.

As the ideology of Marx was used to justify the dictatorship of Lenin and Stalin, the ideology of *Mein Kampf* was used to justify Hitler's.

The French Revolution was a product of ideology. "Man is born free but everywhere he is in chains," wrote Rousseau in the opening line of *The Social Contract*. Both clauses of the most famous line Rousseau ever wrote are nonsense. Man is born dependent, and, to that time, mankind rarely lived freer, better, or longer than in the France of Louis XVI.

"Mankind will only be free when the last king has been strangled with the entrails of the last priest," declared Diderot. His dictum was carried out by Robespierre and Lenin. And were men free in the France of Robespierre and the Russia of Stalin?

Ideology and America's Wars

In every American war, our leaders have invoked higher and nobler ends to persuade the people to sacrifice and suffer and to sanctify the cause. Almost always, it is an ex post facto sanctification. Wars begun for national interests are said to be fought for universal principles.

The Revolution was fought to rid us of British rule—British soldiers, governors, tax collectors. We wanted them out of our country and off our continent. We wanted to rule ourselves, and no longer be subject to the British crown.

To justify what Parliament and King called treason, Jefferson sought to embed the rebellion, the American war of independence from England, in the larger cause of the freedom and equality for all men. Though a slaveholder who thought a "natural aristocracy" was born to rule, Jefferson wrote: "We hold these truths to be self-evident, that all men are created equal, that they are endowed by their Creator with certain unalienable

Rights, that among these are Life, Liberty and the pursuit of Happiness."

From London, Dr. Johnson sneered: "[H]ow is it that we hear the loudest yelps for liberty among the drivers of negroes?" On Johnson's death, the chief beneficiary in his will was his Jamaican servant, an ex-slave. Yet Jefferson, from the way he lived his life, did not truly believe the most famous lines he ever wrote. He did not free his slaves on his death in 1826, fifty years after issuance of his famous declaration, as Washington had done. At Monticello, the Jeffersonian principles of '76 were inoperative.

Even in the declaration he drafted, Jefferson had excoriated George III for having "endeavoured to bring on the inhabitants of our frontiers, the merciless Indian Savages whose known rule of warfare, is an undistinguished destruction of all ages, sexes and conditions."

Did Jefferson believe Indians were "created equal"?

When Tony Blair was making his case for war in Iraq, "the intelligence and facts were being fixed around the policy,"[10] according to an internal document later known as the Downing Street Memo. That is, U.S. and British leaders cherry-picked the intelligence to convince a skeptical public to back a war already decided upon. So, too, did Jefferson fit the ideology of equality—around the policy of rebellion.

Minutemen and colonial soldiers had been fighting the British army at Lexington, Concord, and Boston for fifteen months before Jefferson sat down at his desk in Philadelphia. What he did there was to wrap America's revolt in the cause of the equality of all men, a cause in which Jefferson himself did not believe, and to portray George III as a tyrant in a class with Ivan the Terrible.

Not only the ideas of the Declaration of Independence, but most of the "facts" it contained were being fixed around the policy of rebellion. As Russell Kirk wrote, "The Declaration of 1776 is simply a declaration—and a highly successful piece of immediate political propaganda; such philosophical concepts as find expression therein are so mistily expressed as to mean all things to all men, then and now."[11]

At Gettysburg, too, Lincoln sought to ennoble the Union's war to crush the South's fight for independence by embedding the Union cause in the higher cause of the equality of all men.

> Fourscore and seven years ago our fathers brought forth on this continent, a new nation, conceived in Liberty, and dedicated to the proposition that all men are created equal.
>
> Now we are engaged in a great civil war, testing whether that nation, or any nation so conceived and so dedicated, can long endure.[12]

Yet, as we have seen, while Jefferson's declaration proclaimed that "all men are created equal," Jefferson was preaching a doctrine which he did not believe nor did he practice. Nor was equality the practice or belief of Lincoln or his countrymen, or the policy of the nation he led, when he spoke at Gettysburg.

Nor did Lincoln seek the presidency to free the slaves. When he called for volunteers after Fort Sumter, there were more slave states in the Union than there were in the Confederacy. Like most Americans then, Lincoln was a white supremacist. He believed freed slaves should be sent back to Africa, whence their ancestors had come. In his first inaugural address, Lincoln endorsed a constitutional amendment that would have made slavery permanent in the fifteen states where it existed, and offered to assist the South in running down fugitive slaves. When General John Frémont, the Republican candidate for president in 1856, issued an order emancipating the slaves of Confederates in Missouri, Lincoln angrily revoked his order. Frémont had usurped authority and put Kentucky, a slave state Lincoln wanted to keep in the Union, at risk. When Frémont's wife, the impulsive Jessie Benton Frémont, daughter of Thomas Hart Benton, asked for a hearing, Lincoln directed her to come to the White House. As she wrote in her diary, Lincoln told her, "It was a war for a great national idea, the Union, and that General Frémont should not have dragged the negro into it."[13] As he wrote Horace Greeley with raw honesty,

> My paramount object in this struggle is to save the Union, and is not either to save or to destroy slavery. If I could save the Union without freeing any slave I would do it, and if I could save it by freeing all the slaves I would do it; and if I could save it by freeing some and leaving others alone I would also do that. What I do about slavery, and the colored race, I do because I believe it helps to save the Union; and what I forbear, I forbear because I do not believe it would help to save the Union.[14]

The Union was the cause for which the Union fought. Thus, when Lincoln issued his Emancipation Proclamation, January 1, 1863, it freed only slaves in rebel-held territory, slaves Lincoln had no power to free. The slaves of his generals, political allies, and friends remained their private property.

Lest the point be missed, let it be restated.

Jefferson's Declaration of Independence and Lincoln's Gettysburg Address and second inaugural are splendid, beautiful, and powerful. The words, ideas, and ideals behind them have elevated into America's pantheon the men who wrote and spoke them. Ever since they were put down on paper they have moved men and inspired people all over the world.

But these words were also war propaganda, some of the finest ever written.

For the Civil War was not fought for racial equality. The ideology of egalitarianism was conscripted to sanctify the war to posterity and to make it appear worthwhile to the families of those who had lost sons at Gettysburg. The ideology of egalitarianism Lincoln invoked at Gettysburg may have had immense appeal to the New England Transcendentalists. It had almost none to the Illinois farmers and workers who heard Lincoln's assurances, in his 1858 debates with Douglas, that he did not at all believe in social or political equality for Negroes.

The ideology Lincoln invoked to justify the war—the equality of all men—was neither his belief nor the cause of the war. It was the South's declaration of independence, as intolerable to Lincoln as Jefferson's had been to George III, that was the cause of the war—that, and Lincoln's resolve to march the rebellious states back at the point of a bayonet if necessary.

In *The Gettysburg Gospel*, Lincoln scholar Gabor Boritt writes that while the address has been "granted miraculous powers—'the words that remade America,'" the actual words "do not do that. How could a speech do that, especially one that was not heard distinctly in its own day?"[15]

"[T]he 'Gettysburg Gospel' wasn't quite a gospel in 1863," writes reviewer John Willson in *Chronicles*: "The most interesting feature of Mr. Boritt's book is his description of how it became a gospel."

> Mr. Boritt shows . . . that the Gettysburg Address assumed its gospel status exactly as the Progressives were rewriting our history to save us all through Big Government. And, as Mr. Boritt says, "If in the 1860s the United States was to save the world by saving the democratic example at home through force of arms, in 1917, it would do the same by sending those arms abroad." In general, the Progressive movement, striving for the common man, for democratization, turned the Gettysburg Address into a manifesto. Thus, what was meant as "a war speech" became a 272-word set piece for a progressive ideology. In Wilson's hands, and in FDR's, that ideology became the foundation for empire.[16]

What is Boritt saying?

The Gettysburg Address was a "war speech" heard by but a few standing near Lincoln on the battlefield. Decades later, it was seized upon by the Progressives, who reinterpreted it to persuade the nation that their goal, democratizing not only America but the world, was the cause for which the Union had fought and Lincoln had died. Equality, the Progressives declared, was America's preordained and divine mission—from Concord Bridge to Gettysburg. Now we Progressives are the heirs of Washington, Jefferson, and Lincoln and we are carrying forward to the world the founding mission of America, equality and democracy.

Thus were the words of Jefferson and Lincoln—neither of whom believed in the literal truth of what they wrote—conscripted by the Progressives and declared holy writ, America's gospel, that we were all obligated to carry to mankind, if need be by force of arms.

To make the whole world democratic thus became America's mission, as proclaimed by Woodrow Wilson and George Bush. And any who rejected the mission were "isolationists," faithless to the cause of America as defined in the Declaration of Independence and confirmed in blood at Gettysburg.

This is false history, fabricated history, fictional history, woven to sustain an ideology of interventionism the Founding Fathers rejected again and again as fatal to the republic.

In April 1917, when America plunged into the Great War that had been bleeding Europe since August 1914, Wilson declared that this was "the war to end war" and "make the world safe for democracy."

Wilson had been reelected in November 1916 on the slogan "He Kept Us Out of War." And before the war became a crusade in which the fate of civilization was at stake, Wilson could not fathom what it was all about. With the objects and causes of Europe's war, he had said in 1916, "we are not concerned. The obscure fountains from which its stupendous flood has burst forth we are not interested to search for or explore."[17]

In December 1916, as he sought to mediate between the belligerents, Wilson suggested that the goals for which the Allies and Central Powers both claimed to be fighting were "virtually the same."[18] But once German U-boats began to sink U.S. ships running guns, munitions, and supplies to England, it suddenly became a war for civilization. Wilson's words were uplifting and lovely. They were also war propaganda.

When Wilson arrived at Paris in 1919, his Fourteen Points that the Germans had accepted as the terms of armistice were cast aside by the Allies. Germans, Hungarians, and Austrians were consigned against their will and without their consent to the rule of Poles, Czechs, Romanians, Serbs, and Italians. Promised freedom, Arabs were denied it under the secret Sykes-Picot agreement, whereby France grabbed Lebanon and Syria and the British took Palestine and Iraq. The right of self-determination for all peoples that Wilson had proclaimed was denied by Britain to Irish, Egyptians, and Indians. All were crushed when they rose up to demand the self-determination Wilson had promised. Millions of Chinese in Shantung, formerly under German rule, were consigned to Japan.

Written by Wilson to counter Bolshevik exposure of the secret deals by the Allies to carve up the German, Austro-Hungarian, and Ottoman empires, the Fourteen Points were brilliant war propaganda. To the defeated nations that believed them, they turned out to be a pack of lies. Wilson's rhetoric about the self-determination of all nations was powerful and moving. But this was not the reason why the war began. This was not the reason why the war was fought. And Wilson's words were mocked by the vengeful peace the war produced and he brought home. In refusing to commit American blood to enforce the vindictive terms of Versailles, the U.S. Senate never performed a greater service.

World War II, children are now taught, was a great struggle for the future of mankind between fascism and freedom. Yet the Russians under Stalin, with whom Britain and the United States were allied, were less free than the Italians under Mussolini. America's war on Imperial Japan was not fought for democracy, but as payback for Pearl Harbor. Curtis LeMay did not fire-bomb Tokyo and burn 100,000 civilians to death in a single night to make Japan safe for democracy. Nor does that appear the motivation of his navy colleague Adm. William J. "Bull" Halsey, who declared in a 1944 newsreel interview, "We are drowning and burning the bestial apes all over the Pacific, and it is just as much pleasure to burn them as to drown them."[19]

Herman Kahn once told this writer that for most men there are two times in life when one's beliefs can best be reshaped—when the child is three to seven, and in the college years. This writer turned three a month before Pearl Harbor and the war ended two months before my seventh birthday. We were immersed in that war, from comic books to newspapers, radio, newsreels, movies, magazines, the talk of parents and peers, schoolyard prayers for the war dead. But to kids in our corner of Washington, D.C., this was not a battle of ideas. It was a war to kill "yellow-bellied Japs"—as they were called. We didn't know a fascist from a Fudgesicle. Only after the war was over did we learn it had been an ideological struggle. But that was not what our comic books were about, which painted the Japanese as subhuman and bestial. That was not what *Thirty Seconds Over Tokyo* was about, or postwar films like *The Sands of Iwo Jima*. In the Pacific it was a war of race and revenge, what poet Robinson Jeffers called "our present blood feud with the brave dwarfs."[20] In America's public schools and popular culture, World War II is portrayed as a great ideological struggle between fascism and freedom. And, indeed, the fascist powers went down to deserved and crushing defeat, and democracy did triumph in Western Europe and Japan.

But that is not why the war was fought. Britain did not go to war because Hitler was a National Socialist, but because he attacked Poland, to whose authoritarian regime Britain had given a war guarantee. America did not go to war against Japan because she was fascist, but because Japan attacked us at Pearl Harbor. America did not go to war against Germany or Italy until Hitler and Mussolini declared war on us. Stalin began the war as Hitler's ally, ended it as our ally, murdered fascists and democrats indiscriminately, and was, throughout, the greatest enemy freedom had ever known. And FDR was delighted to divide Europe with him.

World War II was a just war, but America fought it, as we have fought all our wars, for national, not ideological ends.

In his 1941 State of the Union address, Franklin Roosevelt, in the tradition of Wilson and his Fourteen Points, identified the Four Freedoms for which America would fight: freedom of speech and expression, freedom of religion, freedom from want, freedom from fear. In the Atlantic Charter agreed upon at Placentia Bay in August 1941, Churchill and FDR, again echoing Wilson, declared that all territorial adjustments at war's end must be in accord with the wishes of the peoples concerned, and all peoples had a right to self-determination.

This, too, was war propaganda. At Tehran, Yalta, and Potsdam, Churchill, Roosevelt, and Truman yielded to all of Stalin's demands—for slices of Romania and Finland, for the annexation of Lithuania, Latvia, and Estonia, for half of Poland, for control of ten Christian nations and Albania, for the ethnic cleansing of 13 million Germans from lands on which their ancestors had lived for centuries. All were monstrous crimes against humanity. Yet Churchill and Roosevelt acquiesced in these crimes and sold them to their countrymen as triumphs of democracy.

From their conduct at the wartime conferences, Churchill and Roosevelt either did not believe in the democratist ideology they professed, or did not believe in it enough to stand up for it in Stalin's presence. The great goal of World War II, on which the Big Three were in full agreement, was to smash and carve up Germany so she would never rise again.

When Bush declared in his 2003 address to the National Endowment for Democracy, "From the Fourteen Points to the Four Freedoms . . . America has put our power at the service of principle," did he not know of the fate of the Fourteen Points and Four Freedoms at Versailles and Yalta?

Marxism

Totalitarian ideologies are, in Edmund Burke's phrase, "armed doctrines." Among the bloodiest have been Jacobinism, Communism, Nazism, and fascism. Of modernity's ideologies, Marxism has had the longest and strongest hold on de-Christianized man and proved the most murderous. What was the Marxist vision that gave belief, hope, and meaning to so many lives?

Marx believed he had found the key to history and the future. In his atheistic vision, there was no God, no paradise. This life and this world were the only life and world we have. Man was not a spiritual being but an economic animal. Religion was an ideology in which the masses were indoctrinated to maintain the existing order and keep people docile and obedient, while their lifelong labors enriched their indolent masters.

Marx declared that a revolution was coming. Feudalism had given way to capitalism and the coming collision between the capitalist class and the proletariat would bring about socialism. Projecting the trends he saw—men leaving farms to work in factories, a growing surplus of labor driving down wages, impoverishment of the masses as wealth accumulated in the hands of the few, Marx predicted an inevitable and welcome explosion.

The proletariat would one day see it had no stake in preserving the system. The workers would rise and overthrow the ruling class that had grown rich exploiting them. The expropriators would be expropriated. The world would reach its final stage, a golden age where the golden rule would be: "From each according to his ability, to each according to his need." The state would wither away. We would reach the end of history.

The crisis for Marxists came early, for, as the nineteenth century unfolded, events failed to bear out Marx's predictions. There was misery in the "dark satanic mills" of Manchester; striking workers were shot; but there was also steady improvement in the economic and social conditions of the working class. Unions were being formed by workers who wanted higher wages and shorter hours, not revolution. In the summer of 1914 came the great awakening. The German Social Democrats, the party that embodied the hopes of Marxists in every land, voted to a man for the kaiser's war credits. The patriot sons of Germany, France, and England were volunteering in the millions to fight for God and country, worker solidarity be damned. Marx had been wrong. When the Great War came, the workers' cry was not "Unite and fight militarists of all nations!" but "On to Paris!" and "On to Berlin!" Nationalism had trumped internationalism.

The Russian Revolution restored the faith. But soon it was apparent that Lenin's regime was more murderous than that of the czars or any capitalist state. The slaughter of priests, poets, aristocrats, and kulaks, the purge of the old comrades, the contradictions between the promise of socialism and the reality of Stalinism, the Hitler-Stalin pact, shook the faith.

But despite conclusive evidence that the armed doctrine of Bolshevism produced regimes more base, brutal, criminal, and evil than any that had gone before, Marxist ideologues rendered it absolute loyalty, betraying comrades, countries, even families in the name of the revolution. Though the Communists, in pursuing Marx's vision of heaven on earth, had created hell on earth, even today, decades after the horrors of Bolshevism, Maoism, and Castroism have been exposed, men still believe. Such is the hold of ideology over the minds of men. Which bring us belatedly to the point of this chapter.

As Dr. Gerhardt Niemeyer, the Notre Dame professor of philosophy, wrote, "Ideology is not confined to communists and fascists."

> We, too, have our share of it, and it shows in our policies. All modern ideologies have the same irrational root: the permeation of politics with millenarian ideas of pseudo-religious character. The result is a dreamworld. Woodrow Wilson dreamed both of a "world safe for democracy," and of "enduring peace." . . . More recently, our national leaders have talked about "creating" a new society, a "Great Society" and to that end making "war against poverty," "war against hunger."[21]

Not only Jacobinism, Marxism, and Nazism, but anarchism, socialism, and neoconservatism meet the test of an ideology. For each is said to explain the direction in which the world is going, or should be made to go, and has a hold on the imaginations of men that contradictory evidence cannot shake.

And it was the midlife conversion of George Bush, after the national trauma of 9/11, to the ideology of neoconservatism, which held out the promise of a world converted to democracy by the force of American ideas and arms, that killed his presidency. What were the ideas, the ideology, behind the fateful decisions of George W. Bush?

The Democratist Temptation

When the Soviet Empire collapsed in 1989 and the Soviet Union broke apart in 1991, Americans awoke to the realization that the United States was the last superpower standing. U.S. military, economic, financial, cultural, and political power was unrivaled, unprecedented in all of history. No nation had ever had global dominance in so many fields of human endeavor.

Even before the Wall fell, several of us who had been allies in the Cold War were invited by *The National Interest* to outline a foreign policy for an era in which no great enemy threatened the United States. Former LBJ aide Ben Wattenberg called for a worldwide crusade to "wage democracy."[22]

Having worked with neoconservatives in the Reagan White House, I was aware they were as ideologically driven as our Cold War enemies. They believed not just in defeating Soviet ideology but in imposing their own on mankind. In an essay titled "America First—and Second and Third," I warned against "the democratist temptation."

> With the Cold War ending, we should look, too, with a cold eye on the internationalist set, never at a loss for new ideas to divert U.S. wealth and power into crusades and causes having little or nothing to do with the true national interest of the United States.
>
> High among these is the democratist temptation, the

worship of democracy as a form of governance and the concomitant ambition to see all mankind embrace it, or explain why not. Like all idolatries, democratism substitutes a false god for the real, a love of process for a love of country.[23]

Baptism of Fire

To understand how President Bush launched an unprovoked war to democratize Mesopotamia and the Middle East, we must understand the ideology to which he had been converted.

After 9/11, a dramatic change came over him. He seemed to have experienced an epiphany. He began to speak in a different tone and a different way. He began to describe our enemies not as fanatics using terror to advance a cause, as other revolutionaries have done. They were satanic. They personified evil.

By October 2001, Bush had begun to call them the "evildoers" and "the evil ones" who "have no country, no ideology; they're motivated by hate." He told the diplomats at State, "This war is a struggle between good and evil."

This war was not, as Clausewitz would have it, an extension of politics by other means. "From the outset," wrote Andrew Bacevich, "President Bush looked upon that war as something of a crusade and he himself as something of an agent of divine will."[24]

This division of the world into good and evil, angels of light against the angels of darkness in a struggle for the future of mankind, in which one must triumph and the other be extinguished, is the essence of the Manichaean heresy of the third century. To Bush, converted in midlife to evangelical Christianity, the world had taken on a clarity approaching luminosity. He saw clearly now, no longer as through a glass darkly.

The articles of faith of Bush's ideology are best seen by excerpting his exact words, his dogmatic declarations about the world and the war we are in, from the most important speeches of his presidency: at West Point in June 2002, at the American Enterprise Institute dinner on the eve of war in early 2003, to the National Endowment for Democracy and at Whitehall Palace in November 2003, in his second inaugural address in 2005, in his State of the Union address in 2007 justifying the "surge" of 21,500 more troops into Iraq, and in his speech to the Democracy and Security International Conference in Prague in June 2007.

In each address, President Bush speaks ex cathedra of the ideology he has internalized. He is not just bold, but as defiant and dogmatic as any fire-and-brimstone preacher calling sinners in the congregation to stand and take the sawdust trail to the mourner's bench. His remarks reveal the zeal of the convert and the certitude of the True Believer.

"Moral truth is the same in every culture, in every time, and in every place."

So Bush told the cadets at West Point.

Transparently, this is untrue. There may be one truth in the mind of God. But behind the clash of civilizations lies a clash of beliefs about moral truth. Do we not ourselves disagree, vehemently, on the morality of capital punishment, assisted suicide, premarital sex, pornography, abortion, homosexuality, war, drug use, gambling? What many Americans see as the most progressive age in which man has ever lived, others view as a time of decadence and moral decline. What many Americans embrace as the new freedom repels devout Muslims and Christians and Orthodox Jews.

"Licence they mean when they cry libertie,"[25] raged Milton. What is the culture war that has torn us apart about, if not conflicting concepts of moral truth? Even in the Bush family, there are deep disagreements over the morality of abortion.

"The requirements of freedom apply fully . . . to the entire Islamic world," the president told the cadets.

But Islam, the faith of one in five people on earth, does not mean freedom. It means "submission"—to the will of Allah. In the Islamic world, there is no freedom to preach and proselytize for faiths such as Christianity that put the souls of Muslims in mortal peril. Muslims ask, as Christians did five hundred years ago: If we have the true faith that leads to paradise, why tolerate the teaching and preaching of heresies that must lead Muslims to the loss of their souls and damnation for eternity? If there is no god but Allah and Muhammad is his Prophet, why permit disbelievers and deceivers to come among us and preach of false gods and false prophets? The secular Western idea—that all religions should be treated equally and permitted to convert non-believers—is punishable heresy in the Islamic world. Can not we Americans, who once called ourselves a Christian country, understand that?

Their politics, too, are simple. Where you are in power, we accept your rule: religious diversity and equality. Where we are in power, you accept our rule: the preeminence of Islam and only as much toleration of Christianity as we concede. Muslims see Western tolerance of all faiths as indifference to all. To serious Muslims, religion is a deadly serious matter.

We may consider this intolerant. And it is. But Christians, using the same reasoning, once burned and beheaded. And a huge slice of humanity still believes this way. Liberated Afghanistan was almost unanimous in insisting that a lone Muslim convert to Christianity, who would not recant, be executed for apostasy. Had his life depended on a democratic vote in Afghanistan, that Christian convert would have been beheaded.

Much of the Islamic world is less like America in the twenty-first century than Spain in the fifteenth. Many Muslims do not at all wish to be like us. If freedom of speech means freedom to blaspheme the Prophet, that freedom should not exist, as Salman Rushdie can testify. To Muslims, there is no freedom of the press to publish cartoons mocking the Prophet. Indeed, any depiction of the Prophet is regarded as blasphemous, violating the First Commandment proscription against graven images. The 1976 film *The Message*, starring Anthony Quinn, which recounted the life and times of the Prophet in a positive way, but did not show his face, was the object of angry protest and actual violence in the United States, because it broke Islamic law. We set the rules for our own societies. But if we wish to live in peace with Muslims, we had best not use our First Amendment freedoms to insult their deepest beliefs.

Consider again Bush's words: "*The requirements of freedom apply fully . . . to the entire Islamic world.*" How arrogant this must sound to the world of Islam. Imagine the reaction among Americans if Mahmoud Ahmadinejad of Iran, in defiant echo of President Bush, declared from the rostrum of the United Nations: "The requirements of Islam apply fully to the entire Western world."

"*We are in a conflict between good and evil, and America will call evil by its name.*"

Again the recurring theme. But in Bush's Manichaean world of good and evil, which is the evil side in Chechnya, Sri Lanka,

Kashmir? In the war against evil, on whose side is Beijing? In World War II we allied with Stalin, in the Cold War with the Shah of Iran and Chile's General Pinochet, in the Gulf War with Syria's Hafez al-Assad. We put moral clarity on the shelf. Did we act immorally by enlisting fallen angels and even great devils to crush Lucifer? Has the president not heard the injunction to choose "the lesser of two evils"?

If one extracts from Bush's address at West Point its moral claims—that we are good and they are evil; that ours is the "single surviving model of human progress"; that America's idea of freedom must "apply fully to the entire Islamic world"—the president is declaring ideological war. This is the very mirror image of Trotsky's permanent revolution. With the arsenal of democracy at his command, Bush was telling the world's autocracies what Khrushchev told America's anti-Communists: "We will bury you!"

When Nikita Khrushchev declared, "Your grandchildren will live under Communism!" Americans were angered and insulted. Why should not others react with anger when we tell them we are good and they are evil and we will not rest until their children live in a society more like ours and less like theirs? If they think ours a decadent, infidel, imperial power, will they not resist us, as we resisted the Communists to remain who we were?

And if these nations do not threaten us, why are their undemocratic and Islamic societies our concern?

The First Epistle to the Neocons

On February 26, 2003, the eve of the invasion of Iraq, President Bush attended the annual dinner of the American Enterprise

Institute, the think tank out of which many of the architects and promoters of his war had come. The reception was rapturous. The president did not disappoint:

> Human cultures can be vastly different. Yet the human heart desires the same good things, everywhere on Earth. In our desire to be safe from brutal and bullying oppression, human beings are the same. . . . For these fundamental reasons, freedom and democracy will always and everywhere have greater appeal than the slogans of hatred and the tactics of terror.[26]

But the human heart manifestly does not everywhere and always desire "the same good things." Through the ages, men have set their hearts on fame, money, power, glory, conquest, sanctity. As a Christian, President Bush knows man is a fallen being, tempted constantly to the capital sins of pride, covetousness, lust, anger, gluttony, envy, and sloth.

"In our desire to be safe from brutal and bullying oppression, human beings are the same."

But, demonstrably, in this desire, we are not the same.

In the twentieth century, Lenin, Stalin, Hitler, Mao, Ho Chi Minh, Pol Pot, Castro ruled regimes with vast bureaucracies of sincere and dedicated men who murdered tens of millions and brutalized a billion people to hold power and advance their vision. And if in the "desire to be safe from brutal and bullying oppression, human beings are the same," how did slavery endure for millennia?

Where did Bush come by these ideas, contradicted as they are by the history of the human race? Surely not in Midland-Odessa.

Birth of an Ideologue

In Simi Valley in 1999, candidate Bush spoke of humility as a virtue.

> Let us not dominate others with our power . . . let us have an American foreign policy that reflects American character. The modesty of true strength. The humility of real greatness. This is the strong heart of America. And this will be the spirit of my administration.[27]

As stated earlier, during one of the debates with Vice President Al Gore preceding the 2000 presidential election, Governor Bush told the nation: "[T]he United States must be humble and must be proud and confident of our values, but humble in how we treat nations that are figuring out how to chart their own course."[28]

This is the voice of prudence. This is a conservative voice. Contrast it with the vaulting pride of the triumphant war chief at West Point: *"The 20th century ended with a single surviving model of human progress."*

Bush had embraced the vision of Francis Fukuyama in *The End of History,* that liberal democracy had won the war for the world, cleared the field of rivals, and all nations must gravitate to it. But, again, Bush seemed divorced from reality and history.

Even as he spoke, China was into its second decade of 10 percent growth, built on autocracy, mercantilism, and repression, a model other nations have begun to adopt as China's growth continues to run at triple the rate of the United States. If democratic capitalism is the "single surviving model of human progress," why are the populations of so many European democracies shrinking and dying? How can a civilization committing suicide via contraception, abortion, sterilization, and euthanasia be the "single surviving model of human progress"?

Clearly, President Bush sees the West as the archetype of what the world should and shall become. But to many in Asia, the West is the civilization of yesterday. In the Middle East, it is viewed as decadent and dying. Even in America, many see their country as in an advanced stage of moral, social, and political decline.

Profession of Faith

It was in his address to the National Endowment for Democracy, November 6, 2003, that President Bush took final vows in the ideology to which he had been converted. On that twentieth birthday of the endowment, Bush brought down from Sinai the "essential principles common to every successful society, in every culture."[29]

"Successful societies limit the power of the state and the power of the military—so that governments respond to the will of the people, and not the will of an elite."

By this standard, fifth-century Athens, a slaveholding society ruled by an aristocratic elite, was not a successful society. The Roman republic and Roman Empire were never successful societies. The England of Elizabeth I, the France of Louis XIV and Napoleon, the Prussia of Frederick the Great, the Russia of Peter the Great, the Germany of Bismarck, all fall woefully short of being "successful societies" by the Bush standard. For none was responsive "to the will of the people."

By Bush's standard, the Virginia of Washington, Jefferson, and Patrick Henry, run by a propertied elite of white men, was never successful—from Jamestown in 1607 to Yorktown in

1781 to Appomattox in 1865. Nor was the United States, until passage of the Thirteenth, Fourteenth, Fifteenth, and Nineteenth amendments.

"Successful societies guarantee religious liberty—the right to serve and honor God without fear of persecution."

By this standard, the Spain of Ferdinand and Isabella, which expelled the Moors and Jews and countenanced the Inquisition, but built the first of the great Western empires, was an unsuccessful society. As was the Islamic caliphate that lasted more than a millennium after the death of the Prophet, because it persecuted Christians, though at one time it rivaled Rome in its dominance of Iberia, North Africa, Egypt, Palestine, Syria, Mesopotamia, and Arabia and produced a great culture. Was the Roman Empire an unsuccessful society because Christians were martyred from the death of Christ to Constantine?

"Successful societies . . . recognize the rights of women."

But how many societies before the twentieth century recognized the rights of women? Were there no successful societies before 1900?

Has there ever been a greater example of hubris by a president than to lay down the "essential principles for successful societies" and cast into outer darkness every society that does not resemble America after we ratified the Nineteenth Amendment and enlisted in the feminist revolution? The Bush speech at the National Endowment for Democracy was the work of a mind saturated in democratist ideology and devoid of historical perspective.

"Sixty years of Western nations excusing and accommodating the lack of freedom in the Middle East did nothing to make us safe—because in the long run, stability cannot be purchased at the expense of liberty," Bush told his nodding listeners at NED,

thus declaring failures the Middle East policies of eleven presidents, while asserting the moral superiority of his own. Bush was wrong on both counts. During the Cold War, the United States had the support of the Shah of Iran, presidents Sadat and Mubarak in Egypt, the Saudi royal family, the kings of Jordan and Morocco, the Gulf states. Does President Bush believe U.S. support for these monarchs and autocrats "did nothing to make us safe," though we won the Cold War and expelled Moscow from the Middle East? Were the Middle East policies of all his predecessors truly failures compared to his own? Asserting purity of motive when a policy has produced disaster is not a defense usually advanced by presidents who call themselves conservatives. This is Wilsonianism. For no matter that Wilson's war produced Lenin and Stalin, and Wilson's peace produced Hitler and Mussolini, his heart was pure.

"Liberty is both the plan of Heaven for humanity, and the best hope for progress here on Earth," said Bush. One would think that President Bush, as a believing and practicing Christian, would say that salvation was Heaven's plan for humanity, and Christ the way, the truth, and the life.

Neoconservatives have made of democracy a god. But what caused George Bush to fall down and worship this golden calf? If liberty is "the plan of Heaven for humanity," has the King of Heaven not taken his time implementing his plan? And if the world had to wait six thousand years for George Bush to arrive and implement Heaven's plan for humanity, is he a messiah, an instrument of Divine Providence? Wilson, too, believed this of himself. By 1919, he had confided in Felix Frankfurter that the League of Nations was divinely inspired and he, Wilson was "the personal instrument of God."[30] This had come about, said Wilson, "by no plan of our conceiving but by the hand of God who had led us into this way. We can only go forward with lifted eyes and freshened spirit to follow the vision."[31]

Scholar Marvin Olasky describes the astonishment of Lloyd George and Clemenceau at Wilson's messianic view of himself.

Wilson's "most extraordinary outburst," according to Lloyd George, came when he explained the failure of Christianity to achieve its highest ideals. "Jesus Christ so far [has] not succeeded in inducing the world to follow His teaching," Wilson stated, "because He taught the ideal without devising any practical scheme to carry out his aims." In Lloyd George's account, "Clemenceau slowly opened his dark eyes to their widest dimension and swept them round the Assembly to see how the Christians gathered around the table enjoyed this exposure of the futility of their Master."[32]

Not only was democracy God's plan for humanity, Bush assured the acolytes of NED, it is consistent with what the Prophet preached:

It should be clear to all that Islam—the faith of one-fifth of humanity—is consistent with democratic rule.

Democratic rule entails religious freedom. Yet columnist Terry Jeffrey's inspection of the Web site of the Grand Ayatollah Ali al-Sistani, whom *The New York Times* had hailed as a cleric who "adheres to a moderate strain of Shiite Islam that traditionally separates religion and politics," found a few inconsistencies with democratic practice.[33]

What was the ayatollah's ex cathedra pronouncement on dealing with those who "intend to slander" Islam. "The ruling upon them is death."[34]

The State Department report on Iran declared, "Apostasy, specifically conversion from Islam, can be punishable by death." "Under Sharia," said State's report on Riyadh, "a conversion by a Muslim to another religion is considered apostasy, a crime punishable by death if the accused does not recant."[35]

As Bush was declaring the compatibility of Islam and democracy, his man in Baghdad, Paul Bremer, was assuring U.S. audiences the new Iraq would ensure "freedom of worship." But the difference between "freedom of worship" and "freedom of religion" is fundamental. With the latter, all religions are treated equally and all have a right to preach, proselytize, and convert. Under "freedom of worship" Christians are permitted to worship, but if they attempt to convert Muslims they risk execution, along with any Muslim converts who refuse to recant.[36]

By the end of 2007, a million Christians, two of every three in Iraq at liberation, had fled to Jordan, Syria, Lebanon, and Egypt. Twenty-seven churches had been destroyed and Catholic priests were being martyred for their faith.[37]

As his speech to the endowment came to a close, Bush declared to his admiring audience, *"The establishment of a free Iraq at the heart of the Middle East will be a watershed event in the global democratic revolution."*

Four years later, Iraq was in bloody chaos and the "global democratic revolution" was over.

Bush was repeatedly interrupted by applause from the ideologues of the National Endowment for Democracy, whose mission is to intrude in the affairs of nations until all live up to the "essential principles of successful societies." But what has this American Neocomintern, which asserts a right to meddle in the affairs of every country on earth, done for America—to compensate for the enemies it has made?

Were President Bush a pundit, his bromides might not matter. But for seven years, he has made foreign policy for the most powerful nation on earth. And having succumbed to what Kennan called "the evils of utopian enthusiasms," he had plunged us into war to create a democracy in an Islamic country that had never known it. The war, at this writing, has cost 4,000 U.S. dead, 27,000 wounded, brought death to perhaps hundreds of thousands of Iraqis, and isolated America as never before in her history. We are paying a hellish price for not heeding the wise counsel of Dr. Kirk, who warned of this fanatic ideology:

> To expect that all the world should, and must, adopt the peculiar political institutions of the United States—which often do not work very well even at home—is to indulge the most unrealistic of visions; yet just that seems to be the hope and expectation of many Neoconservatives. . . . Such foreign policies are such stuff as dreams are made on; yet they lead to the heaps of corpses of men who died in vain.[38]

Russell Kirk was a prophet.

True conservatism is the antithesis of ideology. It is the negation of ideology. For conservatism is grounded in the past. Its principles are derived from the Constitution, experience, history, tradition, custom, and the wisdom of those who have gone before us—"the best that has been thought and said." It does not purport to know the future. It is about preserving the true, the good, the beautiful. Conservatism views all ideologies with skepticism, and the more zealous and fanatic with hostility.

Wilson's Disciple

Within months of the fall of Baghdad, the cause for which America had gone to war began to change as radically in the president's rhetoric as the cause for which the Union went to war changed in Lincoln's. In November 2003, in Whitehall Palace, Bush declared that the invasion of Iraq was part of a world "democratic movement." He invoked the hallowed name of Wilson, "an idealist, without question," who "vowed that right and justice would become the predominant and controlling force in the world."

"Wilson's high point of idealism," said Bush, was just "one short generation from Munich and Auschwitz." But Bush did not blame Wilson or Versailles for what happened at Munich and Auschwitz. He blamed the League of Nations that "collapsed at the first challenge of the dictators."[39]

What Bush left out of his history lesson was that it was not the League, but Wilson's war that gave birth to Bolshevism. It was not the League, but Wilson's peace that gave birth to Hitler's Reich. Wilson had told America that only by plunging into the European war "to make the world safe for democracy" could our own democracy be made secure. At Whitehall, Bush echoed Wilson. We must help Iraq build a "democratic country in the heart of the Middle East," for, by so doing, "we will defend our people from danger."[40]

But this is a total non sequitur. Iraq has never been democratic, but America has always been among the most secure nations on earth. What was Bush talking about? Far from being vital to our security, Middle Eastern democracy has been irrelevant to American security.

The virus Bush had contracted was not confined to the West

Wing. That same month that he ordered Gen. Tommy Franks to invade and take Baghdad, Sen. John McCain wrote in *The Washington Post*:

> The true test of our power, and much of the moral basis for its use, lies not simply in ending dictatorship but in helping the Iraqi people construct a democratic future. This is what sets us aside from empire builders: the use of power for moral purposes.[41]

But where in law or morality does the United States get the right to invade a country that has not attacked us and kill thousands of its people for the "moral purpose" of guaranteeing them a democratic future? Did the nineteenth-century British have a right to invade the United States and kill us in the hundreds of thousands—for the "moral purpose" of forcing our fathers to free their slaves and stop persecuting the Indians?

Who do we twenty-first-century Americans think we are?

The last time we heard rhetoric like Bush at NED and Whitehall was the last time America was mired in an Asian war. With half a million men in Vietnam, Lyndon B. Johnson declared we were going to build a "Great Society on the Mekong."

"Perhaps the most helpful change we can make is to change in our own thinking," said Bush at Whitehall: "[T]o suppose that one-fifth of humanity is unsuited to liberty . . . is pessimism and condescension, and we should have none of it."[42] Here Bush echoed McCain in March 2003:

> "Experts," who dismiss hopes for Iraqi democracy as naive and the campaign to liberate Iraq's people as dangerously destabilizing, do not explain why they believe Iraqis

or Arabs are uniquely unsuited to representative government, and they betray a cultural bigotry that ill serves our interests and values.[43]

Bush and McCain were here demonizing dissent, accusing of bigotry any who thought it naive to expect Iraqis to embrace U.S.-style democracy carried into their country in Bradley fighting vehicles. But because a statement is culturally condescending does not make it untrue. If not one of the twenty-two Arab states is a true democracy, it is not bigotry to conclude that the Middle East may be less conducive to the cultivation of democracy than Vermont.

What was cultural condescension to Bush and "bigotry" to McCain turns out to have been common sense. But to prove a politically correct point—that all are equally endowed with an aptitude for democracy—Bush and McCain sent thousands of Americans and scores of thousands of Iraqis to their deaths. They forgot what the American historian Daniel Boorstin taught: "The Constitution of the United States is not for export." After five years of bleeding America to build democracy in Iraq, "perhaps the most helpful change we can make" is to help President Bush and Senator McCain change their own thinking.

Second Inaugural

In his second inaugural address, President Bush returned to his themes of liberty as indivisible and of America's freedom in permanent peril if the world is not made wholly free. *"We are led, by events and common sense, to one conclusion: The survival of liberty in our land increasingly depends on the success of liberty in other lands."*[44]

But history flatly contradicts this. America has always been free. The world has never been wholly free. Hitler, Mussolini, Stalin, Tojo ruled almost all of Eurasia in 1941. Yet America was free. In his inaugural, Bush was indulging in hyperbole to set up a dramatic declaration of the mission he would pursue the rest of his presidency:

> So it is the policy of the United States to seek and support the growth of democratic movements and institutions in every nation and culture, with the ultimate goal of ending tyranny in our world.[45]

Wilson was going to make the world safe for democracy. Bush was going far beyond Wilson—to make the whole world democratic. But if our goal is "ending tyranny in our world," we have our work cut out for us.

For there are 194 nations. Fifty African and Arab nations and China may be fairly described as autocratic, despotic, unfree, or tyrannical. Bush had just asserted a right to intervene in the internal affairs of every one, by supporting "the growth of democratic movements and institutions in every nation and culture." And he had just put on America's enemies list every unfree nation on earth—from Azerbaijan to Zimbabwe.

But the reelected president was not done. He declared his intent to hector even friendly foreign leaders on the progress they are making in meeting U.S. standards of democracy:

> We will persistently clarify the choice before every ruler and nation. The moral choice between oppression, which is always wrong, and freedom, which is eternally right. . . . We

90

will encourage reform in other governments by making clear that success in our relations will require the decent treatment of their own people.[46]

"President Bush," I wrote the day after that inaugural, "is launching a crusade even more ambitious and utopian than was Wilson's. His crusade, too, will end, as Wilson's did, in disillusionment for him and tragedy for his country."[47]

So it has come to pass, and so Bush's countrymen have come to believe. In a Gallup poll two years after his second inaugural address, which asked, "Should the United States try to change a dictatorship to a democracy when it can, or should the United States stay out of other countries' affairs?" by 4 to 1 Americans said, "Stay out."[48]

In early 2007, a Penn-Schoen poll David Broder cited confirmed Gallup. By 58 percent to 36 percent, Americans agreed that "it is a dangerous illusion to believe America is superior to other nations; we should not be attempting to reshape other nations in light of our values.

"By an even greater proportion—almost 3 to 1—they say the main goal of American foreign policy should be to protect the security of the United States and its allies, rather than the promotion of freedom and democracy."

By 70 percent to 27 percent, Americans agreed with the statement: "[S]ometimes it's better to leave a dictator in charge of a hostile country, if he is contained, rather than risk chaos that we can't control if he is brought down."[49]

By the end of the Bush era, Americans had had their fill of crusades—and were ready for a foreign policy rooted in the national interest and the politics of the possible, not the utopian.

Bush in the Baltic

Four months after his second inaugural, in Riga, Latvia, on the sixtieth anniversary of V-E Day, May 7, 2005, President Bush returned to the theme that America's security is in permanent peril if other nations are not free.

> We will not repeat the mistakes of other generations, appeasing or excusing tyranny, and sacrificing freedom in the vain pursuit of stability. We have learned our lesson; no one's liberty is expendable. In the long run, our security and true stability depend on the freedom of others.[50]

Latvia, where Bush was speaking, had lost its liberty in 1940 and did not regain it until 1991. Was the United States less free in those years?

Following Bush's assertion in Riga that our freedom depends on the freedom of other nations, there was a military coup in Thailand, the armed forces seized power in Bangladesh and Fiji, and rulers in Malaysia, Singapore, Sri Lanka, Pakistan, and the Philippines took steps to stymie democratic reform. "Across Asia, the Generals Strike Back" was the headline over *The Washington Post* story:[51]

> Once at the vanguard of democratization in the developing world, South and East Asia now find their democracies in peril. . . .
>
> Worst of all for Asia's liberals, these days the men in green have received at least initial support from the region's middle class, which is fed up with corrupt, ineffective democratic leaders and is looking to the military or an

enlightened dictator to clean up politics. In Thailand last year, hordes of young people tossed flowers on grim-faced troops carrying assault rifles as the coup began. In Bangladesh, columnists and other opinion leaders cheered the military's crackdown on corruption.[52]

Whether one agrees with the Asian middle class and young cheering on the soldiers as they boot democratic rulers out of power, the impact upon our freedom is nil. What difference does it make to us if soldiers or civilian leaders are managing affairs in Bangkok or Bangladesh? How is our freedom or security imperiled or impaired in any way?

In the nineteenth century, we coexisted with British, French, Russian, and Japanese empires that controlled most of the world and held hundreds of millions of men and women in colonial captivity. Indeed, in World War I, we were fighting as an "associated power" of all four of those empires. Was our freedom imperiled? At what point in history did the liberty of other nations become indispensable to our own?

Never—save in the ideology of George W. Bush.

The Ideological Struggle

In August 2006, in Salt Lake City, before a convention of the American Legion, President Bush sought to define the war we are in—as he saw it.

The war we fight today is more than a military conflict; it is the decisive ideological struggle of the 21st century. On one side are those who believe in the values of freedom and moderation—the right of all people to speak, and worship, and live in liberty. And on the other side are those driven by the values of tyranny and extremism—the right of a self-appointed few to impose their fanatical views on all the rest.[53]

Certainly, terrorists who massacre innocents are fanatics, and the caliphate that bin Laden's acolytes would establish would be tyrannical. But if the enemy were simply a cabal of terrorists, hell-bent on establishing a tyranny, how is it that they are on the verge of expelling us from Iraq and perhaps Afghanistan? If President Bush has properly defined the ideological struggle, why is it that we appear to be losing?

Answer: It is not so simple as our president presents it. The goals of bin Laden, the insurgents in Iraq, and the Taliban are not so watery and abstract as those of Mr. Bush. The goals of those we fight are concrete, understandable, realizable, and appealing to millions.

In his declaration of war on the United States, bin Laden listed three war aims: Expel U.S. forces from the sacred soil of Saudi Arabia; stop the persecution of Iraqis through U.S.-U.N. sanctions; end the Israeli repression and dispossession of the Palestinian people.

Not only do these goals have broad appeal, bin Laden has achieved partial victory in the first. After 9/11, U.S. forces were pulled out of Saudi Arabia. And while Bush calls this an ideological struggle, a war of ideas, the enemy has allied himself with some historically powerful ideas.

As did Mao and Ho Chi Minh, our enemy has captured the flag of nationalism. That is, we fight to get your soldiers off our land! We fight to end your dominance of our governments! We fight to rule ourselves!

Get out of our country! Was this not the war aim of the boys and men at Lexington, Concord Bridge, Saratoga, and Yorktown?

More important, while Bush's crusade for global democracy is rooted in ideology, ersatz religion, our enemy has rooted his cause in a 1,400-year-old authentic religion that has 1.2 billion adherents, has survived invasions and occupations, and is once again growing in militancy and converts.

Our enemy, be they Shia, Sunni, or Taliban, claims to be fighting for a rule of law, sharia, sanctioned by the Koran, and for a form of government the Prophet mandates for Islamic peoples—not some secular-liberal and permissive democracy.

As for the tactics the enemy uses, decent Muslims the world over are said to be growing disgusted with the slaughter by suicide bombers of innocent men, women, and children. But was terror not the tactic the French maquis and Italian partisans used on the Germans and their collaborators? Was this not the way Israelis expelled the British, Algerians expelled the French, Afghans expelled the Soviets, the African National Congress overthrew apartheid, and Hezbollah drove the Israeli Defense Forces out of Lebanon? Clausewitz would understand: Terrorism is the extension of Islamist politics by other means.

State of the Union 2007

In his 2007 State of the Union address, a chastened George Bush, having lost both houses of Congress, facing possible defeat in Iraq, sought to defend his war again in terms of the ideology whose evangelist he had become: "This war," he said, "is a decisive ideological struggle. . . . To prevail, we must remove the conditions that inspire blind hatred and drove 19 men to get onto airplanes and to come and kill us."[54]

A lack of freedom and social progress in their home countries drove the murderers of 9/11, the president seemed to be saying. Yet as Michael Lind and Peter Burger relate, this is the "myth of deprivation." Members of Al Qaeda "are not the dispossessed, but the empowered. . . . Many studied for high-end careers in medicine and engineering at universities, rather than at some dirt-poor madrassa."[55]

Of seventy-nine known terrorists who carried out the 1993 attack on the World Trade Center, the embassy bombings in Kenya and Tanzania, 9/11, the Bali bombing that killed two hundred Western tourists, and the London subway and bus bombings, 54 percent had attended college, compared to 52 percent of Americans. One-fourth had studied at elite colleges in the United States and Europe, a mark of privilege in the Middle East.

Of the first eight suspects apprehended in the car bombings in London and Glasgow in July 2007, six were doctors—from Iraq, Jordan, Lebanon, and India. A seventh was a medical student.[56] "People often assume that terrorists are poor, disadvantaged people who are brain-washed or need the money. But the ones who actually perpetrate violence without handlers and manipulation are highly intelligent by necessity," said Magnus Ranstorp, a terrorism expert at the Swedish National Defense College. "It is only the smart ones who will survive security pressures in a subversive existence."[57]

In his *Financial Times* series on "Al-Qaeda Recruitment," Stephen Fidler contradicts Bush: "Neither is social deprivation a factor," he writes.[58] A 2004 survey by ex-CIA officer Mark Sageman "showed more than 70 percent of jihadis were from middle or upper class backgrounds. More than 40 percent were like the group allegedly behind last week's [July 2007] attacks in the UK, in the professions: teachers, lawyers and doctors."[59]

Muhammad Atta and his men were neither poor nor repressed, and they plotted mass murder in the richest and freest countries on earth. What motivated them? Hate. If we wish to remove the conditions that caused 9/11, we must remove our forces from the Middle East. For as long as we are seen as imperial occupiers or overlords over there, they will come over here to kill us. Terrorism is the price of empire. If we do not wish to pay it, we must give up the empire.

Every survey of Islamic peoples reveals that they bear a deep resentment of U.S. domination and our one-sided support of Israel. Pace President Bush, intervention is not the solution. Intervention is the problem. Our huge footprint on the sacred soil of Saudi Arabia led straight to 9/11.

What motivates terrorists? "In a word, humiliation," write Burger and Lind. As Hitler and the Nazis were motivated by the humiliation of seeing Germany defeated, disarmed, divided, dishonored, dismembered, "Bin Laden sees the Sykes-Picot Agreement [the British-French carving up of the Ottoman Empire] as the beginning of Arab humiliation."

> For bin Laden, the Sykes-Picot Agreement, like the Versailles agreement for Hitler, is a humiliation that must be avenged and reversed: "We still suffer from the injuries inflicted by . . . the Sykes-Picot Agreement between Britain and France which divided the Muslim world into fragments," he said.[60]

"What every terrorist fears most is human freedom—societies where men and women make their own choices," said President Bush in that 2007 State of the Union address. Very American. And very mistaken. Terrorists detest our societies; they do not

fear them. Terrorists flourish in them. The suicide bombers of 9/11, Madrid, and London all plotted in free societies. From Italy's Red Brigades, who murdered Aldo Moro, to the Baader-Meinhoff Gang that tried to kill Al Haig, to the Basque ETA, free societies are where terrorists do their most effective work. Stalin's Russia, Hitler's Reich, Saddam's Iraq had no serious trouble with terrorists.

"Free people are not drawn to violent and malignant ideologies," said the president.

Why then did 70 million free Germans, under the most democratic government they had ever known, the Weimar Republic, give nearly half their votes to Nazis and Communists in the 1930s? In a 1935 plebiscite, under the auspices of the League of Nations, the Saar voted nine to one to return to a Reich ruled by Hitler. In 1938, the year of *Anschluss* and Munich, Hitler was *Time's* Man of the Year, far more popular than a floundering FDR, who lost seventy-one Democratic seats in the House. Were the Italian people "not drawn" to Mussolini and fascism from 1922 to 1941? Did they not prefer Il Duce to the republic he overturned?

If free people are not drawn to malignant ideologies, why did the free peoples of Latin America vote into power leftist demagogues Hugo Chavez in Venezuela, Evo Morales in Bolivia, Daniel Ortega in Nicaragua, and Rafael Correa in Ecuador, and come close to electing their comrades Ollanta Humala in Peru and López Obrador in Mexico? In the free elections Bush had demanded of Egypt, Lebanon, Palestine, and Iraq, the winners were the Muslim Brotherhood, Hezbollah, Hamas, and Moqtada al-Sadr. If a secret ballot were held in the Middle East on the proposition—America out and Israel into the sea—how does the president think it would come out?

In the 1960s, some of the most privileged young in the freest nation on earth joined terrorist cells of the Weathermen to murder fellow Americans. In the nineteenth and early twentieth centuries, anarchists selected for assassination leaders of the democracies—like President William McKinley.

"The great question of our day is whether America will help men and women in the Middle East to build free societies," said President Bush.

But if we bleed America trying to give the men and women of the Middle East full freedom to choose the society they wish to live in, what do we do if they choose a society where sharia is law? What do we do if they choose, as they have in Iran, Lebanon, and Palestine, leaders and legislators committed to war with Israel? What, other than ideology, persuades George Bush that people the world over want what he wants?

Indeed, it is our friends in Saudi Arabia, Jordan, Egypt, Morocco, the Gulf states, and Israel who seem the most apprehensive about any more free elections among the Arab masses. The Islamists appear to welcome them—and to succeed in them.

Should U.S. soldiers die for democracy in the Islamic world when democracy may produce victory for the political progeny of the Muslim Brotherhood? Is that worth the lives of America's young?

This is the heart of the war we are in. Americans believe in freedom first. Muslims believe in Islam first. We decide for us. Do we also decide for them? Perhaps the best advice we can give our friends in the Middle East is the advice Byron gave the Greeks chafing under Ottoman rule: "[K]now ye not, Who would be free, themselves must strike the blow?"

George Bush seems fated to go down in history like Wilson, a failed and tragic figure. After the 9/11 attack, he tried to do the right thing for the right reason. But between September 11 and his axis-of-evil speech in 2002, he embraced an ideology based on a misreading of reality and an ignorance of history. It drove him straight into the greatest blunder of his presidency—and denied him the sight to see his way back home.

The Democracy Worshiper

Of the Bourbons, restored to the throne after the Revolution, the guillotining of Louis XVI, and the Napoleonic interlude, Talleyrand said, they had "learned nothing and forgotten nothing."

Unfortunately, so shall it be said of George W. Bush.

In June 2007, at Czermin Palace in Prague, President Bush delivered yet another paean to democracy as the salvation of mankind. The speech came four years after the invasion of Iraq that was to bring the blessings of democracy to Mesopotamia and the Middle East. Yet it could have been given on the eve of that invasion, for it was as though Bush had learned nothing and forgotten nothing. The same phrases and thoughts, contradicted by events, came tumbling out.

Cherry-picking his way through history, Bush began by paying tribute to the founding father of Czech democracy.

"Nine decades ago, Tomas Masaryk proclaimed Czechoslovakia's independence based on the 'ideals of democracy.'"

Well, that may be what Masaryk said, but it is not exactly what he did. In 1918, he indeed proclaimed the independence of Czechoslovakia, which was confirmed by the Allies at Paris. But inside the new Czechoslovakia, built on the "ideals of democracy," were 3 million dissident Germans who had wished to remain with Austria and half a million Hungarians who wished to remain with Hungary. Many Catholic Slovaks had wanted to stay with predominantly Catholic Hungary. Against their will, all had been consigned to the custody of Masaryk's Czech-dominated nation.

Query for President Bush? If 3 million Germans were put under alien rule without their consent and against their will, and wished to exercise their right of self-determination as preached by Wilson, did they not have a right to secede peacefully and join their Germanic kinsmen?

Because that is what Munich was all about.

Between 1938 and 1939, Germans, Slovaks, Poles, Hungarians, and Ruthenes—abetted by Berlin, Warsaw, and Budapest—broke free of the multinational democracy of Tomas Masaryk. Yet, rather than let them secede from Prague, Winston Churchill thought Britain should go to war.

Was Churchill right, or were the Sudeten Germans right?

In 1945, liberated Czechoslovakia solved its dissident German problem by the ethnic cleansing of 3 million German men, women, and children, a crime against humanity President Bush politely passed over in his tribute to Czech democracy.

"Freedom is the design of our Maker and the longing of every soul. . . . Freedom is the dream . . . of every person in every nation in every age."

One wonders: Who writes this, and does the president read it before delivery? Again, did Lenin, Stalin, Hitler, Mussolini, Mao, Fidel, Uncle Ho, and Pol Pot long for freedom in their souls? Did Churchill long for freedom, as he fought to preserve the British Empire and British rule in India?

"Expanding freedom," said Bush, "is the only realistic way to protect our people in the long run." That is yet another way of saying that, if we abandon the Bush crusade for global democracy, we can never be secure.

Has invading Iraq to expand freedom made us more secure? For it has gotten more Americans killed than died on 9/11 and served as the number one recruiting cause for Al Qaeda.

"Governments accountable to their people do not attack each other."

This may come as a surprise to descendants of those who fought for Southern independence from 1861 to 1865. Does Bush think Mr. Lincoln's Union or the Confederate States of America were not "accountable" to their people? Yet 600,000 Americans died in that war between two democratic republics.

Half a century before our Civil War, the United States declared war on the most democratic nation in Europe and tried to seize Canada. To teach the republic a lesson, the mother country sent an army over here to burn down the symbols of our democracy, the White House and the Capitol.

Turkey and Kurdistan are democratic, but appear ready to have a go at each other. The summer before Bush spoke in Prague, democratic Israel bombed democratic Lebanon of the Cedar Revolution for five weeks, killing a thousand Lebanese and rendering ten thousand homeless.

Had Bush forgotten? He supported that war.

In 1914, the most democratic nations in Europe plunged into the bloodiest war in history. Free people in European capitals cheered lustily as their sons marched off to die.

Democratic peoples are not immune to blood lust.

"Young people who can disagree openly with their leaders are less likely to adopt violent ideologies."

Again, Weimar was the freest government Germany ever had. Yet Nazis and Communists battled constantly, and in 1932 more than 40 percent of all Germans voted Nazi or Communist.

Puerto Rican terrorists tried to kill Truman, shot up the House of Representatives, and dynamited Fraunces Tavern in New York in the freest country on earth.

"[E]very time people are given a choice, they choose freedom."

Had Bush forgotten that in 2005 the Iranian people freely chose Mahmoud Ahmadinejad? Had he forgotten the electoral victories in 2006 of the Muslim Brotherhood, Hezbollah, Hamas, and, in Latin America, of anti-American radicals in Venezuela, Bolivia, Ecuador, and Nicaragua?

What explains this "divinization of democracy," this unshakable faith that the masses will do the right thing?[61] Rejecting that idea, harboring no such faith, the Founding Fathers created a republic. For, as John Adams warned, "the people have waged everlasting war against the rights of men. . . . The numbers of men in all ages have preferred ease, slumber and good cheer to liberty. . . . The multitude must be kept in check."[62]

It is one thing to believe democracy a superior form of government. It is another to worship it or ascribe to it attributes and powers that God alone possesses. This is idolatry. This is ideology.

Democracy means rule by the people And the people can be as bloodthirsty and corrupt as tyrants and kings. In 1901, a twenty-six-year-old MP warned Parliament, "Democracy is more vindictive than Cabinets. The wars of peoples will be more terrible than those of kings." Was Churchill wrong about the character of the masses or the coming century?

In the twenty-first century, Moscow, Beijing, and Hanoi are all more free than they were under the monsters of yesteryear. Yet Lenin, Mao, and Ho, mass murderers all, still lie in state in their respective capitals.

Before we divinize democracy, let us recall what British historian A. J. P. Taylor concluded, two decades after Hitler's suicide in his Berlin bunker:

> Though the National Socialists did not win a majority of votes at any free election, they won more votes than any other German party had ever done. A few months after coming to power, they received practically all the votes recorded. . . . No dictatorship has been so ardently desired or so firmly supported by so many people as Hitler's was in Germany.[63]

Democracy is not enough. Democracy is but a wineskin into which may be poured wine or poison. As T. S. Eliot warned, democracy does not contain within itself the requisites for a good or moral society.

> The term "democracy," as I have said again and again, does not contain enough positive content to stand alone against the forces you dislike—it can easily be transformed by them. If you will not have God (and He is a jealous God), you should pay your respects to Hitler and Stalin.[64]

John Adams expressed a similar sentiment: "Our Constitution was written for a religious and virtuous people; it will serve no other."

Burke anticipated Eliot when he wrote to his constituents in Bristol: "Believe me, it is a great truth, that there never was, for any long time . . . a mean, sluggish, careless people that ever had a good government of any kind."[65] It is not the system that determines the character of a country, but the character of a people that determines the kind of country it will be. On reading of Sunni insurgents, Shia militias, and Al Qaeda suicide bombers, one recalls Burke's words:

> Men are qualified for civil liberty in exact proportion to their disposition to put moral chains on their own appetites. . . . Society cannot exist unless a controlling power upon will and appetite be placed somewhere, and the less of it there is within, the more there is without. It is ordained in the eternal constitution of things that men of intemperate minds cannot be free. Their passions forge their fetters.[66]

The character of Islamic peoples, formed by their history, beliefs, and faith, has, for centuries, called authoritarians to power. If we dethrone their tyrants, dismantle their states, and disband their armies, when we depart, the character of the people will recreate the institutions we have torn down. Human beings are not clean sheets of paper on which idealistic Wilsonian Man can write his blueprints for a democratic society. As Kipling wrote,

> *East is East, and West is West, and never the twain shall meet,*
> *Till Earth and Sky stand presently at God's great Judgment Seat.*

In Prague, Bush explained why Communism was a god that failed.

"The communists had an imperial ideology that claimed to know the directions of history. But in the end it was overpowered by ordinary people who wanted to live their lives, and worship their God, and speak the truth to their children."

Replace "communists" with "democratists," and one is close to the truth as to why Bush's world democratic revolution failed.

The Bush Vision

When George H. W. Bush ran for president in 1988, he was said to suffer in comparison to Ronald Reagan, as he lacked what he himself called "the vision thing." He seemed not to have a clear and compelling concept of where he wished to lead America, that would inform his decisions and set the course for the country. His son, too, when he came to office, appeared to lack a polestar, a philosophy, a vision of the future toward which he would direct the energies and resources of the nation.

After 9/11, that changed radically. In the half-dozen speeches cited above, Bush spoke to how he saw the world and the war we are in.

In Bush's ideology, we are in a struggle of light and darkness for the future of mankind that must end in the triumph of evil—or the end of evil in our world. In that struggle, we are on God's side, fulfilling Heaven's plan for humanity. Yet, we cannot rely on our own courage and arms to save us. For our freedom and liberty are tied to the freedom and liberty of all peoples. Either we all emerge victorious, or we all go down together.

Therefore, America asserts the right to intrude in the politics of all nations with the "ultimate goal of ending tyranny on earth." This is history's climactic battle in the advance of liberty that began with the American Revolution, triumphed on this continent in our Civil War, and was led into the world by Woodrow Wilson. But where Wilson failed, George W. Bush catches the falling flag and carries it forward to triumph.

Let it be said: This is Manichaean. This is messianic. This is utopian. Investing the blood of our sons and treasure of our nation in pursuit of this vision will bleed, bankrupt, and break this republic in endless crusades and interminable wars. Unless this ideology is purged from power, it will bring an end to the republic. No nation, no matter how great, powerful, or rich, can sustain so apocalyptic and global a struggle.

4

Imperial Overstretch

The commonest error in politics is sticking to
the carcass of dead policies.

—LORD SALISBURY[1]

In 1943, Walter Lippmann wrote *U.S. Foreign Policy: Shield of the Republic.* The thesis of his small book was that foreign policy "consists in bringing into balance, with a comfortable surplus of power in reserve, the nation's commitments and the nation's power. The constant preoccupation of the true statesman is to achieve and maintain this balance."[2]

By Lippmann's accounting, a nation's liabilities were its commitments to defend its vital interests and allies. Its assets were its land, sea, and air forces and the military forces of those allies. If a nation's assets could not cover its liabilities, its foreign policy was bankrupt.

Since the Spanish-American War, Lippmann argued, U.S. foreign policy had been bankrupt. We had annexed the Philippines, seven thousand miles from San Francisco, but permitted Germany, then Japan at Versailles, to occupy the crucial islands between Honolulu and Manila. By the Washington Naval Agreement of 1922, we cut our fleets, ceded naval superiority in the western Pacific to Japan, and agreed to no further fortification of Guam or Manila.

The bankruptcy was exposed on December 7, 1941. The Japanese struck Pearl Harbor, smashed the Pacific fleet, then overran the Philippines, Malaya, Singapore, the Dutch East Indies, and closed the Burma Road. Because we failed to maintain the strategic assets in the Pacific to defend our possessions, Manila was occupied, Corregidor fell, the Bataan Death March commenced, and tens of thousands of Americans endured barbaric captivity as prisoners of the Japanese. Of those forty years during which America bristled at Japan, while neglecting to maintain the forces to back her bellicosity, Lippmann wrote, "At the zenith of our commitments, we were at the nadir of our precautions. Eventually, there is a reckoning for nations, as for individuals, who have obligations that are not covered by their resources."[3]

By Lippmann's definition, U.S. foreign policy is bankrupt. Since the end of the Cold War, the United States has expanded its liabilities, while drawing down the assets required to cover those liabilities. The world has awakened to the bankruptcy of U.S. foreign policy, as it has been exposed in Afghanistan and Iraq.

Consider the asset side of the national security balance sheet.

It remains awesome. America spends more on defense than the next ten nations combined. The U.S. Navy deploys 12 carrier battle groups and 278 warships, giving us a dominance of the sea-lanes and oceans greater than the Royal Navy in Victoria's time, when it was the policy of Lord Salisbury that British fleets would always be larger than the combined fleets of the next two greatest naval powers. Today's U.S. Navy has no rival.

The U.S. Air Force is the world's finest, with thousands of fifth-generation fighters and a strategic bomber force that, with air-to-air refueling, can, with B-52s, B-1s, or B-2 Stealth bombers, equipped with cruise missiles, deliver precision-guided munitions on any nation that might attack the United States.

The U.S. Army and Marine Corps, as we saw in Desert Storm and Operation Iraqi Freedom, maintain a superiority in mobility, armor, and firepower that make them almost invincible on a battlefield.

U.S. military technology is generations ahead of any other nation's. Our nuclear arsenal enables this country to reduce enemy nations in hours to the desolation of Germany and Japan in 1945. With such military assets, how can it be said U.S. foreign policy is bankrupt? To answer this question, we must look at the other side of the balance sheet—the liabilities, the commitments we have made to go to war on behalf of other nations.

Origins of the American Empire

In 1800, John Adams negotiated an end to the undeclared U.S. naval war with France. The agreement terminated our Revolutionary War alliance. Adams regarded that peace and the dissolution of the French alliance as the foremost achievement of his presidency, for this comported perfectly with the wisdom of the great man he had succeeded.

In his Farewell Address of 1796, the greatest state paper in American history, Washington had laid down the first commandment of U.S. foreign policy. "The great rule of conduct for us, in regard to foreign nations, is in extending our commercial relations to have with them as little *political* connection as possible." Pointing to America's distance from Europe, Washington implored us,

> Why forego the advantages of so peculiar a situation? Why quit our own to stand upon foreign ground? Why, by interweaving our destiny with that of any part of Europe, entangle our peace and prosperity in the toils of European Ambition, Rivalship, Interest, Humour, or Caprice?
>
> 'Tis our true policy to steer clear of permanent Alliances, with any portion of the foreign world. So far . . . as we are now at liberty to do it.[4]

Washington released his Farewell Address in September 1796 in order to defeat Jefferson and elect Adams. Jefferson was a zealot of revolutionary France; Washington wished to keep clear of European intrigues and wars. Adams would cause the Farewell Address to be read out in Congress every year until our own time. By the time of his own presidency in 1801, Jefferson's ardor for France, now ruled by the emperor Napoleon, had cooled. In his first inaugural address, Jefferson himself reaffirmed "the great rule," declaring it to be national policy to steer clear of "entangling alliances."

The great rule was the wisest counsel left to his countrymen by the nation's first statesman. It was counsel bred of years as a soldier, first in the British army fighting the French, then leading the American army against the mother country, then as a president who had seen his countrymen at one another's throats over a British-French war.

Washington knew his nation had the potential to be the greatest on earth. He also knew America needed generations of peace to grow to her natural size and strength. The father of his country deemed it essential that young America stay out of old Europe's wars.

On only three occasions in the century and a half that followed would the United States go to war with a European power.

In June 1812 the United States declared war on Great Britain as Napoleon was about to invade Russia. Though the war ended in 1815 with a peace that restored the status quo ante—neither nation gained territory—it was, for the United States, as Wellington would say of Waterloo, a "damn near run thing." Americans were routed in their campaigns to take Canada. The White House, the Capitol, and the Treasury were burned by British troops. New England was on the verge of secession in 1814. Were it not for Britain's desire to end the war in America to concentrate upon Napoleon, and Jackson's victory at New Orleans, the republic might have been torn apart.

In 1898 we declared war on Spain, occupied Cuba and Puerto Rico, and annexed the Philippines, igniting a four-year war with Filipinos who were fighting for their independence. Thus did America become an empire, acquiring colonies she soon did not want, without taking the measures necessary to defend them against an avaricious enemy.

In 1916, Wilson narrowly won reelection on the slogan, "He Kept Us Out of War." The following April he led us into the world war. Bowing to the great rule, however, Wilson specified that America would fight as an "associate," not an "allied power." Further, it strained credulity to contend that the British, French,

Russian, and Japanese empires were fighting beside us—to "make the world safe for democracy."

When Wilson brought home from Versailles a treaty that trampled upon virtually all of his Fourteen Points and committed the United States to help enforce an unjust and unsustainable peace, the Senate rejected it—and with it membership in the League of Nations. Had the Senate approved the Versailles Treaty, America might have been embroiled in all the wars the treaties signed at Paris—Versailles, St. Germain, Trianon, Neuilly, and Sèvres—and such secret Allied deals as Sykes-Picot had scheduled for future decades.

When Americans came to realize that 116,000 doughboys had died, and America had reaped a harvest of ingratitude and worthless debt from the Allies, while the British Empire had annexed yet another million square miles, the nation decided Washington had been right: Stay out of Europe's wars.

Thus, when Hitler invaded Poland, the United States was outside the alliance that drew Britain and France into the most ruinous war in history. That war ended with Europe's democracies bled and broken, their empires collapsing, and their continent divided between triumphant Stalinism and beleaguered freedom.

Because America stayed out of the European alliances of 1914 and 1939, she was the last great power to enter the world wars, and suffered least. U.S. forces saw heavy combat for only the final six months of World War I. While the United States was immediately engaged in combat with Japan in the Pacific after Pearl Harbor, not until November 1942, three years after Hitler occupied Poland, did U.S. forces go ashore in North Africa. Not until mid-1943 did U.S. forces cross the Mediterranean to Sicily. D-day in Normandy, the opening of the Second Front that Stalin had been demanding for three years, did not take place until June 1944, four years after the fall of France and eleven months before the war's end. As America emerged from World War II as the strongest and most secure nation, the counsel of Washington, to steer clear of alliances, had proven wise indeed.

Between 1945 and 1949, however, an unprecedented situation arose.

Stalin had kept his victorious Red Army in Central and Eastern Europe, vassalizing a dozen nations. He dropped an iron curtain across Europe, exploded an atom bomb, and aided Mao in overrunning China. The world's largest nation had turned from a wartime ally of the United States into a Cold War enemy. After a national debate, Americans concluded we must create an alliance to defend Western Europe, or the Red Army might overrun the continent to the Channel and shift the world balance of power against us.

Nor did this historic decision, to create a defensive alliance, violate the great rule. Not only had Washington welcomed the 1778 alliance with France, he had counseled us in his Farewell Address, "Taking care always to keep ourselves by suitable establishments on a respectable defensive posture, we may safely trust to temporary alliances for extraordinary emergencies."[5]

The year 1949 was an "extraordinary emergency." Thus we formed the North Atlantic Treaty Organization. The twelve members were the United States, Canada, Iceland, Britain, and eight nations on the continent: Norway, Denmark, Portugal, France, Holland, Belgium, Luxembourg, and Italy. Under

Article V, an attack on any member was to be "considered an attack against them all." In 1952, Greece and Turkey joined. In 1955, West Germany became a formal member. A cordon of free nations had been placed around the periphery of Stalin's empire and an American tradition since 1778 came to an end.

The first Supreme Allied Commander of NATO, General Eisenhower, said U.S. troops would remain in Europe at most ten years, until Europe got back on its feet. In 1961, Ike urged John F. Kennedy to start bringing the hundreds of thousands of U.S. troops home, lest their continued presence induce a permanent dependency. His advice was not taken. And Europe became an American dependency, unwilling to assume the responsibility for its own defense.

Commitments Without End

NATO was Truman's great achievement. Secretary of State John Foster Dulles sought to replicate it, first, with the Central Treaty Organization, which brought Britain, Iraq, Iran, and Pakistan into an alliance the United States promoted but did not join. Then came the Manila Pact of 1954 and SEATO, the Southeast Asia Treaty Organization, which brought the United States, Britain, and France into an alliance with Australia, New Zealand, the Philippines, Thailand, and Pakistan. East Pakistan (now Bangladesh) was near Southeast Asia and Pakistan was seen as the link between SEATO and CENTO.

NATO proved "the most successful alliance in history," but CENTO and SEATO did not endure. The former collapsed when Iraq's king Feisal was assassinated in 1958, his body dragged through the streets of Baghdad. Iraq pulled out. SEATO failed when France and the Philippines, and, later, Pakistan, prevented a unanimous vote to support the U.S. war in Vietnam. Unlike NATO, SEATO required unanimity to act.

In that same decade, the United States negotiated a series of mutual security pacts that would get Dulles ridiculed for "Pactomania."

South Korea. After the Korean War armistice in 1953, the United States negotiated a mutual security treaty with Seoul in which

> [e]ach party recognizes that an armed attack in the Pacific area on either of the parties in territories now under their respective administrative control . . . would be dangerous to its own peace and safety and declares that it would act to meet the common danger in accordance with its constitutional processes.[6]

The Korean War has been over for half a century. The Chinese left the North fifty years ago. Yet 30,000 U.S. troops remain. Should a new war erupt, Americans would be the first to die under fire from the 11,000 artillery pieces massed north of the DMZ, and any nuclear weapon Pyongyang might use would likely fall on Americans.

Japan. The U.S.-Japan Mutual Security Treaty of 1960 obligates us to treat an armed attack against any territories "under the administration of Japan" as "dangerous to [the U.S.'s] own peace and safety."[7] This would appear to cover the Senkaku Islands, also claimed by China. Japan, however, is not obligated to treat an attack on the United States or its possessions as requiring military action. Sixty-two years after defeat in World War II, Japan, with a $4.5 trillion economy, the world's second largest, spends 1 percent of its GDP on defense and relies on America to deal with Beijing or Pyongyang.

Taiwan. In 1979, Jimmy Carter abrogated the 1954 U.S. security treaty. But under the Taiwan Relations Act of 1979, the United States is obligated "to consider any effort to determine the future of Taiwan by other than peaceful means, including by boycotts or embargoes, a threat to the peace and security of the Western Pacific area and of grave concern to the United States."[8] America almost clashed with China over Taiwan in 1996, and George W. Bush declared he would do "whatever it takes" to defend Taiwan. Yet since the Shanghai Communiqué of 1972, negotiated by Nixon's National Security Adviser Henry Kissinger, the United States has regarded Taiwan as "a part of China."

The Philippines. Under the U.S. mutual security treaty of 1951, any attack on this island nation is declared dangerous to our peace and security.

Though Manila expelled U.S. forces from Clark Air Force Base and Subic Bay, we remain duty-bound to defend her.[9]

Thailand and Pakistan. Under Article IV of the Manila Pact that established SEATO, in the event of an armed attack on any member, each member would "act to meet the common danger in accordance with its constitutional processes."[10] Charles de Gaulle withdrew from military cooperation in 1967. Britain refused to assist the United States in Vietnam. In 1972, Pakistan withdrew. And SEATO was dissolved in 1977. The Manila Pact, however, remains in force and, together with a 1962 U.S.-Thailand communiqué, constitutes the U.S. commitment to Thailand, which remains a treaty ally.

Australia. Under the ANZUS Pact of 1951, the United States is obligated to come to the defense of Australia and New Zealand, but they have no obligation to come to the defense of the United States. During the last crisis in the Taiwan Strait, Australia made clear it would take no part in a war over the island. In 1985, a Labour Government in New Zealand refused permission to American warships to enter Wellington harbor, unless Washington stipulated no nuclear weapons were aboard. The United States declared that New Zealand had decided to "renege on an essential element of ANZUS participation" and suspended its security obligations. The ANZUS Pact with Australia remains in force. Each year, the two nations meet for formal talks at the foreign and defense ministerial level.[11]

Latin America. Under the 1947 Rio Treaty, the United States is obliged to come to the aid of any country in the western hemisphere that comes under attack, except Cuba. Havana withdrew in 1960. By Article 3, signatories "agree that an armed attack by any States against an American State shall be considered as an attack against all the American States," and each signatory "undertakes to assist in meeting the attack."[12]

The United States is duty-bound to defend Argentina, the Bahamas, Belize, Bolivia, Brazil, Chile, Colombia, Costa Rica, the Dominican Republic, Ecuador, El Salvador, Guatemala, Haiti, Honduras, Mexico, Nicaragua, Panama, Paraguay, Peru, Trinidad and Tobago, Uruguay, and Venezuela. Article 4 adds: "This article defines the region to which the treaty refers, which extends from the North Pole to the South Pole, and includes Canada, Alaska, the Aleutians, Greenland, the Falklands, the South Orkneys, and Antarctica."[13]

The Middle East. The United States has no formal alliance with Israel, but it is understood that, in a war threatening Israel's survival, the United States would come to her defense. When the Soviet Union seemed about to intervene on the side of Egypt and Syria in the Yom Kippur War of 1973, President Nixon ordered U.S. nuclear forces on alert.

U.S. troops today sit on Mount Sinai to monitor the Israeli-Egyptian peace. There has been talk that, in return for recognition of a Palestinian state, Israel may be given a security guarantee by the United States, to stand with her in any Israeli-Arab war, of which there have been six. Some have suggested that, if Israel returns the Golan Heights to Syria, the United States station its own forces on the heights to ensure Israel's security.

The Persian Gulf. After the Gulf War of 1991, America adopted a policy of "dual containment" of Iran and Iraq. With the 2003 invasion and the "surge" of 2007, U.S. forces in Iraq numbered 160,000. Thousands more are stationed in Kuwait and aboard warships in the Gulf and the Arabian Sea that make routine visits to the U.S. bases in the United Arab Emirates, Oman, and Bahrain.

Bearbaiting

In 1988, Ronald Reagan, who famously branded the Soviet Union "an evil empire," was striding through Red Square arm in arm with Mikhail Gorbachev. Russians were happily pounding both men on the back. They had just signed the greatest arms reduction treaty in history—eliminating all Soviet SS-20s targeted on Europe in return for U.S. removal of the Pershing and cruise missiles President Reagan had deployed in Europe.

"Bliss was it in that dawn to be alive, But to be young was very heaven!" wrote Wordsworth of his first hearing of the fall of the Bastille. Many Americans felt that way then. The Cold War that we had believed would last our lifetimes, that had brought death to 100,000 of our own in Korea and Vietnam, was coming to a sudden end.

Within three years, the Wall had come down, the Communist regimes of Eastern Europe had been swept away, Germany was reunited, the Red Army had gone home, the Soviet Empire had vanished, the Soviet Union had disintegrated. The Baltic republics were free. Ukraine was free. Georgia and Armenia were free.

How did America respond to these miraculous events? Under Bill Clinton and George W. Bush, America began to treat Russia as a defeated nation whose interests did not matter and whose opinions could be ignored.

- Instead of bringing her into NATO and the European Union, we froze her out of both. In violation of an understanding with Gorbachev, we began to move NATO into the front yard and onto the side porch of Russia. Six former Warsaw Pact nations—East Germany, Poland, Hungary, Romania, Bulgaria, and Czechoslovakia—and three former Soviet republics—Lithuania, Latvia, and Estonia—were brought into a U.S. alliance whose raison d'etre was the containment of Moscow, if necessary by war.

  By 2007, U.S. hawks were pushing to bring Ukraine and Georgia into NATO. This would have committed the United States to war with a nuclear-armed Russia over who has sovereignty over the Crimea and whether

South Ossetia and Abkhazia may secede from Georgia, birthplace of Stalin.

- After Moscow gave a green light to Bush to use the former Soviet republics of Central Asia to base U.S. forces for the Afghan war, we decided to seek permanent bases. To throw us out, Russia and China have united in a Shanghai Cooperation Organization that includes Kazakhstan, Kyrgyzstan, Tajikistan, and Uzbekistan, with India, Iran, Pakistan, Mongolia as observers. Russian-Chinese joint military exercises were held in 2007.

- President Bush junked the ABM treaty Nixon and Brezhnev signed and intends to plant antimissile missiles in Poland and radars in the Czech Republic. We say they are to defend against Iran. Russia responds that Iran has no ICBMs, no nuclear warheads, no nuclear weapons.

- America colluded with Azerbaijan and Georgia to build a Baku-Tiblisi-Ceyhan pipeline to carry Caspian Sea oil across the Caucasus to the Black Sea and Turkey, bypassing Russia.

- The United States bombed Serbia for seventy-eight days to punish that country for fighting to hold its province of Kosovo, which Albanian Muslims were tearing away. Recaptured from the Ottoman Turks in 1912, Kosovo has long been regarded as "the cradle of the Serbian nation." And Orthodox Russia had long seen herself as protectress of the Balkan Christians.

- After helping dump the Milosevic regime in Belgrade, our Neocomintern—the National Endowment for Democracy, Freedom House, and affiliated fronts—helped oust pro-Russian governments in Ukraine and Georgia and install pro-American ones.

- The United States has hectored Russia constantly for backsliding on democracy, though compared to Beijing, Moscow is Montpelier, Vermont.
- When Estonia removed the statue of a Russian soldier and the remains of fourteen Red Army veterans of World War II from the heart of Tallinn to a suburban cemetery, the perceived insult ignited anti-Estonian demonstrations in Russia. Bush invited the Estonian president to the White House.

Even Alexander Solzhenitzyn, to whom America gave sanctuary in the Cold War, accuses the United States of trying to encircle and weaken Russia.

"Instead of treating Russia magnanimously," writes Gordon Hahn of the Monterey Institute for International Studies, "the West declared victory."

The cost of NATO expansion is that Russia has been lost in the medium term—and perhaps in the long term as well—as a powerful committed democracy and Western ally. Moreover, the West has pushed Russia closer to China and Iran. If these are the costs of NATO expansion, what are the advantages?[14]

By February 2007, at the Munich Security Conference, a simmering Vladimir Putin exploded:

What is a unipolar world? No matter how we beautify this term, it means one single center of power, one single center

123

of force and one single master. One state and, of course, first and foremost the United States, has overstepped its national borders in every way. . . . Well, who likes this? Who is happy about this?[15]

Can we not appreciate the sensibilities of Russia, which, just two decades ago, was a superpower rival, but which has since lost an empire, a third of her territory, and half her population?

How would the Union have reacted if, after the Confederacy won its independence, the Royal Navy was establishing bases in Charleston and New Orleans, the British army was training troops in Tennessee, and the South had entered a military alliance with Great Britain? Have we forgotten that Gen. U. S. Grant sent 50,000 U.S. troops to the Mexican border and Secretary of State William Seward warned Napoleon III to get French troops out of Mexico, or we would invade and throw them out? Can we not understand how other great nations might want their own Monroe Doctrine?

Why are Russia's political arrangements any of our business? If we don't like how Putin treats Mikhail Khorokovsky and Boris Berezovsky and the oligarchs who robbed Russia blind in the 1990s, perhaps Putin does not like how we treated Martha Stewart.

Putin reacted as any Russian nationalist would have. He renounced the Treaty on Conventional Armed Forces in Europe that had pulled Russian armored divisions back to the Urals. He began to deploy new land- and sea-based missiles. He sent bombers on patrols in the Atlantic and Arctic as in Cold War days. He is redeploying Russian naval forces in the Mediterranean and rebuilding relations with Syria and Iran. He made a dash into the Arctic to claim the resources under the North Pole for Russia.

Truman is often condemned for starting the Cold War. This is an historic libel. The Cold War was Stalin's work. But if Truman did not start the first Cold War, George W. Bush and his neoconservative accomplices have a powerful claim to having started the second.

Outposts of Empire

In his 2002 *National Security Strategy* President Bush declared, "It is time to reaffirm the essential role of American military strength." But that *NSS* did more than reaffirm. It was a leap forward toward the militarization of U.S. foreign policy. In it the president detailed two new uses for U.S. military power: preemptive strikes on "rogue states" seeking weapons of mass destruction, and preventive wars on nations that might seek military power sufficient to challenge U.S. supremacy in any region of the world.

To back up the new policy, the United States added new bases to its worldwide inventory in Uzbekistan, Pakistan, Qatar, and Djibouti. These are what the Pentagon calls lily pads. From them U.S. forces can deploy to defend friendly regimes. To them U.S. forces can be dispatched to launch preemptive strikes and preventive wars. These new installations, said Paul Wolfowitz, "send a message to everybody, including strategically important countries like Uzbekistan, that we have a capacity to come back in and will come back in—we're not just going to forget about them."[16]

With America adding allies and bases all over the world after its Cold War victory and 9/11, Asia expert and author Chalmers

Johnson (*The Sorrows of Empire*) undertook to inventory U.S. military assets. James Sterngold of the *San Francisco Chronicle* relates what he found:

> Johnson says the Pentagon's calculation that it owns or rents 702 bases in about 130 countries—over and above 6,000 bases in the United States—is a gross underestimate because it fails to include installations in such places as Kosovo and Bosnia, as well as Iraq and Afghanistan, and secret installations in Israel, Australia, and England, among others.[17]

Here are some of the larger commitments of U.S. forces as of 2004.

Iraq	153,000
Germany	75,000
Japan	47,000
South Korea	37,000
Italy	13,000
England	12,000
Afghanistan	11,000
Kosovo	5,000
Bosnia	3,000
Qatar	1,600
Djibouti	1,600
Philippines	1,000

"According to the Pentagon's Manpower Report," writes Sterngold, "before Sept. 11, 2001, there were 255,000 U.S. military personnel in 153 countries. According to GlobalSecurity.org, that number was closer to 350,000, as of early February [2004]."[18] Johnson himself wrote earlier:

> [T]he United States dominates the world through its military power. Due to government secrecy, our citizens are often ignorant of the fact that our garrisons encircle the planet. This vast network of American bases on every continent except Antarctica actually constitutes a new form of empire—an empire of bases with its own geography not likely to be taught in any high school geography class.[19]

While the Pentagon acknowledges the 702 bases abroad, Johnson believes the true number is close to 1,000. For since the end of the Cold War, we have added bases in North Africa, Central Asia, Pakistan and Afghanistan, the Persian Gulf, Balkan peninsula, and Eastern Europe. And we are training government forces in Colombia and Georgia.

The mission of these forces is to fight and win the war on terror. Paradoxically, however, the U.S. military presence on foreign soil is the principal cause of terror. As scholar Robert Pape writes, 95 percent of all acts of terrorism are committed by individuals whose countries are host to Western troops and who see their governments as Western vassals. Osama bin Laden gave the stationing of U.S. troops on the sacred soil of Saudi Arabia as a principal reason for his declaration of war. In his February 2003 testimony to Congress, Wolfowitz "conceded that resentment over the stationing of U.S. forces in Saudi Arabia had been 'Osama bin Laden's principal recruiting device.'"[20] In an interview with Sam Tannehaus for *Vanity Fair* that year, Wolfowitz confided:

> There are a lot of things that are different now, and one that has gone by almost unnoticed—but it's huge—is that by complete mutual agreement between the U.S. and the Saudi government we can now remove almost all of our forces from Saudi Arabia. Their presence there over the last 12 years has been a source of enormous difficulty for a friendly government. It's been a huge recruiting device for al Qaeda.
>
> In fact if you look at bin Laden, one of his principal grievances was the presence of so-called crusader forces on the holy land, Mecca and Medina. I think just lifting that burden from the Saudis is itself going to open the door to other positive things.[21]

That "presence of so-called crusader forces on the holy land, Mecca and Medina," was the probable cause of almost three thousand American deaths on 9/11.

Imperial Overstretch

Between the alliance with France in the Revolutionary War in 1778 and the creation of NATO in 1949, the United States did not enter a formal alliance with any country. Yet we are now treaty-bound to defend sixty nations on five continents, though U.S. forces are half of what they were in the peacetime years of the Cold War.

America has taken on the historic role of Germany in keeping

Russia out of Europe, of the Hapsburg Empire in policing the Balkans, of the British Empire in patrolling the oceans and securing the Gulf, of the Ottoman Empire in maintaining the peace of the Middle East, of the Japanese Empire in defending Korea and containing China, of the Spanish Empire in Latin America. Yet, since 1990, the U.S. Navy and Air Force have been cut almost in half and the army slashed to 507,000 men and women. And that army, tied down in Afghanistan and Iraq, is already stretched close to its limits.

Nothing can destroy this country except the overextension of our resources, said Robert A. Taft. Yet these commitments make the British Empire of Victoria look isolationist. America has passed the point of imperial overstretch. We have crossed the line between republic and empire. Our situation is unsustainable, and retreat inevitable. If we do not shed these commitments now, the American imperium will end as did the French Empire in Algeria, the British Empire in India, and the Soviet Empire in Afghanistan.

Challenges are already being mounted to the Bush Doctrine. Beijing has brushed aside the Bush dictum—that no nation should seek to become a regional or world power rival—by hiking military spending 15 percent a year, threatening Taiwan with 900 missiles, blasting a satellite out of orbit, imperiling the eyes-in-the-sky on which U.S. armed forces depend, and deploying land- and submarine-based ICBMs that can strike the United States from Chinese territory and Chinese waters.

North Korea and Iran have defied Bush warnings not to proceed with nuclear development. Al Qaeda jihadists, Sunni insurgents, and Shiite militias are raising the cost in blood of our commitment to Iraq. There is no end in sight to the war in

Afghanistan. And as the Taliban grow stronger, the resolve of our NATO allies is waning.

Resentful of U.S. meddling in its internal affairs and former republics, and of NATO's move up to her borders, Putin's Russia is reverting to autocracy and colluding with Beijing to expel U.S. power from Central Asia. The heady days of American-Russian amity, when Bill Clinton and Boris Yeltsin dined and drank into the early hours, are history. Moscow is creating its own OPEC, a natural gas cartel to squeeze former republics and remind a gas-dependent Europe that Russia is to be respected. All of which seems to sit well with the Russian people, as Putin in 2007, his two terms ending, enjoyed an approval rating twice that of George W. Bush.

A Need for Retrenchment

"[W]e may safely trust to temporary alliances for extraordinary emergencies," said Washington in his Farewell Address.

The extraordinary emergency of 1949 is over. It ended decades ago. The changes that have taken place in the world since Reagan went home are historic. The Red Army has retreated from Europe. Germany is reunited in freedom. The Soviet Empire has vanished. The Soviet Union has ceased to exist. The Warsaw Pact is history. The Baltic republics and Ukraine are free. China has emerged from Maoist madness. The United States has an ambassador in Hanoi. Only Bolshevik backwaters like North Korea and Cuba remain frozen in time.

As our situation is new, said Lincoln, so we must think and act anew. Yet every alliance, every Cold War commitment, endures. We have not torn up a single trip wire for war laid down in the time of Acheson and Dulles. When the world has changed, why have we not? What is this nostalgia for an era that is over? Why cannot we dissolve alliances created to cope with an enemy who no longer exists? Is America incapable of letting go of the world in which we were born? Was Eisenhower right when he warned of a military-industrial complex that had acquired its own momentum and could not abide an end of the Cold War? Have we become a warfare state?

An Interrupted Debate

In the fall of 1989, before the Berlin Wall fell, this writer was invited by Owen Harries, editor of *The National Interest,* to participate in a symposium. Harries asked each participant to address the question: If the Cold War is ending, what should be the foreign policy of the United States? In "America First—and Second and Third," I wrote:

> If the Cold War is ending, what are the terms of honorable peace that will permit us to go home? Are they not: withdrawal of the Red Army back within its own frontiers; liberation of Central Europe and the Baltic republics; reunification of Germany; and de-Leninization of Moscow, i.e., overthrow of the imperialist party that has prosecuted the Seventy Years War against the West? . . .
>
> The compensating concession we should offer: total withdrawal of U.S. troops from Europe. If Moscow will get out, we will get out. Once the Red Army goes home, the reason for keeping a U.S. army in Europe vanishes.

Forty years after the Marshall Plan, it is time Europe conscripted the soldiers for its own defense.[22]

Jeane Kirkpatrick, a foreign policy voice of neoconservatism, echoed my view. In "A Normal Country in a Normal Time," completed after the Wall had fallen but before Saddam's invasion of Kuwait, she wrote,

A good society is defined not by its foreign policy but by its internal qualities. . . . Foreign policy becomes a major aspect of a society only if its government is expansionist, imperial, aggressive, or when it is threatened by aggression. One of the most important consequences of the half century of war and Cold War has been to give foreign affairs an unnatural importance.[23]

Foreign policy must now take a backseat, Kirkpatrick wrote. "The end of the Cold War frees time, attention and resources to American ends."[24]

In a frontal assault on what has since become neoconservative dogma, about America having a quasi-divine mission to democratize mankind, Jeane noted that the only mention of foreign policy in the preamble to the Constitution is "provide for the common defense."

There is no mystical American "mission" or purpose to be found independently of the U.S. Constitution. . . . There is no inherent or historical "imperative" for the U.S. government to seek to achieve any other goal—however great—except as it is mandated by the Constitution or adopted by the people through elected officials.[25]

Earlier, in his contribution, Charles Krauthammer had urged the United States "to go all the way and stop at nothing short of universal dominion."

How was this "universal dominion" to be achieved? By merging the United States, Europe, and Japan in "a super-sovereign West" that would be "hegemonic in the world." The European Economic Community, where "the single greatest voluntary transfer of sovereignty in world history" was taking place, said Krauthammer, is our "model" for the "larger integration of the New Europe with North America and democratic Asia."[26]

Would this not involve a huge sacrifice of American sovereignty? Indeed, it would, said Krauthammer, and we should embrace that future.

> As the industrialized democracies become increasingly economically, culturally, and technologically linked, they should begin to think about laying the foundations for increasingly binding political connections. This would require the conscious depreciation not only of American sovereignty, but of sovereignty in general. This is not as outrageous as it sounds.[27]

But it was every bit as outrageous as it sounded. For what the neoconservative Krauthammer was calling for was public repudiation of Washington's "great rule." Our greatest statesman had called upon his countrymen to have with foreign nations "as little political connection as possible." Krauthammer, however, was calling for the creation of "binding political connections" involving a wholesale surrender of sovereignty. He was urging America to give up the republic to pursue a global empire.

To the patriot Kirkpatrick, the notion that Americans should give up their independent republic as the price of ruling the world in a triumvirate with Europe and Japan was indeed outrageous.

Kirkpatrick backhanded Krauthammer: "[I]t is not America's purpose to establish 'universal dominance' . . . not even the universal dominance of democracy. . . . It is not within the United States' power to democratize the world."[28] As for NATO's future, she wrote:

> Neither can the U.S. be expected to sustain an expensive role in an alliance whose chief role is to diminish European fear of a resurgent Germany. Americans have more pressing priorities. . . .
>
> We should not spend American money protecting an affluent Japan. . . .
>
> Most of the international military obligations that we assumed were once important are now outdated. . . . It is time to give up the dubious benefits of superpower status and become again an unusually successful, open American republic.[29]

America, Kirkpatrick wrote, "should assume no new obligations in remote places," but become "a normal country in a normal time."

A republic, not an empire, the lady said.

The debate of 1989–90 was interrupted by the Gulf War, the triumph of American arms, the stationing of U.S. ground forces in Saudi Arabia, the Bush declaration of October 1991 of a New World Order. Blowback came September 11, 2001.

Today, the debate is renewed, not in the glow of Cold War victory or Gulf War triumph, but in a dark hour of the worst foreign policy disaster of our lifetimes, a disaster bred of hubris, ideology, and ignorance.

5

Who Shall Inherit the Earth?

If the American Century is over, what will replace it? And if Pax Americana has come to an end, who inherits the earth that America dominated? Who are the claimants? Who are the pretenders to the throne?

Will the twenty-first be an Islamic Century in which the children of the Prophet, one in every five people on the planet, conquer Europe, the citadel of Christianity? Will it be the Chinese Century? The Asian Century? Could it yet become the Second American Century?

Globalists believe we are witnessing the end times of the nation-state and the rise of a world government whose institutions—the United Nations, World Bank, International Monetary Fund, World Trade Organization, World Court, International Criminal Court, and International Seabed Authority—are already in operation. Is Davos World, where transnational companies that constitute fifty of the world's hundred largest economic entities displace the world of nations, our future?

Is the European Union, a supranational regime that grows in power at the expense of the nations of Europe, to be the model, as the United States merges with Canada and Mexico in a new North American Union?

Or is Balkanization the future, where nations subdivide into their racial, ethnic, religious, and tribal components, as we have seen in the Soviet Union, Yugoslavia, Czechoslovakia, the Indian subcontinent, and Ethiopia, and as we are beginning to see in Britain, Spain, Belgium, Lebanon, and Iraq?

Another possibility looms: a Dark Age. If the Pax Americana is history and there is no world power to assemble coalitions to police the planet, might we enter a Hobbesean world where large regions—Darfur, Rwanda, Waziristan, Anbar—are ceded to the forces of darkness as an anemic West refuses to intervene and no one else has the power or will? With the inevitable U.S. withdrawal from Mesopotamia, a Sunni-Shia war looms that could spread, with autocratic regimes falling to Islamists who see America as Satan. A U.S. pullout from Afghanistan would leave a vacuum the Taliban, the warlords, and the drug lords will fill.

Pakistan is one bullet away from an Islamist state of 170 million with an atomic bomb. In Latin America, radicalism and racism are on the rise among the indigenous peoples to whom the demagogues pander. In the cities of Europe, enclaves of Africans, Arabs, and Muslims are not assimilating. April in Paris is not what it used to be.

Decline of the West

The twentieth century was indeed the American Century. Yet Spengler was right. The century also saw the decline of the West. For it was the twentieth century in which the great nations of the West, at the apex of their power, fell upon one another in two savage wars that carried off scores of millions of their best and bravest. It was the century in which all of Europe's monarchies were shaken or fell, all the European empires collapsed, all the European nations saw a dramatic fall in their birthrates, and all experienced mass migrations of formerly subject peoples from the Third World, who will change, radically and forever, their racial, ethnic, religious, cultural, and political character.

No Western leader has yet shown the political self-confidence and moral certitude to halt the invasion, for powerful ideological and economic forces, out of contempt for the West or naked greed, look upon its approaching end as eminently desirable.

From across the Rio Grande they come, millions from Mexico and lands to the south, into the United States, as President Bush explains that we must welcome these desperate millions with open arms and ease their passage to citizenship—else we are not a good people.

By 2007, between 10 and 20 percent of the population of Mexico, the Caribbean, and Central America had come here. And America's political class was covering up its complicity and cowardice in failing to stop the invasion by denouncing as nativists and xenophobes any who demanded the borders be protected and the invaders sent home. We cannot, came the reply, as our economy would collapse without their cheap labor.

From the Maghreb and Middle East, Muslims cross into Europe, joined by millions more from the sub-Sahara. With the native-born populations of Europe dying and shrinking, immigrants, it was said, were needed to do the work Europeans would no longer do, and to take care of the aging childless as they pass from this earth. By 2007, 40 million Muslims were in Europe; millions were not assimilating. And because of their high birthrates and continued migration, they were a rising share of Europe's population.

In 1989, the Soviet Empire had collapsed. In 1991, the Soviet Union had disintegrated. Russia is today not much larger than she was under Peter the Great and Catherine the Great. Only now Russia is no longer young, vibrant, and growing. Russia is dying—by almost a million people a year. By 2050, Muslim Turkey may have replaced Mother Russia as the most populous nation in Europe. Meanwhile, Chinese cross the Amur and Ussuri rivers into Siberia to repopulate lands lost to the czars.

A European Century?

Though the European Union embraces twenty-seven nations and 493 million people and produces 30 percent of world GDP, the hour of Europe appears to be over, forever. Though home to five of the ten largest economies on earth, thirteen of the largest twenty-five, this economic superpower has shrunk to a military pygmy.

Outside of Russia, there is no great power in Europe. Nations that ruled empires and deployed vast armies had to scrimp to find a few battalions to send to Afghanistan and Iraq. To put out a pair of Balkan fires in the 1990s, Europe had to phone America. In the seventh decade after World War II, Europe remains a strategic dependency. East Europeans look for security not to Paris or Berlin, but to Washington.

United by liberal values and economic interests, Europe remains divided by nationality and language. Moreover, Europe is dying. No European nation save Muslim Albania has a birthrate among its native born that will enable it to survive the century in recognizable form. By 2050, the median age of Europeans will be fifty. A third of the population of some EU nations will be over sixty-five. And the dying continent is being invaded by Third World peoples who have never before been assimilated into a First World nation.

Europe's social welfare states have begun to siphon off the vitality of the continent. As the population ages and Europe's baby boomers become eligible for retirement and pension benefits, nations are finding they cannot afford what their politicians promised and legislated.

Much of the political energy is directed toward blocking any further transfer of power from the nations of Europe to the European Union—or to siphoning off power from national capitals to constituent states and ethnic enclaves.

The breakup of the multicultural, multiethnic, multilingual states is under way. Czechoslovakia split in two. Yugoslavia, the Kingdom of the South Slavs born at Paris 1919, is now six and potentially seven nations: Slovenia, Croatia, Serbia, Bosnia, Macedonia, Montenegro, and Kosovo.

Continental elites may no longer see themselves as Spaniards or Brits but as good Europeans. But some Spaniards and Brits are beginning to see themselves as English, Scottish, Welsh, Irish, Basque, and Catalan.

The death of Christianity has cut the taproot of European culture. "The faith is Europe. Europe is the faith," said Hilaire Belloc. But the faith has been discarded and displaced by secularism—and the triumphal return of Islam to the continent from which it was largely expelled centuries ago.

Lastly, the EU dream no longer inspires Europeans or the world. Returning after two years as a *Financial Times* columnist in Asia, Guy de Jonquières wrote, "Most Asians, given the choice, would still opt for the—tarnished—American dream."[1] As for Europe's appeal to Asians, de Jonquières mocked:

Europe is irrelevant in Asia, except as a market and a producer of luxury goods. Those in Europe who envisage Asia basing its future development on the European "model" delude themselves. The only European models that Asia would like to embrace are to be found on catwalks.[2]

The fiftieth birthday of the European Union, which was born in Rome in March 1957, proved a pallid affair. German chancellor Angela Merkel, hostess of the party, drafted a "birthday card," the Berlin Declaration. Yet in the EU's malaise, even that caused dissension and division. Some nations objected to any mention of the new constitution. Vaclav Havel of the Czech Republic called the declaration "Orwellian Eurospeak."[3] Poland objected to its failure to mention Christianity. Pope Benedict XVI called that refusal an act of "apostasy."[4] The Christophobic French establishment had got its way again.

Remarking on the "demographic profile" of the continent, the pope added, "One must unfortunately note that Europe seems to be going down a road which could lead it to take its leave from history. . . . You could almost think that the European continent is in fact losing faith in its own future."[5]

After a committee led by former French president Valéry Giscard d'Estaing drafted a new constitution, setting the EU on course toward its final destination: a United States of Europe, the French and Dutch rebelled and voted it down. Politically, the project is stalled if not going in reverse. Resentment of the "faceless bureaucrats of Brussels," where the executive arm of the union, the European Commission, sits, is widespread and growing.

By one poll of EU states, not half the citizens of its twenty-seven nations think positively of it. Only 28 percent of Britons think well of it. Only a third believe membership is good for Britain.[6] Many in Europe oppose plans to bring in new members, especially a Turkey of 70 million Muslims.

What the malaise of the European Union tells us is what patriots already knew.

Democracy and free markets do not a country make. Constitutions, no matter how eloquent, abstract ideas no matter how lovely, do not create a nation. A nation writes its constitution. A nation drafts its own birth certificate. What makes a people and a nation is a common and unique homeland and people, history and heritage, language and literature, song and story, traditions and customs.

The European Union is an intellectual construct, a thing of paper. Unlike a nation, it has no heart and no soul. And when it passes into history, because of some irreconcilable squabble, many may regret it, few will weep. "Europe is doomed to relative decline. Let it decline magnificently," writes Martin Wolf of the *Financial Times.* "That would seem the best of all possible worlds for Europe in the 21st century."[7] No, the twenty-first century will not be the Century of Europe.

An Islamic Century?

Among devout Muslims the belief stirs that Islam is the future, not only of the Maghreb and Middle East, Iran and South Asia, but of Europe and the world. Not a few are prepared to sacrifice, suffer, and die to bring the world into submission to Allah, as their ancestors, fourteen centuries ago, sought to do. The dream is of a resurrected caliphate and Islamic empire like the empire that once ruled from Iberia to India and made converts all the way to the Philippines. An impossible dream?

Surely Belloc has been proven prophetic with his warning in that year of Munich: "It has always seemed to me possible, and even probable, that there would be a resurrection of Islam and that our sons or our grandsons would see the renewal of that tremendous struggle between the Christian culture and what has been for more than a thousand years its greatest opponent."[8]

"That tremendous struggle" has been renewed.

After World War II, Muslim peoples quickly threw off the yoke of Western imperialism. Indonesia, the most populous Muslim nation on earth, with perhaps 200 million, achieved independence in 1946. The Asian subcontinent that embraces India, Pakistan, and Bangladesh—collectively home to 400 million Muslims—became independent in 1947. By 1962, when Algeria broke free of France, the Muslim Maghreb and Middle East were free of European and Christian rule.

With 1.2 billion people now professing the faith, Islam is the largest religion on earth—having surpassed Catholicism—and the dominant faith of fifty-five countries, more than one-fourth of all the nations on earth. The numbers are sufficient for Islamic peoples to play a great role in the destiny of mankind.

But a hegemonic role? A dominant role?

That is difficult to see. While the population of the Islamic nations is huge and growing and the bravery of Islam's sons, who have driven every occupying power out of their world at a high price in blood, is impressive, it is hard to see the Islamic world becoming the decisive force in world history the West was for four hundred years. We had a Pax Britannia in the nineteenth century and a Pax Americana in the twentieth. A Pax Islamica is impossible to see. Why not?

First, the absence of unity. Other than their faith, there is little that unites Muslims. What do Indonesians have in common with Mauritanians? What do the Uighurs of China have in common with the *beurs* of the *banlieues* of Paris? What do Turks, anxious to join the European Union, have in common with Sudanese, or Saudis with Somalis across the Red Sea? Islamic peoples may be united by a common faith, but they are separated by ethnicity, nationality, culture, and race. If faith is their strength, diversity is their weakness.

Zionism unites them. But Muslims have fought more wars with each other than with Israel. Morocco battles for hegemony over Western Sahara. Shia and Sunni fight, murder, and massacre each other in Lebanon and Iraq. Hamas and Fatah kill each other to gain control over Gaza and the West Bank. Kurds have lost more men in wars with Turks than Palestinians have in wars with Israel. Black September commemorates King Hussein's shelling of the Palestinian refugee camps and expulsion of the Palestine Liberation Organization from Jordan. The Ayatollah's Iran and Saddam's Iraq fought the longest, bloodiest war of the 1980s, in which a million perished. Hafez al-Assad leveled his own city of Homa, killing thousands of sympathizers of the Muslim Brotherhood. Nasser used poison gas in Yemen to establish an Egyptian base on the Arabian peninsula. Islam may be "a religion of peace," in President Bush's oratory. The late twentieth century suggests otherwise.

Of the world's Muslim population of 1.2 billion, only a fourth is Arab. Most Muslims are Asians. Indonesia is the most populous Islamic country, followed by Pakistan, China, India, and Bangladesh.[9] And as Muslims are now Asian, Arab, African, European, and American, it is difficult to see how they unite, except around issues such as the Israeli-Palestinian conflict, where Muslims are seen as persecuted by non-Muslims, or religious issues such as Salmon Rushdie's *Satanic Verses* and the

Danish cartoons, where the Prophet was seen as being mocked by the West.

Not only do Muslim nations lack unity, they lack power.

Of the top twenty nations in GDP, only one is Muslim. Turkey, a land of 70 million, the most secularized Muslim state in the Middle East, ranks nineteenth, with a GDP the size of Sweden's, a nation of 9 million. Among the next twenty largest countries, measured by GDP, are four Muslim states: Saudi Arabia (21), Indonesia (24), Iran (30), and Malaysia (37).[10]

Thus, only one of twenty-two Arab nations, Saudi Arabia, is among the top forty in GDP. The United Arab Emirates is forty-sixth, Algeria forty-seventh. Oil and natural gas explain the presence of all three in the top fifty. Egypt, with 70 million people, is fifty-first, but its GDP is smaller than New Zealand's, with a population of 4 million. Taken together, the twenty-two Arab nations have a combined GDP smaller than that of Spain.[11] Should the world find a substitute for oil, the Muslim world would suffer most, and many Muslim nations would sink toward destitution and dependency.

And though Islamic peoples from Algeria to Afghanistan have shown perseverance and courage in expelling Western powers, there is a world of difference between a Battle of Algiers and a conventional war. The Islamic way of war in the modern era has been to let the imperial power invade, then use guerrilla warfare to bleed the occupier until it wearies of the carnage and departs. Thus, the Algerians expelled the French, the Shia in Lebanon expelled the Americans and Israelis, the Afghans expelled the Russians. It is how Iraqi Sunnis and Afghan Taliban fight America, and how the Palestinians fight the Israelis.

In a conventional war, Western powers have overwhelmed

Islamic nations with technology and firepower. The British, French, and Israelis walked into Sinai and Suez in 1956. The Russians and Americans took Kabul in days. The Americans routed the Iraqi army in lightning wars in 1991 and 2003. The Israelis were victorious in 1948, 1956, 1967, and 1982—though the Yom Kippur War of 1973 showed that Egypt, its numbers growing and weaponry improving, had become a formidable adversary. In 2006, Hezbollah held off the Israeli Defense Forces for five weeks, as Israel was unwilling to pay the price in blood of close combat with dug-in guerrillas in terrain where superiority in weaponry was only of marginal advantage. If any nation faces an existential threat from the Muslim world, it is Israel.

While Europe's nations will never again field million-man armies or project power on distant continents, all the Muslim nations depend for their weapons on foreign suppliers. No Muslim country produces artillery, armored vehicles, tanks, or planes as Russia, China, Europe, and the United States do, though some, like Syria, Iran, and Pakistan, are reproducing missiles first purchased from the Soviet Union, China, or North Korea.

Does militant Islam pose a mortal threat to America?

In a word, no. September 11 showed that Islamic terrorists can kill thousands in a day, but no coalition of Islamic nations or terrorists presents remotely the threat to the United States the Soviet Union did. If Japan, a nation with 5 percent of the U.S. landmass, could survive the destruction of Tokyo, Hiroshima, and Nagasaki and be restored to prosperity in a decade, no terrorists are going to destroy the United States. As for America being forced to submit to the dictate of a restored caliphate by nuclear blackmail, that is beyond parody.

This is not to minimize the damage that could be done to our economy and freedom, were a series of mass terror attacks to take place on American soil. It is to say simply: They cannot destroy us and they cannot conquer us.

The deep hostility to the United States in the Islamic world that has bred terrorism has four roots: the Iraq war, seen by Muslims as an imperial war to impose America's rule and system on a Muslim nation; the presence of U.S. troops in Arab lands ruled by regimes seen as American puppets; the lavish aid and uncritical support the United States renders to Israel for what Muslims see as the repression and dispossession of the Palestinians; and the decadence of American culture, associated as it is with hedonism, sensuality, promiscuity, alcohol, and drugs.

Dinesh D'Souza, author of *The Enemy at Home: The Cultural Left and Its Responsibility for 9/11,* is not wrong when he writes,

> What angers religious Muslims is not the American Constitution but the scandalous sexual mores they see on American movies and television. What disgusts them are not free elections but the sights of hundreds of homosexuals kissing each other and taking marriage vows. The person that horrifies them the most is not John Locke but Hillary Clinton.[12]

Is militant Islamism a mortal threat? Strategically, no. None of our radical Arab adversaries has the military power to challenge the United States. The three states that have adopted Islamism—Afghanistan under the Taliban, Iran, and Sudan— have all proven incapable of making social and economic progress or of meeting the needs and demands of their people.

Iran could make life even more hellish for U.S. soldiers in Iraq and Afghanistan and pose a terror threat in the Middle East and here at home. But any attack by Iran, a nation with a GDP 5 percent of that of the United States, on U.S. forces or our homeland, would trigger retaliation that could set Iran back decades. For there is nothing of strategic value in Iran that is not vulnerable to U.S. power. Mahmoud Ahmadinejad is said to believe a war with America would bring the return of the twelfth imam, the Mahdi. A theory that is probably best left untested.

While the Islamic terror threat will be with us as long as we maintain a military presence in the Middle East—and perhaps beyond, for the hatred of America is great and Al Qaeda has reconstituted itself in Pakistan—that threat must be put in perspective. From 9/11 to the writing of this book, 100,000 Americans were victims of homicide. Not one died in an Islamic terror attack. We should be braced for the inevitable, but we ought not frighten ourselves with our own propaganda that they can defeat or destroy us. Where the threat of militant Islam is a danger to the West is in Europe. There the native-born populations are dying and 40 million Muslims are growing in numbers and militancy. And there is no tradition of assimilation as there is in the United States.

Though a clear and present demographic danger to Europe, Islamism is not an existential threat to the United States—unless we open our borders and permit it to become one.

A Chinese Century?

"Let China sleep, for when she awakes, she will shake the world," Napoleon warned. If the American Century is to give way to an era dominated by another nation, the lone credible claimant is

China. Not only is China comparable in size, her population, 1.3 billion, is four times that of the United States, and her economic growth has been three times as rapid for over a decade. China's savings rate runs as high as 50 percent, and her GDP is now the fourth largest on earth and closing on Germany.

Hoover Institution scholar Alvin Rabushka contends that, measured by purchasing power parity (PPP), China is the world's second economy, valued at $10 trillion, fast approaching the $13 trillion U.S. economy.[13] Beijing's cash reserves are growing by 20 percent a year, as is tax revenue.[14] As it is inevitable, Rabushka writes, that the U.S. share of global output and world influence must decline, he calls for "a worldwide Monroe Doctrine" where the United States remains dominant in the western hemisphere, and China and India assume greater responsibility for stability in Asia:

"It is time for some serious thinking and strategic dialogue between China and the United States aimed at developing an increasingly cooperative relationship in trade, politics, and military affairs, rather than treating China's growing prosperity and military power as a threat."[15]

Great before, China is becoming great again. Many believe her the nation of the future and America the nation of the past. Evidence exists to support the thesis. In research and development, China has surpassed Japan and is second only to the United States. Her R&D investment increases by 20 percent a year, America's by 4 percent. In the last decade, the U.S. economy grew 40 percent, China's 140 percent. Where Americans save 1 percent of GDP, Chinese save 35 percent to 50 percent.

Of China's trade surplus with the United States, $233 billion in 2006, computers and electrical equipment accounted for almost half. Outside of the $6 billion surplus we ran up in aircraft and spacecraft, we had trade surpluses with China only in oil seeds, soybeans, cotton, yarn, wood pulp, copper, raw hides, skins, ores, slag, ash, base metals, meat, chemicals, fertilizers, aluminum, nickel, tobacco, cigarettes, dairy products, birds' eggs, honey, animal and vegetable fats, wadding, agricultural foods—and other such high-tech goods. China's exports to America read like those of an industrial economy and manufacturing power. Aircraft apart, U.S. exports to China read like those of a colony providing raw materials to the mother country.

While the U.S. trade deficit with China was $233 billion, the current account deficit with China in 2006 was $275 billion. In that additional $42 billion are the tax dollars the U.S. government transfers yearly to China as interest on the vast and growing slice of the U.S. national debt that Beijing holds.

Having abandoned the Maoist madness of 1949–76, China's rulers have chosen the path to world power of autocratic capitalism, refusing to renounce the legacy of the Great Helmsman, whose remains yet lie in state in a crystal sarcophagus in Tiananmen Square.

China's growth of 10 percent for nearly two decades refutes *The End of History* thesis that democracy has won the struggle for the future. Though a one-party dictatorship and the most protectionist great power on earth, China has experienced an economic miracle that eclipses the postwar Germany of Ludwig Erhard. Beijing is showing the world that mercantilism and autocracy are compatible with dynamism. For two decades, no democracy has matched China's growth.

Because of its immense and growing trade surpluses with the

United States, Beijing's cash reserves have passed the $1.3 trillion mark and are the largest on earth. What does Beijing do with its hoard of dollars?

First, China creates ties of dependency in Asia by buying more from her neighbors than she sells to them. Australia, whose natural resources pour into the Middle Kingdom, is becoming dependent upon China for prosperity.

Second, China invests strategically in energy projects in nations the United States has declared off limits: Sudan, Iran, Burma.

Third, China buys weapons and armaments technology from Russia, Israel, and Europe to modernize her armed forces. Beijing's military budget has grown by double digits for years, the most recent increment being 18 percent, in 2007.[16] "Since no nation threatens China, one must wonder: Why this growing investment? Why these continuing large and expanding arms purchases?" asked Donald Rumsfeld.[17]

The configuration of Chinese forces provides the answer. China has deployed nine hundred missiles opposite Taiwan—either to intimidate or attack it. China is also investing in warships, submarines, antiship missiles, attack aircraft, and space technology. As there is only one sea power off the coast, there is little doubt at whom this buildup is directed.

Diplomatically, Beijing is drawing close to nations in conflict with the United States—from Russia to Burma to Iran to Sudan to Venezuela.

China's challenge to America recalls the challenge of the kaiser's Germany to Great Britain. As Wilhelm II and Admiral Tirpitz built a high-seas fleet to rival the Royal Navy, China builds up her naval forces to counter the U.S. fleet in the western Pacific. As the kaiser saw British plots to isolate and deny Germany her place in the sun, China sees the United States thickening its ties to Japan, Taiwan, Australia, Vietnam, India, Pakistan, and the former Soviet republics of Central Asia. Like Germany then, China today sees the specter of encirclement.

There is no greater work for U.S. and Chinese leaders than to ensure that what happened between Germany and Britain in the first half of the twentieth century, ten years of the bloodiest warfare in history that drove both forever from the ranks of great powers, is not replicated by us in this century.

Will the twenty-first century be the Chinese Century? The possibility exists. But a China that seeks to displace America as first power faces limitations.

Mighty as the Middle Kingdom is, it is vulnerable and dependent.

First, unless Professor Rabushka is right, China's economy is still only half that of Japan and a fourth that of the United States. By the eve of World War I, Germany had surpassed Great Britain.

Second, China's growth is dependent on the United States. For U.S. imports from China represent 10 percent of her GDP and 100 percent of her growth. In 2006, China sold us seven times what she bought from us. If China were shut out of the U.S. market, she would plunge into a depression. But if the United States were locked out of China's market, we would lose sales equal to one-fourth of 1 percent of GDP. Free Asia would fill the vacuum. A 35 percent U.S. tariff on Chinese-made goods would put Beijing into an instant recession, creating unemployment and social unrest.

Third, China has a long and unprotected lifeline to the Persian Gulf upon which she depends for oil, a lifeline easily cut by the U.S. Navy.

Fourth, China is bordered by nations deeply wary of her ambitions for expansion and hegemony, nations with no reason to fear the United States. Beijing has laid claim to 38,000 square kilometers of Kashmir, to 90,000 square kilometers of India's northeastern state of Arunachal Pradesh that borders Bhutan and Tibet, to all the islands in the South China Sea down to the Philippines, to Taiwan, and to the Senkakus held by Japan.[18] Nor has Beijing forgotten that Imperial Russia joined in the rape of China in the nineteenth century, seizing a California-sized slice of land north of the Ussuri and Amur rivers. Moscow makes an historic mistake if it believes this a closed question.

Fifth, Beijing is seen as antidemocratic and repressive by tens of millions of her own people—religious minorities such as Catholics, Falun Gong, and Muslims, and national minorities like the Uighurs, Mongols, and Tibetans.

Sixth, after uprooting Confucianism and shedding Maoism, China has no prevailing and unifying faith, moral code, or ideology. Minority faiths—Islam, Christianity, Falun Gong, Tibetan Buddhism—are seen as suspect and separatist. Other than tradition and custom, which the Maoists sought to eradicate, nothing prevents China's deracinated young from defying Beijing and looking to secular America as a model.

Seventh, Beijing has a crisis of legitimacy. Mao seized power in a revolution to expel the "foreign devils," unite the nation, and place China in the vanguard of the world revolution. But how does the Chinese Communist Party defend its absolute monopoly of power, when the world Communist revolution is over and China is capitalist? As a Chinese middle class develops, the regime will face the same crisis as the one that ended the Communist Party's monopoly of power in Moscow.

To hold the nation together, Beijing is playing the tribal card with appeals to nationalism and racial solidarity—as a people that has suffered at the hands of Japan and the West, but whose time has come to command the world. "China has stood up!" said Mao in 1949. China's time of humiliation was over. The Germans said the same in 1933. And as the Olympic Games were held in Berlin in 1936, they will be held in Beijing in 2008. And as the Berlin Games were followed by a clamor for return of the Sudetenland to Germanic rule, so the Beijing games may be followed by a clamor for the return of Taiwan to the "embrace of the motherland."

The Asian Century

With the combined Asian economies now as large as that of the United States or European Union, there is talk of an Asian Economic Community, knitting together East and Southeast Asia. At present levels of GDP and population growth, an AEC could soon become the dominant economic bloc. Could this be the way to an Asian Century?

The difficulties with an AEC are immediately apparent. Who leads?

Japan or China? They are fierce rivals. Would Taiwan be included? India? Russia? Australia and New Zealand? Or would it be a club closed to all but Asians? As the United States holds the security umbrella over Japan, South Korea, Taiwan, the Philippines, and Australia, would America be excluded? How might America respond to her exclusion? With the United States running trade deficits of $700 billion to $800 billion—and China and Japan the largest beneficiaries, with a combined $321 billion in trade surpluses with America in 2006—an Asian bloc that excluded the United States would cause a nationalistic reaction on this side of the Pacific. Asia's free nations would be cutting their own throats. For the United States still has the largest single bloc of affluent consumers on earth and the world's most open markets. For Asians to put this at risk would seem suicidal.

Given the fears in India, Vietnam, Taiwan, Japan, and the Philippines of the growing power and hegemonic and territorial ambitions of Beijing, an AEC, with China at its helm, would seem less like an Asian copy of the European Union than a Chinese copy of the Greater East-Asia Co-Prosperity Sphere of Hirohito's Japan. Put down an Asian Economic Community leading the world in the twenty-first century as improbable at best.

World Government

In 1795, Immanuel Kant set down the ideas and principles he believed would lead to an end to war among civilized peoples. As his title, Kant chose "Perpetual Peace."

> [T]here must be a league of a particular kind, which can be called a league of peace (*foedus pacificum*), and which would be distinguished from a treaty of peace (*pactum pacis*) by the fact that the latter terminates only one war, while the former seeks to make an end of all wars forever. . . .
>
> The practicability . . . of this idea of federation, which should gradually spread to all states and thus lead to perpetual peace, can be proved.[19]

In his preamble, Kant conceded he had lifted the phrase "perpetual peace" from an inscription on a Dutch innkeeper's sign, on which a church burial ground had been painted. Only the dead know the end of war, said Plato. Yet Kant's vision captured the imagination of philosophers and poets. In "Locksley Hall," Tennyson wrote of a coming age where "the wardrum throbbed no longer, and the battle-flags were furled."

For I dipped into the future, far as human eye could see,
Saw the Vision of the world, and all the wonder that would
* be;*

Saw the heavens fill with commerce, argosies of magic sails,
Pilots of the purple twilight, dropping down with costly bales;

Heard the heavens fill with shouting, and there rained a
* ghastly dew*
From the nations' airy navies grappling in the central blue;

Far along the world-wide whisper of the south-wind rushing
* warm*
With the standards of the peoples plunging through the
* thunder-storm;*

Till the war-drum throbbed no longer, and the battle-flags
* were furled*
In the Parliament of man, the Federation of the world.

There the common sense of most shall hold a fretful realm in
* awe,*
And the kindly earth shall slumber, lapped in universal law.[20]

This vision of a Parliament of Man, a Federation of the World, to usher in a time of universal peace and universal law took form at Versailles, where Wilson discarded, one by one, his Fourteen Points and yielded his first principles for Allied assent to a League of Nations to ensure that the "war to end all war" had not been fought in vain.

About the interwar era 1919–39, a great myth has been propagated and is believed: That it was American isolationism that caused World War II, that it was America's refusal to ratify Versailles and join the League of Nations that led to the democracies' capitulation to the fascist dictators—Imperial Japan in Manchuria in 1931, Mussolini in Abyssinia in 1935, Hitler in the Rhineland, Austria, and the Sudetenland in 1936 and 1938—that led to the most terrible war in history.

This myth aided FDR and the New Dealers in their fight at war's end for a United Nations to succeed the failed League, that would police the planet and keep the peace.

Companion institutions were created: an International Monetary Fund to protect the new economic order, the International Trade Organization to bring the benefits of free trade to all nations, the International Bank for Reconstruction and Development (now the World Bank) to assist in the rebuilding of war-torn Europe, and an International Court of Justice, which would take up where the Permanent Court of International Justice, a child of the League, had left off. The architects were New Deal Democrats, one of whom, Dean Acheson, would title his memoirs *Present at the Creation*.

The ITO was stillborn. But a substitute General Agreement on Tariffs and Trade, GATT, evolved into the World Trade Organization in 1994, when the national establishment closed ranks against Middle America's protest against any further surrenders of sovereignty to global institutions.

For decades, Americans, protective of their liberty, have resisted the accretion of power by institutions of "global governance." But like the guns of Singapore that pointed out to sea,

America's patriots may be guarding against a danger stealthily advancing from another direction.

For the EU, China, Russia, and the United States are never going to submit to the authority of a United Nations dominated by Third World regimes and global bureaucrats. The exposure of corruption in the oil-for-food program, corruption that led to the office door of the secretary general, and charges of sexual abuse of women by U.N. peacekeepers have terminally ravaged the organization's reputation. And as the United Nations has evolved into an anti-American and anti-Israel forum, receptive to the rants of Hugo Chavez and Mahmoud Ahmadinejad, it has forfeited the favor it enjoyed among the founding genera-tion of Americans. Few today describe the United Nations as what many called it not so long ago, "the last best hope of earth." The child of so much love—has been lost.

Under Reagan, America rejected the Law of the Sea Treaty and the International Seabed Authority. Under George W. Bush, America refused to submit to the authority of the International Criminal Court and repudiated the Kyoto Protocol. Under the 1946 Connally Reservation, the United States denies the Inter-national Court of Justice jurisdiction over disputes to which America is party, unless we agree to accept its ruling. At his confirmation hearings, Zalmay Khalizad, President Bush's nominee to replace John Bolton as U.S. ambassador to the United Nations, threatened the United Nations with a cutoff in U.S. funds: "[T]he absence of reform is a mortal threat to the United Nations. . . . The issue of funding has to be on the table, but it has to be . . . a kind of last resort."[21]

"Lawmakers from both parties effusively praised Khalizad," said the press reports. In times past, a public threat to drive the United Nations into bankruptcy if it failed to reform would have gotten one branded a John Bircher. No more. Skepticism toward, even opposition to the United Nations, is mainstream.

The real threat to the liberty and sovereignty of the United States comes from another quarter: Washington, D.C. As Pogo said, "We have met the enemy and he is us."

The North American Union

Of all the potential commitments of the United States, the most perilous to its survival as an independent republic is the North American Union. It already exists on paper. It would entail a merger of the United States, Canada, and Mexico into one economic unit, with all borders open to travel, tourism, and trade, from Prudhoe Bay to Chiapas. America's immigration crisis would be ended by the erasure of America's borders. This would be the decisive step in uniting the three nations in a new transnational entity and be as fateful as our Constitutional Convention. America would be on course to a destination where her sovereignty and independence would forever disappear. Final goal: 450 million Mexicans, Americans, and Canadians as dual citizens of the North American Union.

The North American Free Trade Agreement is the foundation of the NAU. The model is the EU, where crucial decisions have passed out of the jurisdiction of national parliaments. The EU imposes hate-crimes laws, dictates human rights policy for Europe, and prohibits the death penalty, no matter the will of peoples or parliaments. The EU has its own central bank and prints its own money. The EU constitution calls for a European president and foreign minister. No nation in the euro zone may run a deficit in excess of 3 percent of GDP. The EU seeks to harmonize the rules, regulations, and laws of twenty-five nations to enable Europe's transnational companies to compete with U.S. corporations, which face a single set of federal laws and standards from Maine to Maui. All is done to facilitate commerce and trade.

On March 23, 2005, President Bush hosted a summit at his ranch in Crawford with Mexican president Vicente Fox and Canadian prime minister Paul Martin. After signing an agreement to form a Security and Prosperity Partnership of North America, "the three amigos" drove to Baylor University to issue a press release. The ostensible purpose of SPP is to upgrade the NAFTA tribunals into a transnational court like the WTO, to decide disputes among the three nations and to review the laws of the fifty states to see that they do not conflict with the higher laws of transnational trade.[22] The denizens of Davos see a world where the economic nationalism of Hamilton is dead and buried.

Among the major projects of the NAU is the NAFTA superhighway. With six lanes each way and rail lines and oil pipelines in the center corridor, this highway would run from the Mexican port of Cardenas through Texas and Oklahoma into Kansas. Kansas City would become the port of entry for the containers from the Far East and China, which would pass through Mexico and into the United States without inspection. From Kansas City, the NAFTA superhighway would proceed north to Winnipeg and Fairbanks, Alaska, with branches spreading east and west throughout the United States and Canada. The idea is to weld the three nations together by bonds of steel railway and concrete highway, as the United States was brought together by the Northern Pacific, Union Pacific, and Southern Pacific railroads and the Interstate Highway System.[23]

With this difference: Americans will never be permitted to

vote on whether they wish to see the erosion of their sovereignty, the abolition of America's borders, and a shotgun marriage of their republic with a Third World nation of 110 million that is on its way to becoming a narco-oligarchy.

Many questions puzzle even the most reliable friends of George W. Bush: Why, when our bleeding border is causing terrible social problems and destroying his party's base in Middle America, does he refuse to enforce the immigration laws as he is constitutionally obligated to do? Why does he not build the fence, halt the invasion, secure the border, and send the illegal aliens back home—beginning with felons, gang members, and scofflaws? Support for enforcing the law and securing the border is so overwhelming even open-borders advocates talk the talk.

Answer: President Bush may not want the border secured because he wishes to see it erased one day, except as a line on a map. For President Bush, as is surely true of ex-president Fox, may see NAFTA as the first historic step in a journey of decades that is to end with the United States and Mexico, with resource-rich Canada, become one economic, social, and political bloc: the North American Union.

In a 2006 article in *The National Journal*, "Beyond Hegemony," Paul Starobin cited Samuel P. Huntington's essay in *The National Interest*, in which the Harvard professor wrote of an "emerging global superclass" that is "fixated on the world as an economic unit."[24]

Comprising fewer than 4 percent of the American people, these transnationalists have little need for national loyalty, view national boundaries as obstacles that thankfully are vanishing, and see national governments as residues from the past whose only useful function is to facilitate the elite's global operations. In the coming years, one corporate executive confidently predicted, "the only people who will care about national boundaries are politicians."[25]

Such men call to mind the words Sir John Harrington spoke half a millennium ago, "Treason doth never prosper: What's the reason? For if it prosper none dare call it treason."

A New Dark Age?

"For seven days last May the city of São Paulo, Brazil, teetered on the edge of a feral zone where governments barely reach and countries lose their meaning. That zone is a wilderness inhabited already by large populations worldwide, but officially denied and rarely described. It is not a throwback to the Dark Ages but something new—a companion to globalization, and an element in a fundamental reordering that may gradually render national boundaries obsolete. It is most obvious in the narco-lands of Colombia and Mexico, in the fractured swaths of Africa, in parts of Pakistan and Afghanistan, in much of Iraq. But it also exists beneath the surface in places where governments are believed to govern and countries still seem to be strong."[26]

So wrote William Langewiesche in "City of Fear," his *Vanity Fair* depiction of the panic that seized São Paulo, a metropolitan area of three thousand square miles and 20 million people, when the anarchic young in May 2006 went on a rampage and murder spree against police. Seventy-three prisons containing 140,000 felons, all directed by the Primeiro Comando da Capital or "First Command of the Capital," which controls the jails and prisons and runs an "antigovernment," rioted in solidarity. In forty-eight hours, forty police and prison guards had been killed, with many times that number injured and wounded. Reprisals followed. By the end of the first week, police units and death squads had killed 450 civilians and inmates.[27]

Langewiesche describes how the P.C.C. came to wield such power in the prisons and concludes: "São Paulo is not alone. Consider all the other Third World cities, consider Moscow, consider L.A. The P.C.C. is just another inhabitant of the feral zones."[28]

Feral zones are the subterranean regions of Thomas Friedman's flat world, where pundits sip their Starbucks at their workstations and create their Brave New Worlds on their Dells. For it is not only tourists and immigrants that cross borders. Criminal cartels move narcotics from Bolivia and Colombia through Mexico into the United States. Gangs like MS-13, Mara Salvatrucha, that boast tens of thousands of members, reach across borders and commit atrocities that make Al Capone look like The Fonz. Islamic terrorists move money across borders for bombings the way bright young stockbrokers do on Wall Street.

As scholars Steven Weber and Ely Ratner write, Friedman's flat world has a dark underbelly that globalists ignore.

> The post–Cold War world is an increasingly dangerous place in which to live in part because of the dark side of globalization. New diseases roam across national borders; trade in drugs and women flourishes; pollutants spread to less-polluted jurisdictions; deadly weapons find their way easily into the hands of anyone with hard currency.[29]

Religious and political fanaticism also crosses borders more easily now, in the hearts and minds of travelers.

President Bush celebrates our "undocumented workers" from Mexico and Latin America. He does not mention that Hispanic youth are joining criminal gangs at nineteen times the rate of white Americans, and the children of Asian immigrants are joining gangs at nine times the rate. Only China and South Africa rival America in the share of their population in jail or prison.

Europeans once looked down on Americans as a gun-crazy, lawless lot. They now find that in their new multiethnic, multiracial, multicultural Europe violent crime rates are matching those of the United States. From South Central, where Crips and Bloods fight a losing battle with Mexican gangs, to the *banlieues* of Paris, where police fight a losing battle to second- and third-generation children of North African and sub-Saharan immigrants from lands France once ruled, there are "no-go zones." Parts of countries, parts of continents, are being ceded to those beyond the reach of civilization.

Maoist guerrillas took a share of power in Nepal and now fight in India. Genocide beckons in Darfur as it did a decade ago in Burundi and Rwanda. Islamists fight police and the army in the Philippines, Thailand, Chechnya, Nigeria. Drug cartels engage in guerrilla war in Colombia against a regime whose troops have colluded with death squads. Criminal cartels fight in Nuevo Laredo for control of the drug corridor into the United States. As NATO draws down its forces, Afghanistan is being re-conquered by the Taliban and the drug lords they once opposed. Both are receptive to sanctuary for Al Qaeda—at the right price.

A U.S. defeat in Iraq would lead to America throwing its badge into the dust like Gary Cooper in *High Noon,* refusing to serve any longer as sheriff to an unappreciative world. If so, writes Michael Mandelbaum in *The Case for Goliath,* "The world would become a messier, more dangerous, and less prosperous place." If the U.S. role as Globocop ends, Mandelbaum concludes, they "will miss it when it is gone."[30]

Nor can a renewal of race conflict be dismissed. From the Andean nations of Bolivia and Peru through Chiapas to South Central, there arises a clamor that the "European invaders" must restore to the "indigenous peoples" the land, power, and wealth they stole in the sixteenth and seventeenth centuries. From Evo Morales in La Paz to Ollanta Humala in Lima to Hugo Chavez in Caracas to Manuel López Obrador in Mexico City to the MEChA militants of the barrios and American campuses, the Chicano movement to liberate "Aztlan," all politics is not local. All politics is tribal.

The Indian peoples of the Americas are beginning to echo the demands of militant African Americans and Third World regimes for "reparations"—for all the sins, alleged and real, of the West, from colonialism to imperialism, racism, slavery, and genocide. We may be looking at what Hobbes called "bellum omnium contra omnes"—the war of all against all.

Second American Century?

There is another credible claimant to the twenty-first century: the United States of America. For though Pax Americana is over and America is no longer hegemonic on every continent, America remains militarily, politically, economically, and culturally the first nation on earth. And while America now has rivals and competitors, and enemies who defy her, she has no peer. And there remain many around the world who prefer that America, for all her flaws and failings, shape the future. For they fear the rival claimants.

Can there be a Second American Century? Does America have a Second Chance to get it right, as Dr. Zbigniew Brzezinski argues in his 2007 *New York Times* bestseller of that title?

To answer that question, we must take a closer look at our country, and how it has changed, for better and for worse, from the nation Henry Luce called on to lead the world in the twentieth century.

6

Deconstructing America

Yet at present, the United States is unwinding strand by strand,
rather like the Soviet Union.
—WILLIAM REES-MOGG, 1992[1]

The histories of bilingual and bicultural societies that do not assimilate
are histories of turmoil, tension and tragedy.
—SEYMOUR MARTIN LIPSET[2]

In 2007, on the 400th anniversary of the Jamestown settlement,
Queen Elizabeth II arrived to commemorate the occasion. But
it took some fancy footwork by Her Majesty to run the
Powhatan gauntlet.

For the queen had been there before, fifty years ago, for
the 350th anniversary, in a less progressive era. As the Associated Press reported, "the last time the queen helped Virginia
mark the anniversary of its colonial founding, it was an all-
white affair in a state whose government was in open
defiance of a 1954 Supreme Court order to desegregate public
schools."[3]

That was the time of massive resistance to integration in Virginia. And the queen was quick to recognize and embrace the
change: "[S]ince I visited Jamestown in 1957, my country has

become a much more diverse society just as the Commonwealth of Virginia and the whole United States of America have also undergone a major social change."[4]

Both nations are indeed more diverse. But the most recent reminder of diversity in Virginia, to which the queen alluded, was the massacre of thirty-two students and teachers at Virginia Tech by an immigrant madman.

And now that London is Londonistan, Muslim imams preach hatred of the West in mosques, and Pakistani subway bombers find support in their madrassas. Race riots are common in the northern industrial cities. Crime rates have soared. In parts of London, people fear to walk. Yes, the Britain of Tony Blair and Gordon Brown is more diverse than the Britain of Victoria and Lord Salisbury, Lloyd George and Churchill. Is it also a better, lovelier, stronger, more respected nation than the Britannia that ruled the waves and a fourth of the world?

The prevailing orthodoxy demands that we parrot such platitudes. And Her Majesty was careful to conform. "Fifty years on, we are now in a position to reflect more candidly on the Jamestown legacy," said the queen, as she began to reflect less candidly on that legacy.[5]

Here, at Jamestown, "Three great civilizations came together for the first time—western European, native American and African."[6]

Well, that is certainly one way of putting it.

Even Her Majesty must have smiled inwardly as she delivered this comic rendition of history. For the Jamestown settlers were not Western Europeans but English Christians. They despised French Catholics and the great event in their lives had been the sinking of the Spanish Armada. And the first decision taken at Jamestown was to build a fort to protect them from

Chief Powhatan's tribe, whom they thought might massacre them, as they suspected Indians had massacred the Roanoke colony. Their leader, Capt. John Smith, would escape being clubbed to death by Powhatan, thanks only to the princess Pocahontas. Or so Smith liked to tell the tale. In 1622, the Indians succeeded in massacring a third of all the inhabitants of Jamestown.[7]

As for the Africans, they arrived in 1619 in slave ships, and were not freed for 246 years. Then they were segregated for a century.

Jamestown was no coming together of "three great civilizations." It was the beginning of centuries of imperial conquest by British Christians who drove the pagan Indians westward, repopulated their lands, and imposed their own faith, customs, laws, language, and institutions upon their New World. Jamestown was the beginning of America—and of the British Empire.

"With the benefit of hindsight, we can see in that event [Jamestown] the origins of a singular endeavor—the building of a great nation, founded on the eternal values of democracy and equality," said the queen.[8]

A great nation did indeed arise from Jamestown, but, intending no disrespect to Her Majesty, democracy and equality had nothing to do with it. The House of Burgesses, formed in 1619, was restricted to white males, men of property. The American Revolution was not fought for equality, but to be rid of British rule. Four of the first five presidents—Washington, Jefferson, Madison, and Monroe—were Virginia slaveholders. Exactly two and a half centuries after Jamestown, in 1857, came Chief Justice Roger B. Taney's *Dred Scott* decision declaring that slaves were not Americans and that none of them had any of the rights of American citizens. Few Americans then, certainly not Abe Lincoln, believed in social or political equality.

Now, if, in 1957—350 years after Jamestown, 100 years after *Dred Scott*—the state of Virginia had a declared policy of massive resistance to racial integration, how can the queen claim that Jamestown or Virginia or America were always about "the eternal values of democracy and equality"?

History contradicts the politically correct version the queen had to recite about the Jamestown settlement—and raises another question.

If Jamestown and Virginia were not about democracy, equality, and diversity for the 350 years between 1607 and 1957, who invented this myth that America was always about democracy, equality, and diversity? And what was their motive?

At Jamestown the queen performed a service to America of which she was surely unaware. By radically revising her views of fifty years ago, about what Jamestown was, the queen revealed the real revolution that occurred between the era of Eisenhower and that of George W. Bush.

It is a revolution in thought and belief about who we are as a nation. In the half century since massive resistance, Virginia has indeed become a radically changed society. No longer does Richmond proudly call herself the Capital of the Confederacy. Lee-Jackson Day is out. Martin Luther King Day is in. The Confederate flag flies nowhere. On Monument Avenue, which features the statues of Robert E. Lee, "Stonewall" Jackson, J. E. B. Stuart, and Jefferson Davis, a statue of Arthur Ashe, an African-American tennis player, has been added.[9] "Carry Me Back to Old Virginny" was retired by the legislature as the state song ten years before the queen's return. Within days of her arrival in 2007, the Virginia legislature apologized for slavery.

Virginia 2007 is ashamed of who she was in 1957. But how then can Virginia be proud of what Jamestown was in 1607? For the first Jamestown was not some multicultural village but the first outpost of an imperial nation determined to settle and conquer North America for English Christians, to wipe out or drive out Indians who got in its way, and to bring in Africans as slaves to do the labor English settlers would not do.

An Inconvenient Truth

The point here is unpleasant to modernity but critical to recognize: The United States, the greatest republic since Rome, and the British Empire, the greatest empire since Rome, may be said to have arisen from that three-cornered fort the Jamestown settlers began to build the day they arrived. But that republic and that empire did not rise because the settlers and those who followed believed in diversity, equality, and democracy, but because they rejected diversity, equality, and democracy. The English, the Virginians, the Americans were all "us-or-them" people.

They believed in the superiority of their Christian faith and English culture and civilization. And they transplanted that unique faith, culture, and civilization to America's fertile soil. Other faiths, cultures, and civilizations—like the ones the Indians had here, or the Africans brought, or the French had planted in Quebec, or the Spanish in Mexico—they rejected and resisted with cannon, musket, and sword. This was *our* land, not anybody else's.

But today America and Britain have embraced ideas about the innate equality of all cultures, civilizations, languages, and faiths, and about the mixing of all tribes, races, and peoples, that are not only ahistorical, they are suicidal for America and the West. For all over the world, rising faiths like Islam, rising movements like the indigenous peoples' movement rolling out of Latin America to Los Angeles, rising powers like China reaching for Asian and world hegemony—ignore the kumbaya we preach, and look to what our fathers practiced when *they* conquered the world.

What the queen said at Jamestown 2007 was that we are not the same people we were in 1957. She is right. For we now reject as repellent and ethnocentric the idea that the British who founded our republic and created the British Empire were not only unique but superior to other peoples and civilizations. And to show the world how resolutely we reject those old ideas, we threw open our borders in the last forty years to peoples of all creeds, cultures, countries, and civilizations, inviting them to come and convert the old America into the most multicultural, multilingual, multiethnic, multiracial nation in history—"The First Universal Nation" of Ben Wattenberg's warblings. But if the Jamestown settlers had believed in equality and diversity, and had shared their fort with the Indians, the settlers would never have been heard from again.

No matter the lies we tell ourselves and teach our children, no great republic or empire—not Persia, Rome, Islam, Spain, France, Britain, Russia, China, the United States—ever arose because it embraced democracy, diversity, and equality. None. The real question is not whether the values the queen celebrated at Jamestown created America—they had nothing to do with it—but whether America can survive having embraced them. In his farewell address, President Reagan warned, "We've got to teach history based not on what's in fashion but what's important. . . . If we forget what we did, we won't know who we are. I'm warning of an eradication . . . of the American memory that could result, ultimately, in an erosion of the American spirit."[10]

Reagan's fear on leaving office, that forgetting the great things we have done in the past could lead to an erosion of the national spirit, was echoed by the incoming president of France, Nicolas Sarkozy, who said in May 2007: "I'm going to make the French proud of France again. I am going to bring an end to repentance, which is a form of self-hatred."

If France was ever to be great again, Sarkozy was saying, France must cease to grovel and apologize for sins committed in the days when she was great.[11] And it is true of us. The truth about Jamestown, Her Majesty's syrupy recital of history notwithstanding, is that a great and brave people with a superior faith, culture, and civilization conquered this continent and created something historic and wonderful. Others did not do it; others could not have done it. And if we lose that unique culture and civilization, we will cease to be what we were—a great people and a great nation.

The Real Revolution

Nothing in the above is written to suggest that slavery was not evil, or that everything done to the Indians was morally righteous. But it is to say that we must learn and speak the truth about who our ancestors were, and what they did, if we wish to preserve the best of what they created. Here we must separate the civil rights movement of the 1950s and early 1960s from the broader and deeper social, moral, and cultural revolution of the 1960s.

The civil rights movement of A. Philip Randolph, Roy Wilkins, and Dr. Martin Luther King Sr.—as opposed to that of his son, who became more radical in the mid-1960s—was not a movement to overthrow the system but to secure for black

Americans equality of rights within the system. It was not a new revolution but the continuation of an evolutionary process that had lasted for a century. It was not about overturning the social or moral order. It did not have its roots in radicalism. Many among the Negro elites of the 1950s were conservative on social, cultural, and moral issues. They were patriots. They had fought for the right to bear arms in World War II. Their movement was about improving the schools black children attended, ending segregation in federal housing and public accommodations, and the right to vote and to participate equally in politics. With the Civil Rights Act of 1964 and the Voting Rights Act of 1965, their movement had triumphed.

The real revolution of the last half century began in the 1960s and drove wedges through society that endure today. This revolution involved the repudiation of America's past as racist, sexist, imperialist, and genocidal in its treatment of women, Indians, Africans, and all peoples of color.

This revolution involved the rejection and overthrow of traditional Christian morality and Christianity itself as bigoted and repressive, and the conversion of the young to a sensuality, self-indulgence, and promiscuity condemned by all Christian faiths.

This revolution involved the overturning of all laws rooted in Christian doctrine regarding divorce, homosexuality, abortion—and the purge of all Christian symbols, books, and practices from public schools. This revolution was about de-Christianizing and secularizing America.

This revolution involved treason, siding with the enemies of the United States in Vietnam and in the Cold War by marching under Viet Cong flags, blowing up ROTC buildings, disrupting troop trains, going to Hanoi and Havana to denounce Amerika and celebrating the triumphs of Fidel and Ho Chi Minh.

This revolution involved the rewriting of history texts used in schools and colleges to demonize men previous generations of Americans had been taught to revere—Columbus and the explorers, the Founding Fathers, the pioneers, Custer and the 7th Cavalry, the men who won the West, Lee and Grant—and replacing them in the pantheon with new heroes drawn from among those who had resisted our forefathers.

This revolution involved the rejection of authors and writers whose poetry and prose we had all learned and loved as "dead white males" and propagandists who had nothing to teach the new generation.

This was a true social, moral, and cultural revolution that changed the way Americans think about their country and civilization. It captured and converted not only many of the young, but most of the academy, media, and Hollywood, who went over to the revolution because that is where popularity lay and because they despised the America they had grown up in.

It is not necessary for this book to trace the roots of this revolution, which hit the campuses with the arrival of the baby boomers in 1964.

But what must be recognized is that the revolution happened, that it has divided us deeply and permanently—over what is good, true, beautiful, right and wrong. It has made us two peoples. A husband and wife who disagreed as deeply as we Americans do over our most basic beliefs would have divorced and gone their separate ways. A family that differs as much as we Americans do would no longer be on speaking terms.

While the young have known no other America than the one in which they were raised, to many in the older generation, the changes in society have been revolutionary and dispiriting.

"[S]ince the end of World War II, American society has been suffering decomposition and deconstruction," wrote the late professor of theology Harold O. J. Brown. "Consider what we have come to in seven decades."

> The distinctiveness of marriage has been abolished (*Baird v. Eisenstadt*); prayer and Bible reading in schools has been stamped out (*Abington, Schemp, et al.*); the mother's womb has become the most dangerous place for a baby (*Roe v. Wade, et al.*); the rights (but not the duties) of fathers and parents of minor girls have been voided (*Planned Parenthood v. Danforth*); divorce has become easier than marrying; the Ten Commandments have been banned from public view; and now the natural distinction between male and female is being abolished (*Goodridge, Lawrence*, etc.). The Pledge of Allegiance is forbidden; the Boy Scouts are under attack; and Christmas carols are banned. Pornography is everywhere.
>
> The structure of American society is being demolished brick by brick. Within a few short years, Americans will have reached the "liberty" desired by Jean-Jacques Rousseau, the abolition of every particular dependency. This is what Hannah Arendt called "the atomistic mass," a precondition for the establishment of totalitarianism.[12]

But there is another America that looks back on the 1960s as a decade of liberation from the racially, socially, sexually repressive 1950s, and an even worse America before. Freedom from all external constraints on matters of morality, on how and with whom one chooses to live one's life, on how and when one wishes to end it, is a cardinal value for this post-Christian America. This

America believes that morality is subjective, that the good life consists of living according to the beliefs and values one freely chooses, that no state or society has a right to tell us how to live or to punish the choices we make. It is not the duty of government to uphold the commandments of any church or faith, but to protect people from all legislation rooted in religious belief.

One America believes (or hopes) that America is still a "Christian country." The other regards the phrase itself as bigoted.

This was a revolution. And it is far along toward creating a society devout Christians feel obligated to resist. And it raises the most fundamental questions about America's future. If we cannot agree on what is right and wrong and moral and immoral, and we cannot agree on whether America is a great and good country with a heroic and honorable past, as compared to all other countries, how can we agree on what we shall fight to defend?

The Disuniting of America

America is today less a nation than an encampment of suspicious and hostile tribes quarreling viciously over the spoils of politics and power. We live on the same land, under the same set of laws, but we are no longer the one people of whom John Jay wrote in *Federalist* No. 2.

> Providence has been pleased to give this one connected country to one united people—a people descended from the same ancestors, speaking the same language, professing the same religion, attached to the same principles of government, very similar in their manners and customs, and who, by their joint counsels, arms, and efforts, fighting

side by side throughout a long and bloody war, have nobly established their general liberty and independence.[13]

"This country and this people seem to have been made for each other," Jay wrote, calling his countrymen "a band of brethren." Even before the Constitution had been ratified, Jay regarded Americans as "one united people," "one connected country," "brethren," of common blood.[14]

But what held this "one united people" together—a common heritage, history, faith, language, manners, customs, and culture—today pulls us apart.

Are we united by language? Children in Chicago are taught in two hundred languages. Our fastest growing media are Spanish speaking. Half the 9 million in Los Angeles County speak a language other than English in their homes. Today's vile talk on radio and television, in the movies, magazines, and books, would have been an embarrassment in a marine barracks fifty years ago.

Are we united by faith? While 99 percent Protestant in 1789, we are now Protestant, Catholic, Jewish, Mormon, Muslim, Hindu, Buddhist, Taoist, Shintoist, Santería, Sikh, New Age, voodoo, agnostic, atheist, Rastafarian. The mention of the name of Jesus by the preachers President Bush chose to give invocations at his inauguration evoked cries of "insensitive," "divisive," "exclusionary." A *New Republic* editorial lashed out at these "crushing Christological thuds" from the inaugural stand.[15]

Many of the Christian churches have split asunder over abortion, female bishops, homosexual clergy, and gay marriage.

In 2007, after a court battle by the American Civil Liberties Union, the U.S. Department of Veterans Affairs agreed to add the five-point star of the Wiccan neo-pagan religion to the list of thirty-eight "emblems of belief" allowed on VA grave markers.

The thirty-eight include "symbols for Christianity, Buddhism, Islam and Judaism, as well as . . . for . . . Sufism Reoriented, Eckiankar and the Japanese faith Seicho-No-Ie."[16]

Are we united by a common culture? To the contrary. We are in a raging culture war in which peaceful coexistence is a myth.

In the nineteenth century, America was torn apart by slavery and the tariff. Those issues were settled in a civil war that resulted in 600,000 dead. Today, America is divided over issues of race, ethnicity, religion, language, culture, history, morality, the very things that once defined us and united us as a people and a nation.

Protestants and Catholics, a hundred years ago, disagreed passionately over whether beer, wine, and spirits were wicked. Today, we Americans disagree over whether annihilating 45 million unborn babies in the womb since *Roe v. Wade* is a mark of progress or a monstrous national evil causing us to echo Jefferson, "I tremble for my country when I reflect that God is just."

In the 1960s, to do penance for all her sins, from Jamestown on, the United States threw open its doors to peoples of all colors, continents, and creeds. And today, the America of John F. Kennedy, 89 percent white and 10 percent of African descent, an essentially biracial country united by a common culture, creed, history, and tradition, is gone. We threw it away.

Today, America is twice as populous as in 1950—with 300 million people. Instead of 1 to 2 million Hispanics, there are 45 million, with 102 million expected by 2050, concentrated in a Southwest that 58 percent of Mexicans say belongs to them. Our population is down to 67 percent European, and falling; 14.5 percent Hispanic and rising rapidly, 13 percent black and holding, and 4.5 percent Asian and rising. By 2040, Americans of European descent will be less than half the population, when, as President Bill Clinton told an audience of cheering California students, we will all belong to minorities. White Americans are already a minority in California, New Mexico, Texas, Hawaii. Twelve to 20 million illegal aliens are in the country. We may not have believed in diversity in the old America, but we are practicing it now. But has all this diversity made us a stronger nation than we were in the time of Eisenhower and Kennedy?

In October 2006, the *Financial Times* reported the findings of Robert Putnam, author of *Bowling Alone,* on diversity in America.

> A bleak picture of the corrosive effects of ethnic diversity has been revealed in research by Harvard University's Robert Putnam, one of the world's most influential political scientists.
>
> His research shows that the more diverse a community is, the less likely its inhabitants are to trust anyone—from their next-door neighbour to the mayor.
>
> The core message . . . was that, "in the presence of diversity, we hunker down," he said. "We act like turtles. The effect of diversity is worse than had been imagined. And it's not just that we don't trust people who are not like us. In diverse communities, we don't trust people who do look like us."
>
> Prof. Putnam found trust was lowest in Los Angeles, "the most diverse human habitation in human history. . . ."[17]

The city Professor Putnam references, Los Angeles, was the scene of the Academy Award–winning film *Crash,* which portrayed a feral zone in which whites, blacks, Asians, and Hispanics clashed violently again and again, as they could not understand one another or communicate with one another.

Wrote columnist John Leo, after perusing the report, "Putnam adds a crushing footnote: his findings 'may underestimate the real effect of diversity on social withdrawal.'"[18]

With another 100 million people anticipated in the United States by 2050, most of them immigrants and their children, legal and illegal, Putnam's findings are ominous. If the greater the diversity the greater the mistrust, Balkanization beckons—for all of us.

Is diversity a strength? In the ideology of modernity, yes. But history teaches otherwise. For how can racial diversity be a strength when racial diversity was behind the bloodiest war in U.S. history and has been the most polarizing issue among us ever since?

Our most divisive Supreme Court decision, *Dred Scott,* was about race. The War Between the States was about race. Reconstruction was about race. Segregation was about race. The riots in Harlem, Watts, Newark, Detroit, then Washington, D.C., and a hundred other cities after the assassination of Dr. King were about race. The riot in Los Angeles following the Simi Valley jury's acquittal of the cops who beat Rodney King was about race. Forced busing, affirmative action, quotas, profiling are about race. The O.J. trial, the Tawana Brawley and Duke rape-case hoaxes, and the Don Imus affair were about race. When Gunnar Myrdal wrote his classic *American Dilemma,* about the crisis of our democracy, the subject was—race.

All Americans believe slavery was evil and the denial of equal justice under law was wrong. But because they were wrong, does that make what we are doing—inviting the whole world to come to America—right or wise?

Today, tens of thousands of corporate and government bureaucrats monitor laws against discrimination and laws mandat-
ing integration in housing and employment. To achieve equality,
Americans are sacrificing freedom. Police are ever on the look-
out for hate crimes. Hardly a month passes without some con-
troversy or crime rooted in race being forced through cable TV
and talk radio onto the national agenda. How does all this make
us a more united, stronger people?

Among the educated and affluent young, resegregation is in
vogue. Columnist Leo writes that at UCLA, racially separate
graduations have become the norm. "The core reason," he
writes, "is the obvious one."

> On campus, assimilation is a hostile force, the domestic
> version of American imperialism. On many campuses,
> identity-group training begins with separate freshman
> orientation programs for nonwhites, who arrive earlier
> and are encouraged to bond before the first Caucasian
> freshmen arrive. Some schools have separate orientations
> for gays as well. Administrations tend to foster separatism
> by arguing that bias is everywhere, justifying double stan-
> dards that favor identity groups.[19]

Leo concludes on a note of despair, "As in so many areas of
national life, the preposterous is now normal."[20]

Quo Vadis, America?

Again, history teaches that multiethnic states are held together either by an authoritarian regime or a dominant ethnocultural
core, or they are ever at risk of disintegration in ethnic conflict.

The Soviet Union, Czechoslovakia, and Yugoslavia, artificial nations all, disintegrated when the dictatorships collapsed.

In democracies it is an ethnocultural core that holds the country together. England created a United Kingdom of English, Scots, Welsh, and Irish, with England predominant. Now that Britain is no longer great, the core nations have begun to pull apart, to seek their old independence, as the English have begun to abandon the land they grew up in.

In "Vanishing England," in August 2007, columnist Cal Thomas reported a startling fact: Between June 2005 and June 2006, 200,000 British citizens (the equivalent of a million Americans) left their country for good, as more than a half million legal immigrants and unknown thousands of illegals entered. "Britons give many reasons for leaving, but their stories share one commonality," Thomas wrote; "life in Britain has become unbearable for them."[21] There is the lawlessness and the constant threat of Muslim terror, but also

the loss of a sense of Britishness, exacerbated by the growing refusal of public schools to teach the history and culture of the nation to the next generation. What it means to be British has been watered down in a plague of political correctness that has swept the country faster than hoof-and-mouth disease. Officials says they do not wish to "offend" others.[22]

Intellectuals deceive themselves if they believe the new trinity of their faith—democracy, equality, and diversity—can replace the old idea of what it meant to be a Briton, what it meant to be an Englishman.

In the thirteen North American colonies, the ethnocultural

core was British-Protestant, with a smattering of Germans whose growing numbers alarmed Ben Franklin. After the wave of Irish from 1845 to 1849, and the steady German influx, and then the great wave from Southern and Eastern Europe between 1890 and 1920, America was no longer British-Protestant, but a European-Christian nation whose institutions, language, and culture remained British. Bismarck said the most important fact of the twentieth century would be that the North Americans spoke English. Indeed, that is why we fought on Britain's side in two world wars. Despite our eighteenth- and nineteenth-century quarrels and wars, the Brits were still "the cousins."

By 1960, 88.6 percent of our nation was of European stock and 95 percent Christian. America had never been a more united nation. African Americans had been assimilated into the Christian faith and national culture if not fully into society. While Jews, perhaps 4 percent of the population, were non-Christians, their parents or grandparents had come from European Christian nations.

Since the cultural revolution of the 1960s and the Immigration Act of 1965, however, the ethnocultural core has begun to dissolve. Secularism has displaced Christianity as the faith of the elites. The nation has entered a post-Christian era. There is no longer a unifying culture. Rather, we are fighting a culture war. And the European ethnic core is shrinking. From near 90 percent in 1960, it is down to 67 percent today, and will be less than 50 percent by 2040.

Here we come to the heart of the matter.

Quo Vadis, America? Where are you going?

If we have no common faith and are divided by morality and culture, and are separated by ethnicity and race, what holds us together? Especially in light of Putnam's report that "diversity" dilutes "social capital," erodes community, and engenders mutual mistrust.

Realizing we are divided on the things that constitute a true nation—blood and soil, tradition and faith, history and heroes—intellectuals have sought to construct, in lieu of the real nation, the nation of the heart that is passing away, an artificial nation, a nation of the mind, an ideological nation, a creedal nation, united by a belief in the new trinity: diversity, democracy, and equality. As Christianity is purged from the public schools, this civil religion is taught in its stead. The dilemma of those who conjured up this civil religion and creedal nation, liberals and neoconservatives, is that it has no roots and does not touch the heart. Americans will not send their sons to fight and die for such watery abstractions.

To Die for Diversity?

Wilson declared in April 1917 that we were going to war "to make the world safe for democracy." That was nonsense. If saving democracy was why we fought, why had we stayed out of the war from August 1914 to April 1917, while millions of French, Germans, Russians, Italians, Austrians, and Britons had gone to their deaths? The truth: We only entered the war when U-boats began sinking our ships and killing American sailors, and German Foreign Secretary Arthur Zimmermann was caught secretly urging the Mexicans to stab us in the back and occupy the Southwest if the U.S. Army was sent to France. And Woodrow Wilson concluded he could not save the world if we did not get into the war.

The slogans that have rallied Americans—"Remember the Alamo!" "Fifty-Four Forty or Fight!" "Remember the *Maine!*" "Remember Pearl Harbor!"—had nothing to do with ideology.

Lincoln, in his cry from the heart to his "dissatisfied countrymen" not to take the path of civil war, did not appeal to principles of democracy, but to "bonds of affection," and "mystic chords of memory" that tied us together, and to our patriot fathers who had fought side by side.

I am loath to close. We are not enemies, but friends. We must not be enemies. Though passion may have strained, it must not break our bonds of affection. The mystic chords of memory, stretching from every battlefield, and patriot grave, to every living heart and hearthstone, all over this broad land, will yet swell the chorus of the Union, when again touched, as surely they will be, by the better angels of our nature.[23]

During the run-up to the Iraq war, we were told that Saddam may have been behind 9/11, was in league with terrorists, had weapons of mass destruction, and was seeking nuclear weapons and that U.S. inaction risked a "mushroom cloud over an American city." So the nation backed the president's decision to invade, because the nation was told, and the nation believed America was in peril.

Only after Baghdad fell did we learn that Iraq was part of a "world democratic revolution." Had the American people been told in March 2003 that building democracy in Iraq was the reason we had to go to war, we would not have gone to war.

Where are we now?

Having gone through a social, cultural, and moral revolution, we Americans have ceased to be the one people and one nation we once were. Our differences are too deep and they are about the most basic of beliefs—God and man, good and evil, right and wrong. With the Cold War over, we no longer even agree on who our enemies are, or what we should fight for.

Disillusioned by a bloody mess of a war undertaken for other than vital interests, we will not soon again unite around a cause that cannot be tied to America's security. We are in no mood for any more crusades to "make the world safe for democracy" or "end tyranny in our world." The only foreign policy around which this deconstructed nation can unite is one designed to defend the vital interests of the United States. The crusades are over. As Lippmann wrote,

> we must consider first and last the American national interest. If we do not, if we construct our foreign policy on some kind of abstract theory of our rights and duties, we shall build castles in the air. We shall formulate policies which in fact the nation will not support with its blood, its sweat, and its tears.[24]

7

Colony of the World

Give us a protective tariff, and we will have the
greatest country on earth.
—ABRAHAM LINCOLN, 1847[1]

Free trade results in giving our money, our manufactures,
and our markets to other nations.
—WILLIAM MCKINLEY, 1892[2]

Pernicious indulgence in the doctrine of free trade seems
inevitably to produce fatty degeneration of the moral fibre.
—THEODORE ROOSEVELT, 1895[3]

I'm concerned about protectionism.
—GEORGE W. BUSH, 2007[4]

"Trade is all very well in its way, but Trade has been put in the place of Truth. Trade which is in its nature a secondary or dependent thing, has been treated as a primary and independent thing: an absolute. The moderns, mad upon mere multiplication, have even made a plural out of what is essentially singular.... They have taken what all ancient philosophers called the Good, and translated it as the Goods."[5]

Chesterton captured a truth little understood. To many economists, free trade is not a policy option to be debated but a dogma to be defended. As Joseph Pearce observes in *Small Is Still Beautiful,*

> Global free trade has become an unquestionable moral dogma enshrined at the heart of modern economic theory. As such, politicians and economists are reluctant to question its presumptions and are failing to confront or even comprehend the effects of free trade on a world economy that is changing. . . .
>
> [H]ere in America conservatives who speak against unrestrained free trade are consistently marginalized and reviled.[6]

When the Nobel Prize–winner in economics Maurice Allais declared, heretically, that free trade produces beneficial effects only when conducted between regions at comparable levels of development, Jacques Attali, president of the European Bank for Reconstruction and Development, denounced all such negative reflections on free trade as *"stupides."*[7]

When, after thirty years as a devout free trader, this writer lapsed in the faith, after witnessing the impact of globalism on communities and towns across America, my friend, the late Nobel Prize–winner Milton Friedman, wrote to me that I was "doing the devil's work."[8] I was not just wrong. I was an apostate leading the faithful away from the true church.

Dr. Friedman was the most influential economist of the last century, with the exception of J. M. Keynes. Indeed, the late J. K. Galbraith wrote toward the end of his life, unhappily, that "the age of John Maynard Keynes gave way to the age of Milton Friedman."[9]

When I wrote my friend that I had converted to Hamilton's philosophy, Milton wrote back.

> Among the Founding fathers, Hamilton was a great sinner. In his Report on Manufactures he praised Adam Smith to the sky and then proceeded to urge a policy strictly inconsistent with Smith's arguments. Recall that he proposed a tariff on steel on the grounds of protecting an "infant industry." That infant has apparently never grown up.[10]

Milton was referring to the quotas Ronald Reagan slammed on steel imports to prevent foreign dumpers from taking down the U.S. industry. But was it a sin to protect a U.S. steel industry that became the greatest on earth, capturing world markets from Great Britain, making America self-sufficient, and enabling us to build the weapons that won two world wars? If free trade is one's religion, it may be a mortal sin to put quotas or tariffs on imported steel. But if a statesman's goal is to make his nation self-sufficient and build up its industry so it can capture the world's markets, tariffs make all the sense in the world. What is decisive here is what one believes is crucial—faithfulness to ideology, or putting America first.

And if Hamilton was a sinner, was not Adam Smith also a sinner? From 1778 to his death in 1790, he served as commissioner of customs and enforced Britain's protectionist policy. "To expect . . . that freedom of trade should ever be entirely restored in Great Britain," said Smith, "is as absurd as to expect that an Oceana or a Utopia should ever be established in it."[11]

Smith believed in the selective use of tariffs to defend national interests. He was a patriot first, a free trader second.

In his 1979 bestseller *Free to Choose* Dr. Friedman dismissed all arguments against free trade, in Smith's phrase, as the "interested sophistry of merchants and manufacturers," declaring, "We should move unilaterally to free trade . . . over a period of, say, five years."[12]

> We could say to the rest of the world: we believe in freedom and we intend to practice it. . . . Our market is open to you without tariffs or other restrictions. Sell here what you can and wish to. Buy whatever you can and wish to. In that way cooperation can be worldwide and free.[13]

Milton Friedman was a great economist, but this is pure ideology.

Not all who believe that the interests of the nation come first, before the commands of free trade, are hired men of the Business Roundtable or Chamber of Commerce. Indeed, corporate lobbyists today endlessly prowl the halls of Congress promoting free trade. In whose interest do they toil?

Dr. Friedman noted with chagrin that while almost all economists preach free trade, few statesmen practice it. True, but why? Because a statesman is responsible to the nation, while economists are, by and large, responsible for nothing. Devising an ideal world while sitting in an upholstered chair in the privileged sanctuary of a Beltway think tank or tenured professor's office is easier than dealing with the real world from the Oval Office.

Making the case for free trade from history, Dr. Friedman wrote, "From Waterloo to the First World War . . . Britain was the leading nation of the world and during the whole of that century it had nearly complete free trade."[14]

My friend cherry-picks his history. True, Britain was the first nation on earth when the Corn Laws were repealed in 1846. And in 1860, when free trade was embraced, Britain boasted an economy twice that of ours. But by 1914, Britain's economy was not half the size of the high-tariff U.S. economy, and Britain had been surpassed by a protectionist Germany that did not exist before 1871. The Britain that had emerged as the world's first and greatest manufacturing power in the eighteenth century did so under the mercantilist Navigation Acts. Under free trade, Britain's preeminence passed away forever. Free trade left her so dependent on imports that German U-boats would have forced her surrender in the Great War had it not been for the industrial and shipping capacity of the United States. An America built on protectionism rescued free-trade Britain.

"International free trade fosters harmonious relations among nations that are different in culture and institutions," Dr. Friedman assured us.[15] But no nations were ever more intertwined by trade than the European countries that plunged into the bloodiest war in history in 1914. And the two that traded most intensively with each other were the Britain of George V and the Germany of his cousin, the kaiser.

If free trade is best for nations, how is it that every modern state that rose to preeminence and power—Britain before 1846, the United States from 1860 to 1914, Germany from 1870 to 1914, Japan after World War II, China today—was protectionist? Not one followed the model of Milton Friedman. All adopted the economic nationalism of Alexander Hamilton. All four presidents on Mount Rushmore—Washington, Jefferson, Lincoln, Theodore Roosevelt—were economic nationalists. All believed in tariffs to finance the government, spur industry, and give U.S. manufacturers an advantage over foreign manufacturers in the American market. And what is wrong with preferring your own? Does not every family?

Origins of a Cult

From its birth in the early nineteenth century, the free-trade movement had aspects of an ideology, indeed, of a religious cult. When its great evangelist Richard Cobden rose in Free Trade Hall in Manchester on January 15, 1846, the year of repeal of the Corn Laws, he declared:

> I believe that the physical gain will be the smallest gain to humanity from the success of this principle. I look farther; I see in the Free Trade principle that which shall act on the moral world as the principle of gravitation in the universe— drawing men together, thrusting aside the antagonism of race, and creed, and language, and uniting us in the bonds of eternal peace.[16]

Free trade, like God's grace, had salvific power to cause men to cast aside malice, envy, and greed and embrace one another in love. From birth, utopianism was a feature of the movement. "It would be well to engraft our free trade agitation upon the peace movement," declared Frédéric Bastiat. "They are one and the same cause."[17] Bastiat urged France to adopt unilateral disarmament, proclaiming in 1849, "I shall not hesitate to vote for disarmament . . . because I do not believe in invasions."[18]

Unfortunately, France's German neighbors did believe in invasions.

Jean-Baptiste Say was another free-trade evangelist and utopian: "All nations are friends in the nature of things."[19]

Their great antagonist was Friedrich List, a German immigrant who provided supporting fire for the America-first economics of Madison, Jackson, and Henry Clay. List mocked the "cosmopolitanism" of the free traders who seemed to care more about the world than their own countries. To List the world did not command love and loyalty. The nation did.

> Between each individual and entire humanity . . . stands *the Nation*, with its special language and literature . . . origin and history . . . manners and customs, laws and institutions . . . with its separate territory; a society, which, united by a thousand ties of mind and of interests, combines itself into one independent whole.[20]

In the real world, Europe's nations were rivals and antagonists. Where the classical liberals declared that the choices of consumers should determine what was best for the country, List dissented furiously:

> The foreign trade of a nation must not be estimated in the way in which individual merchants judge it . . . the nation is bound to keep steadily in view all these conditions on which its present and future existence, prosperity, and power depend.[21]

Where the nineteenth-century liberals declared consumption the sole purpose of production, List retorted that production "renders consumption possible." The "power of producing wealth is therefore infinitely more important than wealth itself."[22]

The forces of production are the tree on which wealth grows. . . . The tree which bears the fruit is of itself of greater value than the fruit itself. . . . The prosperity of a nation is not . . . greater in the proportion in which it has amassed more wealth (i.e. values of exchange), but in the proportion in which it has more developed its powers of production.[23]

List would be appalled watching rich Americans grow richer on the soaring stock prices of companies whose profits are exploding because they had moved their factories overseas and outsourced American jobs to Asia.

List carried the day in America and the Germany of Bismarck, who ordered List's works used as texts in the schools of the Second Reich. But the free traders won the debate in England—and the inexorable decline of Great Britain as first industrial power began.

As late as 1923, John Maynard Keynes was still writing of free trade in lyrics as rhapsodic as those of Cobden and Say:

We must hold to free trade, in its widest interpretation, as an inflexible dogma, to which no exception is admitted, wherever the decision rests with us. We must hold to this even where we receive no reciprocity of treatment and even in those rare cases where by infringing it we could in fact obtain a direct economic advantage. We should hold to free trade as a principle of international morals, and not merely as a doctrine of economic advantage.[24]

This is the authentic voice of the ideologue, the true believer. In 1930, however, Keynes, his country wracked by depression, recanted. He came out for tariffs to protect British industry then under assault from U.S. and continental imports. And Keynes was attacked for his apostasy. But he had come to understand, as had Jefferson, Madison, and John Adams, that it does matter immensely where a nation's goods are produced. As this writer argued a decade ago,

> Manufacturing is the key to national power. Not only does it pay more than service industries, the rates of productivity growth are higher and the potential of new industry arising is far greater. From radio came television; from television, VCRs and flat-panel screens. From adding machines came calculators and computers. From the electric typewriter came the word processor. Research and development follows manufacturing.[25]

Alan Tonelson of the U.S. Business & Industrial Council echoed this view in the *Financial Times* in 2007:

> In the US . . . manufacturing is the economy's most productive sector, the engine of most of the technological progress, the employer of most of its scientists and technicians, and the creator of its best-paying jobs on average. An economy that simply watched as its manufacturing shriveled would be like a sports team that simply watched as its star players departed for rivals.
>
> . . . a world-class manufacturing base located in country is essential for a world-class military and for acceptable levels of national security. Countries that lose these assets lose considerable control over their national destinies—as should be obvious to any European.[26]

Manufacturing is the nation's muscle. In the perpetual struggle of nations, the manufacturing powers always rise to the top. When the Industrial Revolution began in England, England vaulted to the forefront. The Navigation Acts kept her there. William Pitt, architect of victory in the Seven Years' War, knew it. He supported the colonies' demand, "No taxation without representation!" But Pitt warned that if he ever caught Americans engaged in manufacturing—exclusive province of the mother country—he would send his ships and blow their factories off the map.

It is the mark of an ideologue to take a simple, plausible statement—"International free trade fosters harmonious relations among nations"—elevate it to an absolute and universal law, declare it dogma, and attack as infidels or apostates any who question it. To Milton Friedman, all impediments to free trade should be abolished *unilaterally*. If other nations dump goods here to kill our manufacturers and capture our markets, not to worry, the consumer benefits. Trade deficits are better than trade surpluses because U.S. consumers get goods from foreign producers in exchange for little green pieces of paper, dollars.

If a foreign government subsidizes exports, Dr. Friedman asks,

> Who is hurt and who benefits? To pay for the subsidies the foreign government must tax its citizens. They are the ones who pay for the subsidies. U.S. consumers benefit. They get cheap TV sets or automobiles or whatever it is that is subsidized. Should we complain about such a program of reverse foreign aid?[27]

Following Friedman, our country lost its TV industry. We lost half of the world's market for civilian airliners because of decades of European subsidies of Airbus; and we are losing our automobile industry. Is America better off?

What Friedman and the free traders fail to understand or ignore is that the transfer of production abroad is *not free trade.* Unlike the export of goods, which adds to GDP, the transfer of factories subtracts from U.S. GDP and adds to Asian and Chinese GDP. When factories closed in the North and reopened in the Sun Belt, the North became a Rust Belt. The same happens to a nation when production is transferred overseas. As Ralph Gomory, coauthor of *Global Trade and National Conflicting Interests,* argues, there is no basis in economic theory for saying it is good to shift a factory overseas.

If you want to do anything about the transfer of capabilities, you're labeled as interfering with free trade. But it isn't free trade. In fact, it is almost certainly bad. But people just blindly mix that with trade. That piece of confusion is very hard to overcome.[28]

It needs to be said again and again: Exporting factories is not free trade.

"The Asians countries have figured this out," says *Manufacturing & Technology Report*; "they are exploiting the divorce between a country's GDP and its companies' desires for profit."[29] Unfortunately, Gomory adds, "The people in our government still are treating the companies as if they represent the country, and they do not."[30]

"What is best for the consumer is best for America" is a maxim that might sum up Milton's philosophy. But is what is best for consumers really what is best for America? The statesmen who converted thirteen rural colonies into the greatest technological and manufacturing power the world had ever seen, through protectionism, believed otherwise. They regarded free trade as utopian folly.

Our Founding Fathers did not oppose trade. From birth, America was one of the great trading nations. But there were more important things than foreign trade. Economic independence was one. Self-sufficiency in the vital necessities of our national life was another. Making America a manufacturing power was a third. Taxes on imports, Washington, Hamilton, and Madison agreed, were the way to finance the government. Taxes on incomes and exports were prohibited by the Constitution. Our Founding Fathers wanted foreigners to carry as much of our tax load as possible. Is this discrimination? Of course. But the first bill out of Congress was the Tariff Act of 1789.

What explains the mass conversion of American conservatives to a free-trade ideology their fathers held in contempt? What caused the Republican Party to turn its back on the philosophy of Lincoln, Theodore Roosevelt, and Calvin Coolidge, and begin to recite the catechism of Wilson and FDR? What explains the refusal of thinking men to question free trade when it has gutted our industries, outsourced the jobs of Middle America, deepened our dependence on an unreliable world, and sent the Reagan Democrats home to the party of their fathers? Why are so many conservatives willing to be martyred for an ideology and dogma their fathers regarded as the utopian absurdity of free trade?

And what are the fruits of Friedmanite free trade? In 2006,

- The U.S. trade deficit reached a record $764 billion.
- The trade deficit in goods hit $836 billion, 6 percent of GDP.

- The trade deficit in manufactures rose to $536 billion from $504 billion in 2005, a record.
- The trade deficit in autos, auto parts, and trucks hit $145 billion, another record.
- The trade deficit with China rose 15 percent to $233 billion, largest ever recorded between two nations.
- The trade deficit with Japan rose to $88 billion, a record.
- The trade deficit with Mexico hit $60 billion, a record.[31]

Between January 2002 and January 2007, the gargantuan U.S. trade deficit set five straight world records, as did the U.S. trade deficit in autos, auto parts, and trucks. If this is the fruit of a successful trade policy, what would a failed trade policy look like?

From 2001 to 2007, America ran $4 trillion in trade deficits, $2.6 trillion in manufactured goods. Three million manufacturing jobs, one in every six, vanished. By January 2007, wages in manufacturing had fallen 3 percent in three years—during a recovery when the stock market had risen every year.[32]

Since NAFTA passed in 1993, America has run fourteen straight trade deficits with Mexico. Grand total: over $500 billion. In 2006, Mexico exported more than 900,000 vehicles to the United States. The United States exported fewer than 600,000 to the entire world.[33]

Where did Mexico get an auto industry? Is it good that the U.S. auto industry is being exported? Has the price of a new car plummeted because Mexicans are paid a fraction of what U.S. autoworkers earn?

In 1943–44, at the height of World War II, 40 percent of all U.S. jobs were in manufacturing. In 1950, a third of our labor

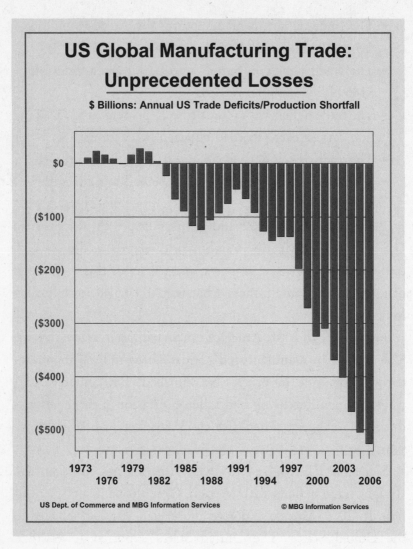

US Global Manufacturing Trade: Unprecedented Losses

$ Billions: Annual US Trade Deficits/Production Shortfall

US Dept. of Commerce and MBG Information Services

© MBG Information Services

force was still in manufacturing. Today it is 10 percent and falling.[34] For the first seventy years of the twentieth century, we ran trade surpluses every year. We have now run trade deficits for thirty-five years. We used to export twice as much as we imported. Now we import twice as much as we export. Is it good for America that our dependence on imports has risen from 4

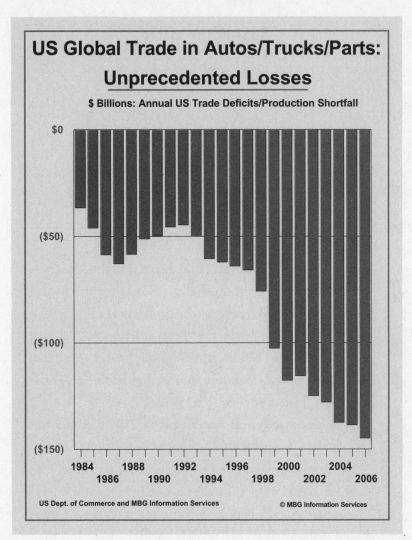

US Global Trade in Autos/Trucks/Parts: Unprecedented Losses

$ Billions: Annual US Trade Deficits/Production Shortfall

US Dept. of Commerce and MBG Information Services

© MBG Information Services

percent of GDP to 16 percent? Is it good for America that we import a third of our manufactured goods? Is it good that American workingmen and women make fewer and fewer of the things their countrymen need, while corporate chiefs bank billions of dollars for shipping American jobs overseas?

History and common sense teach otherwise.

Runt of the Litter

Responding to voter anger over lost jobs and closed factories, the Republicans point to the 3.6 percent growth in 2006 and full employment. But even graded on a curve, the Bush administration is at the bottom of the class.

- In President Bush's first six years, an average of 47,000 nonfarm payroll jobs were created each month—compared to 150,000 a month under Reagan, and 237,000 under Clinton.
- From the end of the recession Bush inherited, in November 2001, through mid-2007, wages for the lowest 80 percent of U.S. workers rose by 0.6 percent per year. And average real wages for those workers were lower than they were in 2003.[35] Bush himself finally conceded: "[O]ur dynamic economy is leaving working people behind. . . . Income inequality is real."[36]
- Average income for all Americans in 2005 was still below the last year of the Clinton administration.[37]
- "For . . . men 25 years and older working full time, median real weekly earnings were not only below their level of August 2003," said *The Washington Times* in mid-2007, "these median real weekly earnings were less than they were when Bill Clinton left the White House."[38]
- By mid-2007, median household income had fallen $1,300 below what it was in Bill Clinton's final year.[39]
- Between January 2001 and January 2007, the United States added 4.79 million jobs, weakest six-year performance in fifty years. Of the 3.5 million created in the

private sector, all could be accounted for by the 2.74 million new jobs in private education and health services and the 1.29 million in food services and drinking places. Of 3 million manufacturing jobs lost, 558,000 were in computers and electronic products.

But not everyone is treading water.

The Fortunate Few

"Greed is right. Greed works. Greed clarifies, cuts through, and captures the essence of the evolutionary spirit," said Gordon Gecko in the movie *Wall Street*.[40] Indeed, it does.

"Yea, they are greedy dogs which can never have enough," said Isaiah. In Christian teaching, covetousness stands between pride and lust as the second of the seven capital sins to which men are tempted. Especially, it would seem, in twenty-first-century America.

When his salary was raised in 1930 to $80,000, Babe Ruth was asked how it felt to make more than the president of the United States. Well, the Babe retorted, "I had a better year than he did."

In 2006 the head of Citigroup earned $26 million, forty-seven times the salary and benefit package of the president of the United States, writes Joseph Becker in *The New Republic*. Citigroup's chief executive may have had a better year than George Bush, but can anyone say he had as tough a job?[41]

In 2006, the average CEO saw his compensation package rise by almost 10 percent to $14.78 million.[42] As middle-class wages stagnate and the costs of health care, education, gasoline, and heating oil rise, the superrich have wildly prospered. The average CEO of a major company earns more in a day than the average American in a year. Many CEOs earn the annual pay of their workers before lunchtime. And being a CEO can mean rewards, even for failure.

Robert Nardelli of Home Depot and Henry McKinnell of Pfizer each walked away with a severance package of nearly $200 million, despite producing declines in the value of their companies. Richard Grasso, head of the New York Stock Exchange, a nonprofit, quasi-public body, earned $140 million and $48 million in added payments in a year when the NYSE earned $28 million. One member of the board thought the salary a typing error. Grasso reportedly got a bonus of $5 million for getting trading going again after 9/11. Meanwhile, almost half of all Americans reported salaries of less than $30,000 and two-thirds salaries of less than $50,000.[43]

In 2006, for the first time, one had to be a billionaire to make the Forbes list of America's richest 400. Together, that Forbes 400 had assets of $1.25 trillion, a sum greater than the gross national product of all but seven nations.[44]

In September 2007, the newest Forbes 400 list arrived. Where, a year earlier, it took $1 billion to make the list, now it required $1.3 billion, and eighty-two disconsolate billionaires did not make the cut. The total wealth of the Forbes 400 had risen from $1.25 trillion to $1.54 trillion. The combined wealth of the 400 Forbes fortunates is now greater than the GDP of Canada, a member of the G-8. Two of the top ten on the Forbes list had compiled their wealth in the gambling industry, once considered a vice and once outlawed in the United States.[45]

"Top money managers," notes *The New York Times*, "earn such huge incomes that even when their compensation is mixed with the much lower pay of clerks, secretaries and others, the average pay in investment banking is ten times that of all private sector jobs."[46] Some 173,000 Americans work in investment banking. The average wage in the private sector in the USA is $841 a week; in investment banking it is $8,367 a week. For the six thousand folks in investment banking in Fairfield County, Connecticut, the average annual pay is $1.24 million.[47] In 2006, at Goldman Sachs, the *average* bonus for each of its employees was $622,000.[48]

In the twenty-first century, greed and corruption appear endemic at many of our great companies, Enron being one, and the accounting firm that audited its books, Arthur Andersen, another. Global Crossing, Tyco, WorldCom, have become household words, as have the names of their disgraced CEOs. In 2006, the Securities and Exchange Commission was investigating 160 companies for fraud in the backdating of stock options to enlarge the compensation of corporate executives.

America has always had robber barons, we are told. Look at the nineteenth and early twentieth centuries. And it is true. Many of Teddy Roosevelt's malefactors of great wealth were avaricious men. But they were also something that few of our superrich are today. They were nation builders.

Cornelius Vanderbilt gave New York steamships and railroads. E. H. Harriman and James J. Hill laid down the rails that pulled America together. John D. Rockefeller created Standard Oil, the parent of the world's great oil companies. Andrew Carnegie and Henry Clay Frick made us the world's greatest steel producer. J. P. Morgan could walk onto the floor of the New York Stock Exchange and stop a panic with an order of stock. Henry Ford put America on wheels. Thomas Edison gave us the inventions that helped bring light and heat to America's homes. These men were giants. Other than a few like Bill Gates, how many of our nouveaux riches are in that league? How many will warrant biographies anyone wants to read? How many made their money simply by being more clever at studying financial reports and trading paper?

The age of the robber barons was also a time of stunning growth and soaring prosperity for almost all Americans. Between 1869 and 1900, the gross national product quadrupled, prices fell 58 percent, real wages rose 53 percent, though population doubled.[49] That is not the story of the American middle and working class in the twenty-first century.

"The very rich are different from you and me," Scott Fitzgerald said to Hemingway, who reportedly quipped, "Yes, they have more money."

They have something else as well—privileged access to such exotic instruments as derivatives and investment opportunities as hedge funds that most Americans can neither understand nor participate in.

Through loopholes in the tax laws, operators of these hedge funds have been able to have their income taxed at the capital gains rate of 15 percent, a lower rate than some of their secretaries pay.

Many of our superrich have something else most Americans do not have. Pleonexia. That is the word for unbridled greed, and the recurrence of the disease in America has done much to alienate the middle class from the system and convert ours into a land where the inequalities of wealth and disparities of sacrifice are as great as in any advanced nation on earth. America was not that kind of country when we were growing up.

High-Tech Deficit

Traditionally, the United States has run trade surpluses in advanced-technology goods. But in 2002 that surplus disappeared, and since 2004 the nation has run a trade deficit both in technology goods and services and intellectual property.

Alan Tonelson and Pete Kim of the U.S. Business & Industrial Council undertook a study of the import penetration of vital U.S. industries, "the kinds of high-value, capital-intensive sectors that make up the industrial and technological backbone of any advanced economy."[50]

What did Tonelson and Kim find?

- In 24 of the 114 key industries, such as telecommunications hardware, heavy-duty trucks, broadcast and wireless communications gear, imports, by 2005, had seized more than 50 percent of the U.S. market.
- In eight industries, including autos, environmental controls, and aircraft engines and parts, imports had captured 60–69 percent of the U.S. market.
- In six sectors, including machine tools and electric resistors and capacitors, imports controlled more than 70 percent of the American market.

Of the 114 U.S. industries investigated by Tonelson and Kim, 111 had lost customers to imports.[51] In President Bush's first term alone, the era of the dot-com bust, the United States lost a million technology jobs, most of which it has never regained.[52] By 2007, America was again adding jobs in the tech sector. But the disaster of the first five years of the new century had contributed to a plunge of 70 percent in the number of college freshmen planning to major in computer science.[53]

Consider one of America's great high-tech manufacturers, Boeing, which is said to have recaptured the lead from Airbus in the building of new commercial jets. As the *Financial Times* reported on the 2007 roll-out of the 787 Dreamliner, the manufacturing "is almost entirely out-sourced."[54]

> Most of the 787 will in fact be made far from the Everett facility, which will in effect snap together the parts in a move that has left some observers wringing their hands over potential skill losses and the long-term impact of technology transfer. While Boeing and Airbus have enjoyed a virtual duopoly on larger aircraft manufacturing for twenty years, Russia, Japan, and China may launch aircraft makers of their own.[55]

No wonder the Chinese have been so welcoming to U.S. aircraft manufacturing plants, and the Japanese so receptive to buying Boeing planes—if they can build the crucial parts.

Downhill Racer

Before World War I, America was a debtor nation. By Armistice Day 1918, however, the United States had become the greatest creditor on earth. Germany and Russia were prostrate. Borrowing from America to finance the war, Britain and France had gone into a black hole of debt.

Today, the United States has again become the world's greatest debtor nation. But now we borrow to finance consumption.

A current account is a country's profit-and-loss statement.

To measure it, one adds all the earnings from exports and all the dividends, interest, and capital gains received from abroad. One subtracts the cost of all imports, and all dividends, interest, capital gains, and foreign aid that have gone overseas.

In 1992, the current account deficit was $50 billion, less than 1 percent of GDP. In 2006, America ran a current account deficit of $857 billion, 6.5 percent of GDP, twice the 3.4 percent of the Reagan decade, when America was said to be in a "competitiveness crisis."[56] America is today borrowing $2.3 billion every day in order to consume more foreign goods than we can cover with our sales abroad. Foreigners are using these huge surpluses to snap up U.S. assets—T-bills, stocks, bonds, companies, and real estate. Foreign ownership of U.S. assets now exceeds U.S. ownership of foreign assets by $2.7 trillion.[57]

When one hears of a couple spending more than they earn, drawing down savings, selling off assets, one concludes that the couple is either in financial straits or has entered their sunset years. Both are true of us.

At the close of the Philadelphia convention, Franklin rose to remark that he had observed on the back of Washington's chair the image of a sun on the horizon. I had long wondered, said Franklin, whether it was a rising—or a setting sun. "Now I see it is a rising sun."

For America the sun is no longer rising.

The Selling of America

In his 1950s "Sixteen Tons," "Tennessee Ernie" Ford sings of a coal miner who, weak of mind but strong of body, works himself to death, but begs St. Peter not to call him, because "I owe my soul to the company store."

That coal miner is a metaphor for us. Foreigners are now using the dollars we ship abroad to take control of U.S. highways built by American taxpayers.

The 157-mile Indiana toll road that connects the Ohio Turnpike to Chicago has been leased for seventy-five years to a Spanish company, Cintra, and Australia's Macquarie. Indiana got $3.85 billion for letting the toll road go, and Goldman Sachs $19 million for brokering the deal. Cintra and Macquarie have leased the Chicago Skyway for ninety-nine years. In 2005, Macquarie acquired the Dulles Greenway in Northern Virginia. Centra is a partner in the Trans-Texas Corridor, a 4,000-mile road network of 400-yard-wide superhighways, with separate lanes for cars and trucks, and high-speed commuter rail, and infrastructure for utility lines and oil and gas pipelines. The first leg would run from Laredo to Oklahoma. In 2006, Virginia leased the Pocahontas Parkway near Richmond to an Australian consortium for ninety-nine years.[58]

Other states are rushing to lease their roads and grab the money. We are selling our country for cash now. And any kid who ever played Monopoly knows how the game ends.

"What's in it for the foreign companies?" Daniel Gross of *Slate* asks, and answers:

Huge potential profits. Gigantic, steady profits. Toll roads are an incredible asset class. They're often monopolies. They can support debt, since they provide a recurring guaranteed revenue stream that is likely to rise over time, as more people take to the roads and tolls increase . . . the heavy lifting has already been done: The state or federal governments have acquired the land and rights of way,

built the roads and maintained them for years, and enacted toll increases. All the private companies have to do
is deliver the cash upfront, maintain the roads, and collect
the windfall.[59]

Piece by piece, we are selling off the homestead we inherited
so we can consume at the expense of our children. And Gross
asks a basic question:

How is it that in the richest nation on earth, localities simply don't have the cash to do necessary maintenance on
basic infrastructure, the political will to raise such funds,
or the competence to run such easily profitable operations? Why are they being forced to sell off long-term
cash cows for short-term cash?[60]

The great auction of America's national assets has begun.
And like companies that do this, countries that do it are usually
going out of business. Americans sense what is happening. Gov.
Mitch Daniels touted his lease of the toll road as a bargain for
Indiana, but bumper stickers began to appear on the eighteen-
wheelers on the venerable highway: "Keep the Toll Road, Lease
Mitch."[61]

As the firestorm from the Dubai ports deal revealed, the
global elites are playing with nationalist nitroglycerine.

New Masters of the Universe

In the artificial world of the global economy, the newest creatures
to evolve may prove the most menacing. They are sovereign

wealth funds (SWFs), huge capital funds controlled by governments. They are the new giants in the world of global finance.

Consider. In 2002, foreign governments held $1.9 trillion in currency reserves. By mid-2007, the figure was $5.4 trillion, triple the total in the world's hedge funds.[62] China had $1.3 trillion in reserves, Japan $900 billion, Russia $315 billion. According to Stephen Mallaby of *The Washington Post,* "The Kuwaiti Investment Office is rumored to manage $500 billion, and the United Arab Emirates has an investment fund worth perhaps $1 trillion. . . ."[63]

These SWFs are mutants that have sprung up out of the massive trade deficits America has been running and the surpluses foreign regimes have been piling up. Rather than keep their reserves in U.S. Treasury bonds earning 4 to 5 percent, nations have begun to create SWFs to seek higher rates of returns and control of Western companies to advance their strategic interests.

By mid-2007, the UAE had $500 billion in SWFs, Norway over $300 billion, Singapore and Saudi Arabia $200 billion, China $66 billion, Russia $122 billion. Worldwide, SWFs held $2.5 trillion, an amount that is expected to double to $5 trillion by 2010, and double again to $12 trillion by 2015. Morgan Stanley projects that SWFs could grow to $17.5 trillion in ten years.[64]

For America, the dangers are immense.

Since the Reagan-Thatcher era, the privatization of publicly owned assets has been a worldwide trend. Airlines, railroads, mines, utilities, telephone, and telegraph companies have been sold off by governments to private investors who, to make them profitable, have made them efficient.

The SWFs reverse the trend. For they are owned, operated by, and answerable to regimes whose agents can direct this immense wealth into the acquisition of assets for strategic advantage.

Suppose China with its $1.3 trillion in reserves begins to invest, through its SWFs, in Boeing, GM, Microsoft, IBM, GE, and the American companies that build our submarines, Stealth bombers, satellites, and missiles. Will the United States rope off the industries that build the weapons of our national defense from ownership by SWFs? If foreign investors can buy stock in these companies, why cannot foreign countries—through SWFs?

What percent of a defense contractor will China be permitted to hold? Will Japan be allowed to buy stakes in companies responsible for what remains of our lead in high tech? Will the Japanese be allowed to extract the technology? Who will decide what companies constitute vital national assets that SWFs will not be allowed to take over or even invest in?

The new corporate raiders are going to be a tougher lot than the old, for this game is now about bigger stakes than where someone ranks on the Forbes list of the 400 richest.

Former treasury secretary Lawrence Summers writes,

In the last month [June 2007] we have seen government-controlled Chinese entities take the largest external stake . . . in Blackstone, a big private equity group that indirectly, through its holdings, is one of the largest employers in the U.S. . . . Gazprom, a Russian conglomerate controlled by the Kremlin, has interests in the energy sectors of several countries, even a stake in Airbus. Entities controlled by the governments of China and Singapore are offering to take a substantial stake in Barclays, giving it more heft in its effort to pull off the world's largest banking merger, with ABN Amro.[65]

Is it a good idea to allow Beijing to acquire part ownership of Western banks, and access to all the information they contain?

Should Rupert Murdoch retire, and his successors decide to divest media properties, will sovereign wealth funds be allowed to buy shares in NewsCorp? One recalls the hysteria in the 1980s, when it was learned that South Africans might use a front group to buy *The Washington Star*.

Auto Graveyard

The Detroit of the 1940s was the forge and furnace of the arsenal of democracy. Studebaker, which built the wagons the pioneers used to cross the plains, built the Weasel armored personnel carrier. Willys built the Jeeps that carried Allied armies across Europe. Ford built Sherman tanks. Packard produced the engines for the PT boats and the P-40s of the Flying Tigers. Buick manufactured engines for the B-24 Liberator bomber; Chevrolet the engines for the "Flying Boxcar." Oldsmobile built the B-25 Mitchell bomber Jimmy Doolittle used in his raid on Tokyo from the carrier *Hornet* in early 1942—in retaliation for Pearl Harbor.[66]

Nash-Kelvinator produced the Navy Corsair, America's first 400-mph fighter. Hudson helped build the Helldiver that succeeded the Dauntless, made famous in the Battle of Midway where four of the Japanese carriers that had put planes over Pearl Harbor went to the bottom. And GM led all manufacturers in war production.[67] For every shell Krupp sent our way, it was said, General Motors sent four back.

Fast forward to 2007.

On Valentine's Day, Chrysler, a subsidiary of Daimler-Benz, sent a bouquet to its North American workers. Eleven thousand manufacturing jobs would be abolished—9,000 in the States, 2,000 in Canada—and 2,000 white-collar workers would be let go. The SUV assembly plant in Newark, Delaware, would be closed. The Warren, Michigan, truck plant and South St. Louis assembly plant would each eliminate one of two shifts. In May, Daimler paid Cerberus Capital Management "$650 million to take 80 percent of Chrysler, which less than a decade earlier Daimler had paid $36 billion to purchase."[68] So begins the final chapter of the once-mighty U.S. auto company.

All Detroit is in trouble. In 2006, Ford posted a loss of $12.7 billion, largest of any company in history, breaking GM's record loss of $10.6 billion in 2005. By 2007, Toyota was reaching for first place in world sales, which GM had held for seventy-six years. In the first quarter 2007, Toyota became number one.[69]

How has Japan succeeded?

First, Japan makes fine cars. Second, Japan has protected her home market and repelled imports for decades. Third, Japan manipulates the yen to keep it cheap against the dollar, so the price of her cars is below that of comparable U.S. models. Fourth, Tokyo imposes a value added tax (VAT) on imported American cars, but rebates the VAT on Japanese autos and parts sent to America. This double subsidy gives Japanese cars a price advantage over Ford or GM in both markets. Fifth, the Japanese assembly plants in the United States are free of the legacy costs of pensions and health insurance for retired autoworkers. For Japanese companies in the USA have almost no retired U.S. autoworkers.

Finally, there is the venerable practice of transfer pricing. Japanese manufacturers have overcharged U.S. subsidiaries for auto parts. This cuts the profits of their subsidiaries and reduces the subsidiaries' income taxes. The real profits are repatriated to Japan.

Thus is Japan capturing the U.S. auto market and bringing down the companies that built the machines that brought down the Japanese Empire.

Revenge is a dish best eaten cold.

To stay competitive, U.S. auto manufacturers are being forced to close plants here, lay off U.S. workers, re-site plants abroad, and export to the USA. That is why Mexico exports half again as many cars to us as we ship to the world. By moving plants to Mexico, U.S. automakers rid themselves of high-paid U.S. workers and relieve themselves of the cost of Social Security taxes, health benefits, and pension contributions.

To see what is happening to Chrysler, Ford, and GM, one need only glance at the trade figures. In the auto sector, the total U.S. trade deficit since 1991 exceeds $1.5 trillion. The U.S. share of the U.S. market, 98 percent fifty years ago, has fallen below 50 percent and is sinking.[70]

Mexico and Britain now export to the United States three times what they import from us in trucks, autos, and parts. Germany exports to us four times as much as we export to her in autos. With Korea and Japan the ratio of sales to us, over U.S. truck, auto, and parts sales to them, is 16 to 1 and 20 to 1.

Are these folks that much more efficient? Are American

autoworkers simply unable to compete with Japanese, Germans, Koreans, Mexicans, Brits?

No. The problem is not the American autoworker. The problem is the American politician. Taxes are factored into the price of goods. Half the sticker price of a U.S.-made car goes for taxes—the Social Security and Medicare taxes, state and federal income taxes withheld from the wages of workers and salaries of executives—and to pay the company's corporate tax, property taxes on offices, factories, and dealerships, and state sales taxes.

As Ronald Reagan used to say, companies don't pay taxes, they collect them.

When we buy U.S.-made cars, we contribute to Social Security, Medicare, homeland security, and national defense. We pay for roads, schools, teachers, cops, parks. When foreigners buy U.S.-made cars, they help underwrite the cost of American government. But when we buy foreign cars, we pay taxes to the governments of the nations where those cars were produced. And when we buy goods made in China, we subsidize the regime in Beijing.

All that was warned about for decades—mammoth trade deficits, a falling dollar, deindustrialization, growing dependence on foreign nations for the necessities of our national life and the weapons of our national defense—has come to pass. This generation is witnessing the passing of America as the greatest industrial power and most self-sufficient republic the world had ever seen. But to free-trade ideologues, it does not matter. For whatever result free trade produces is the right and best result.

After having watched our nation imbibe for thirty years, we

can see clearly now that free trade does to a nation what alcohol can do to a man. It saps him first of his energy, then of his self-reliance, then of his independence. America today exhibits all the symptoms of an alcoholic in late middle age. We save next to nothing. We consume more than we produce. We spend more than we earn. We have left physical labor behind, for leisure time.

Free trade says what is best for me is best for America. Free trade puts the claims of consumers ahead of the duties of citizens. And history has proven free trade to be both a serial killer of manufacturing and the Trojan horse of transnational government.

Why Do We Take It?

If we were to cast aside ideology and begin to look out for our country and countrymen first, consider the leverage we have.

Mexico's trade surplus with the United States, $60 billion, was equal to 150 percent of her economic growth. Add the $23 billion in remittances from Mexicans working in the United States to the trade surplus Mexico ran with us, and one comes to $83 billion. That is two times the dollar growth of the Mexican economy. Add the billions spent each year by our tourists and one gets an idea of Mexico's dependence on U.S. goodwill—a goodwill rarely reciprocated on issues vital to America, like the invasion across our Southern border.

Japan's trade surplus with the United States, $88 billion in 2006, was 100 percent of her growth. China's trade surplus, $233 billion, accounted for nearly 100 percent of her growth. Canada's trade surplus, $72 billion, accounted for over 100 percent of her growth.

As these nations depend on the U.S. market for the growth they enjoy, why do we not use our leverage to advance our interests?

For example, while China exports to us nearly 10 percent of her entire GDP, U.S. sales to China account for one-fifth of 1 percent of our GDP. If we gave up all sales to China, it would be a pothole in the road. But if China lost all sales to the United States, China's growth would come to a screeching halt. Beijing would go through the windshield. Foreign investment would dry up. U.S. companies would pull out.

Why, then, did Treasury Secretary Henry M. Paulson, Fed Chairman Ben Bernanke, and six cabinet officers go kowtowing to Beijing in December 2006 to plead with the mandarins to revalue their currency, when a 20 percent U.S. tariff would have brought Beijing bolt upright, asking what it was we wanted. Hamilton would have solved our Chinese problem in a single meeting with their trade minister.

Why do we allow factories to be exported and our manufacturing supremacy to be siphoned off? What is the matter with this feckless generation?

Answer: Ideology and greed.

Free-trade zealots are like militant Christian Scientists who will not undergo surgery, even if the malady is killing them. Second, there are the obtuse who cannot believe our so-called trade partners have found a way around the rules to skin us alive. Third, to win and hold office, candidates of both parties depend on the political contributions of corporate America and its K Street auxiliaries whose salaries, bonuses, stock options, and golden parachutes depend on a rising share price. And a rising share price means cost cutting. And cost cutting means shifting production out of the United States—to be rid of high-wage American workers with their pensions and health benefits.

"The country and the companies are going off in two different directions," says Ralph Gomory. "That is something most people feel intuitively."[71] And as the companies succeed, the country fails. But rich are the rewards of economic treason.

Inscrutable Americans

Washington remains wedded to globalism, but it has a problem.

China. The flood of Chinese goods into the USA, the $233 billion trade surplus Beijing ran up at our expense in 2006, the paltry U.S. exports to China, swamped 7 to 1 by imports, the competition of goods made by $10-a-day Chinese labor driving off the shelves goods made by $100-a-day U.S. labor—that is our China problem.

According to free-trade ideology, there is no problem. We should welcome our trade deficits with China, for this amounts to a Chinese subsidy of American consumers. This is "reverse foreign aid" to us, wrote Milton Friedman. China sends us all these quality goods in exchange for those little green pieces of paper.

Americans are skeptical. They see the factories closing, the jobs going offshore, China growing at four times the rate of the United States—and they sense that something irreplaceable is slipping away. And they are right. We are selling off the family estate, so we can live the high life in the city. A Paris Hilton nation.

The Chinese understand what Friedrich List taught. Production comes before consumption. What matters most is not who consumes the apples today, but who owns the orchard. For those who only consume are eventually dependent on those who produce. Nor is it only low-skill jobs that China is sucking out of the United States. Writes William Greider of *The Nation*:

> Microsoft and Google opened rival research centers in Beijing. Intel announced a new, $2.5 billion semiconductor plant that will make it one of China's largest foreign investors. China's industrial transformation is no longer about making shirts and shoes, as some free-trade cheerleaders still seem to believe. It is about capturing the most advanced processes and products.[72]

How did China achieve her extraordinary growth? How did China manage to run a trade surplus of $233 billion with the United States?

In 1994, China devalued her currency by 45 percent. This cut the price of Chinese-made goods 45 percent in world markets while almost doubling the cost of imported goods. China gained an instant comparative advantage over Japan, South Korea, Taiwan, Singapore, Thailand, and Malaysia. By tying her currency to the dollar, refusing to let it float upward, China can offer her goods at fire-sale prices to U.S. consumers, while keeping U.S. goods overpriced and out of her market.

Despite blustery U.S. protests, the looting of U.S. industry continues—because both nations see it serves their interests. Buyers for Wal-Mart in China are no more concerned about wages and working conditions there than were British manufacturers concerned about the wages and working conditions of the slaves who hoed and picked and baled and toted the cotton they bought in America.

U.S. consumers want quality goods at the cheapest price. American businesses want to produce at the lowest cost. China meets both demands.

In China the nation comes first. Voters do not decide policy. There are no voters. National goals are set by national leaders. What are those goals? China's trade policy and monetary policies are designed to suck jobs, industry, and technology out of the United States and displace America as the factory of the world and first nation on earth. Like the grasshopper of the fable, the Americans spend all they earn and borrow to consume more. Like the ants, the Chinese work and work and save and save.

When we demand they let their currency float and rise in value, they reply: Why should we abandon a trade policy that is succeeding for us for a trade policy that is failing for you? Why should a nation growing by 12 percent from exports adopt the trade policy of a nation running the largest deficits in history? Why, when China's reserves exceed $1.3 trillion, should China take the advice of an America whose savings rate is zero and is bleeding $2 billion a day to finance imports? Why should winners adopt the policy of losers?

And, by the way, what is wrong with fixed rates of exchange, which you Americans preached and practiced for generations?

No, it is not the Chinese who are inscrutable.

Like the Americans of the nineteenth century, China accepts the truth of what List wrote: "The power of producing wealth is infinitely more important than the wealth itself."[73] We sacrifice the future to the present. China sacrifices the present for the future. We own today. They will own tomorrow.

China runs up huge trade surpluses with us in computers, electrical machinery, toys, games, footwear, furniture, clothing, plastics, articles of iron and steel, vehicles, optical and photographic equipment. Our trade surpluses with China are in soybeans, corn, wheat, animal feeds, meat, cotton, metal ores, scrap, hides and skins, pulp, wastepaper, cigarettes, gold, coal, mineral fuels, rice, tobacco, fertilizers, glass.

Which country has the trade profile of a First World manufacturing power, and which of a colony?

The one advanced industry where America runs a trade surplus with China is aircraft. In March 2007, the *Financial Times* reported: "China plans to mount a head-on challenge to the dominance of Boeing and Airbus in the global market for big passenger jets by setting up a state-owned company to build the aircraft."[74] If state subsidies are needed to create an industry to capture a market, Beijing does not let ideology stand in the way.

By mid-2007, even the fabled tolerance of the free-trade *New York Times* seemed to have been exhausted. The sudden death of American dogs from Chinese pet food had finally got the *Times*'s attention: "Washington needs to have what diplomats call a frank discussion with Beijing about its irresponsible export of poisonous toothpaste, dog food and toys and its piracy of American-produced software, movies and other goods."[75]

Liberals and Libertarians

Most inscrutable of all is the liberals' enthusiasm for free trade.

Liberals take pride in the social reforms that their forebears enacted into law. Liberals wrote the minimum wage law. Liberals led the fight for civil rights, requiring equality of treatment in the workplace. Liberals enacted environmental laws to curb the pollution of air and water. Liberals passed health and safety laws to make the factory floor clean and reduce the dangers to workers. Liberals passed laws to make it easy for workers to organize, so unions could fight for higher pay and benefits, and pensions for retirees.

Having passed historic legislation to make the American factory the fairest, cleanest, safest, and finest place on earth for industrial workers, liberals then turned around and backed free-trade agreements that say to U.S. manufacturers: "If you want to get out from under all these liberal laws, if you want to be rid of those demanding U.S. workers and unions, shut down your plant here, lay off your U.S. workers, move to China, make your goods there, and export, free of charge, to the USA. Pocket all the money you save and put it into executive bonuses and stock options and laugh at us liberals on the slopes of Teluride and Vail."

The free-trade treaties of the twentieth century were a Magna Carta for corporate greed, enabling acts for the avaricious who have no God but Mammon, and who saw clearly that deserting the nation that nurtured them, and firing Americans and hiring Asians would be good for business. No wonder more and more of corporate political contributions are finding their way into the campaign funds of progressive Democrats.

Why, too, are libertarians clamoring for unrestricted imports when the result is that Chrysler, GM, and Ford lay off autoworkers who, having lost their company health insurance, demand national health insurance?

Why are conservatives casting Reagan Democrats into a Darwinian competition with $10-a-day Mexican labor and $5-a-day Chinese labor? When imports close factories and kill high-paying American jobs, the Reagan Democrats who held those jobs may go to work at Wal-Mart, but they will also go back to the Democratic Party of their fathers, which will vote government benefits to replace the company benefits they have lost.

Every man seeks security for himself and his family. Kill the corporate welfare state, as free trade is doing, and you increase the constituency and clamor for the government welfare state.

By freezing and cutting the pay of American workers, free trade is forcing the middle class, which moved rightward in the Nixon and Reagan years, back to the left. Karl Marx was not wrong when he wrote in 1848:

The Protective system . . . is conservative, while the Free Trade system works destructively. It breaks up old nationalities and carries antagonism of proletariat and bourgeoisie to the uttermost point. In a word, the Free Trade system hastens the Social Revolution. In this revolutionary sense alone, gentlemen, I am in favor of Free Trade.[76]

Globalism Versus Patriotism

What caused the GOP to abandon the economic nationalism that had made America the greatest industrial power in history and the Republican Party America's party for seventy years?

First, in the postwar era, the economics departments of universities and colleges were dominated by New Deal Democrats, socialists, and Marxists. Like isolationism, protectionism was now a dirty word. Republicans of the Harding-Coolidge era, who had slashed income taxes, raised tariffs, and created the Roaring Twenties, were demonized and, with Smoot-Hawley, indicted for the Great Depression. The Keynesian economics of the New Deal, it was said, had cured the Depression. Both myths are gospel today.

After World War II, the economic philosophy summed up in the GOP motto "Prosper America First!" came to be regarded as capitalistic, nationalistic, crude, and selfish. Protecting American industry was unfair to foreign competitors.

Second, at the end of the Cold War, China abandoned Maoism, India dumped socialism, Eastern Europe broke free, and the Soviet Union collapsed. These epochal events freed up hundreds of millions of workers and put them into a world labor pool with the American working and middle classes, whose wages were ten and twenty times their own.

Third, then came the Internet, enabling companies to acquire intellectual property instantly from anywhere on earth.

Fourth, there was a sea change in the mind-set of the Fortune 500. Protecting the home market became less important than assuring access to foreign markets. The National Association of Manufacturers converted to free trade—to be free of its American workers, free to move its factories abroad, free to export back to the United States, free of charge. To hold their American consumers and be rid of their American workers became a corporate obsession.

Finally, the trade deals of the late twentieth century were enabling acts for companies to shed national identities and loyalties and reinvent themselves as global companies, the new masters of the universe.

Hamilton's vision was history. Patriotism yielded to globalism. Our old cherished independence was to be set aside for a new and higher "interdependence." All nations must now engage in the mutual sacrifice of sovereignty to create the New World Economic Order. Rich nations must annually transfer a slice of their wealth to poor nations. First World workers must compete fairly with Third World workers. There will be pain, but these are the birth pangs of the brave new world we are about to enter.

Behind this vision lies a dirty little secret. The designated beneficiary of the global economy is the global company. The hidden agenda of the global economy is the empowerment of the global company.

In the global economy, the Middle American worker politicians once courted with promises of "a chicken in every pot" and a "full dinner pail" has become the unwanted American—except as a consumer.

U.S. workers must now compete for jobs in their own country with tens of millions of immigrants, legal and illegal. Meanwhile, their factories are shut down and moved to Mexico and China. Knowledge-industry jobs are outsourced to South Asia. Corporate America has been empowered to go abroad and hire bright young men and women to come and take the jobs of middle-aged Americans at half their salaries. Mexican trucks now roll on American roads, and in India, long-haul truck drivers are being trained to come to America and take the jobs of American truckers.[77]

There was a time when an American could, on a single income, support a wife and half a dozen kids and look forward to a secure retirement. In the new America, where the commands of globalism trump the call of patriotism, the American dream is receding. For many it has already died.

Princeton economist Alan S. Blinder, a former vice chairman of the Federal Reserve, contends that, with millions of educated and talented young Indians and Chinese earning advanced degrees, millions of U.S. jobs will be moved offshore electronically—"not only low-skill services such as key-punching, transcription and telemarketing [but] . . . high-skill services such as radiology, architecture and engineering—maybe even college teaching."[78]

After the exodus of manufacturing jobs, how many U.S. knowledge-industry jobs could be lost?

"I estimated that 30 million to 40 million U.S. jobs are potentially offshorable," wrote Blinder. "These include scientists, mathematicians and editors on the high end and telephone operators, clerks and typists on the low end."[79] Blinder also mentioned Indian accountants who will "happily work for a fraction of what Americans earn."

Recently, an accountant in the United States earned an average of $3,000 to $4,000 a month, while the average Indian accountant earned $300 to $400 a month. Is there any doubt about where H&R Block will be turning for employees to prepare the tax returns of American wage earners? For challenging free-trade ideology, Blinder was accorded the customary treatment. "What I've learned is anyone who says anything that even obliquely sounds hostile to free trade is treated as an apostate."[80]

In the global economy, old ties among Americans are cut and replaced by new bonds—to foreign producers, foreign suppliers, foreign employers, foreign lenders. The work of Hamilton is undone. We now depend on foreign nations for a third of our steel, half our autos and machine tools, two-thirds of our textiles and apparel, almost all of our shoes, bicycles, motorcycles, cameras, toys, tape recorders, TVs, radios. America has become again a dependent nation.

In the land of Bill McKinley, Theodore Roosevelt, and Cal Coolidge, the interests of American producers coincided with loyalty to country. In the global economy of the new century, the interests of American producers clash with loyalty to country.

For in the global economy, the $13.5 trillion U.S. market may be the most desirable on earth to sell to, but it is among the least desirable to produce in.

If we are to remain one nation and one people, we have to change that.

8

Day of Reckoning

Is the best of the free life behind us now?
Are the good times really over for good?
—MERLE HAGGARD[1]

Is America on a path to national suicide?

Native-born Americans are no longer reproducing them-selves. And our leaders seem incapable of securing our border against an endless invasion from the Third World. As a people we save nothing. We spend all we earn.

Our dependence on foreign goods for the necessities of our national life, and on foreign loans to pay for them, deep-ens with each year. Social Security and Medicare are headed for bankruptcy, as our politicians appear incapable of impos-ing the sacrifices needed to save them. The annual U.S. trade deficit in manufactures alone is half a trillion dollars. We have become the world's leading debtor. The dollar has sunk to all-time lows against the euro, a twenty-six-year low against the pound. The Canadian dollar has reached parity with the U.S. dollar for the first time in thirty years. Yet we borrow hundreds of billions of dollars every year to fight wars and defend nations as though these were the flush times of the fifties.

When the Interstate 35W bridge between Minneapolis and St. Paul fell into the Mississippi, we learned that 70,000 U.S. bridges are "structurally deficient." Our infrastructure—bridges, tunnels, sewers, ports, airports, electrical grids—is crumbling. We depend on imported oil for 60 percent of our consumption, but have not built a refinery in twenty-five years or a nuclear power plant since the accident at Three Mile Island almost thirty years ago. Our politicians prattle of energy independence, then outlaw drilling in the Arctic tundra and off the coast of California or Florida. The great dams like Hoover and Grand Coulee have all been built. Now we tear them down. Where nation building is going on, with U.S. dollars, is China.

The 4,000 U.S. dead in Iraq are the same number we lost putting down a Filipino insurgency a century ago, when our nation was one-third as populous as today. Yet with victory nowhere in sight, a U.S. retreat from Iraq appears imminent. Was bin Laden right? The superpower cannot stand the pain? For clearly, we have begun to exhibit the unmistakable symptoms of an empire in terminal decline.

With armed forces of 1.4 million, and an army of 500,000 men and women, we are committed to defending nations from Europe to the Middle East to Asia and the Pacific. Few of these commitments are vital to our security. Almost all are the residue of a Cold War that ended two decades ago.

We are frozen in yesterday. To any suggestion that America is overextended comes the patriotic retort: Preposterous! The United States is the world's only superpower. We spend more on national defense than the next ten nations combined. Our economy is 30 percent of the world's economy.

All true. But the European Union also controls 30 percent of the world's wealth. Is there any doubt that Europe is in decline, that Europe is dying? Moscow's power once rivaled that of Washington. And where is the Soviet Union today?

Twenty-five years ago, Ronald Reagan said the Soviet Empire was headed for the "ash heap of history." Is it impossible that the American Empire is finished, that the American Century is over, that America is herself in an existential crisis she will not survive? Can we not see the downhill slide we are on, or is it that we do not care, as Europe seems not to care? "Carpe diem!"—Seize the pleasure of the passing day!—seems the attitude.

However, as we saw in the national uproar and grass-roots uprising against the Bush-McCain-Kennedy amnesty for 12 to 20 million illegal aliens in 2007, which sent the political and corporate establishment down to stinging defeat, Americans wish to preserve the country they grew up in. They want the border secured and illegal aliens deported. With Theodore Roosevelt they yet believe, "We are a nation, not a hodge-podge of foreign nationalities. We are a people, and not a polyglot boarding house." Americans do not want to go gentle into that good night. But they lack the unity and resources of a corporate-political-media iron triangle that works ceaselessly to embed our republic irretrievably in their New World Order.

"I think the nation-state is finished," said Robert Bartley, for thirty years the editorial page editor of *The Wall Street Journal,* which considers itself the voice of American conservatism.[2] All nations are artificial, echoes Strobe Talbott of *Time*. "[W]ithin the next hundred years . . . nationhood as we know it will be obsolete; all states will recognize a single, global authority."[3]

Most powerfully and prominently, the forces working for an end to American sovereignty and independence are the transnational corporations that make up fifty of the world's hundred largest economic entities. Their agenda?

They intend to create a new world where capital, goods, and people all move freely across borders. Indeed, national borders disappear. They seek the "deep integration" of the United States, Mexico, and Canada in a North American Union modeled on the EU, tied together by superhighways and railways where crossing from Mexico into the United States will be like crossing from Virginia into Maryland. They are about the merger of nations into transnational entities and, ultimately, a world in which national sovereignty and national identity disappear.

Their agenda is about globalism, and it is about greed. *Radix omnium malorum est amor pecuniae.* Love of money is the root of all evil. The last obstacle standing in the way of the brave new world of the transnationals is the American people's will to preserve the free, independent, sovereign, self-sufficient republic they inherited from their fathers and wish to hand down to their children.

And they must fight on, for, as Euripides said, "There is no greater sorrow on earth, than the loss of one's native land."[4]

Second Chance

"There are simple answers," Ronald Reagan used to say. "There are just no easy answers."

And Reagan proved the point. He thought that the cure for a sick economy was to unleash the engines of private enterprise, that the cure for a national malaise was a leader who believed in his people. He looked at the Soviet Empire and saw through the façade of military might to the rot at the core—the lack of faith, the lack of freedom, the lack of loyalty of its subjects, the lack of a moral code, the lack of energy and dynamism of its sclerotic system. Confident in his own country, Reagan relished the challenge of Communism and the Soviet Empire that seemed so awesome in the Carter years. By the time he went home to California, the Soviet Union was being administered last rites and Communism was finished.

That Cold War is over. But since Reagan went home, America has been led by men who do not understand their time as he understood his. The truth is as it was: There are simple answers. There are just no easy answers.

Consider the Social Security and Medicare crisis, the dimensions of which Robert Samuelson outlined in August 2007 in *The Washington Post*:

> From 2005 to 2030, the 65-and-over population will nearly double, to 71 million; its share of the population will rise to 20 percent from 12 percent. Social Security, Medicare and Medicaid—programs that serve older people—already exceed 40 percent of the $2.7 trillion federal budget. By 2030, their share could hit 75 percent of the present budget, projects the Congressional Budget Office.[5]

"These projections are daunting," writes Samuelson.

> To keep federal spending stable as a share of the economy would mean eliminating all defense spending and most other domestic programs (for research, homeland security, the environment, etc.). To balance the budget with existing programs at their present economic shares would require, depending on assumptions, tax increases of 30 to 50 percent—or budget deficits could quadruple.[6]

We all know what caused this crisis and we know how to cure it. Our politicians voted benefits for the baby boomers for which they refused to vote the taxes. Rather than indexing Social Security to prices, protecting the income of seniors from inflation, they indexed them to wages, giving retired seniors pay hikes every year. The unfunded liabilities run into the scores of trillions of dollars. If we do not deal with the crisis now, it will deepen. It will kill the economy. The Social Security surplus will begin to shrink in the first term of the new president. It will disappear in a decade, and Social Security and Medicare will have to draw on the general revenue, which means the federal deficit will explode into the trillions and the U.S. government will consume an ever-increasing share of GDP. The fuse is lit and is burning toward the dynamite.

What needs to be done? Simple, but not easy. Either tax rates will have to be raised. Or the wage base that is taxed will have to be raised. Or the eligibility age for Social Security and Medicare will have to be raised. Or benefits will have to be capped or cut. Or all the above. And the Social Security crisis is a bookkeeping error alongside the Medicare crisis, which was worsened by the prescription drug benefit that is George Bush's legacy. This is a situation where either the patient undergoes surgery and painful recuperation, or the patient dies.

Culture War

As for the culture war—ignited by the social and moral revolution of the 1960s that converted a vast slice of the nation—no president can win it or end it. It will be with us forever. But we can agree upon where and how the issues that divide us so deeply can best be settled.

In the 1648 Treaty of Westphalia that ended the Thirty Years War that took the lives of a third of the German people, it was agreed that the prince of a province would decide its religion, and the adherents of other religions would be free to practice their faith. The principle *"Cuius regio, eius religio"*—Whose region, his religion—had come out of the Peace of Augsburg (1555) and brought an uneasy truce to the Catholic-Protestant wars.

This generation of Americans is never going to agree on abortion, gay rights, school prayer, public display of the Ten Commandments, homosexuality, Darwin, creationism, medical marijuana, racial quotas, or assisted suicide. But perhaps there can be a Geneva agreement on where and how these culture wars should be fought, and how temporary truces are to be reached.

Essentially, a modus vivendi, a way to live together, can best be found in this morally disparate society in four principles. The first is republicanism. These issues are best decided by elected representatives, not unelected judges. The second is federalism. These issues are best decided by the fifty states, not the federal government. A third is the principle of localism or subsidiarity. Decisions are best taken by the smallest unit of government able to decide and implement them. A fourth is participatory democracy. Let the voters decide these issues by initiative and referenda.

For Americans believe deeply in self-rule. It is part of our nature. We may bridle at it, but we accept majority decisions. We rebel at minority dictation. When the Massachusetts supreme court ordered the state to begin issuing marriage licenses to homosexuals, a firestorm erupted. Governor Mitt Romney had an historic opportunity to act as Jefferson did in the case of the Alien and Sedition Acts, declare the court's 4–3 decision unconstitutional, and refuse to issue state marriage licenses to gays. But he and the legislature backed away from confrontation with the renegade court. Rather than accept Massachusetts' marriages of homosexuals, however, thirteen states swiftly introduced ballot propositions restricting marriage to a man and a woman. Turnout was heavy in 2004 and probably cost John Kerry the presidency. But when the Connecticut legislature, elected by the people, voted to allow civil unions, there was no national reaction. What Connecticut did democratically was Connecticut's business and the people could repudiate their representatives at the next election.

It was *Roe v. Wade*, the U.S. Supreme Court's diktat stripping the states of their right to perform the first duty of any state—protecting innocent life—that tore the nation asunder as no other decision since *Dred Scott*. The way out is the overturning of *Roe* and the return of this issue to the states and the people, whose elected leaders can then write new laws, as can Congress. Then the people can work to persuade their countrymen a constitutional amendment guaranteeing the right to life is as right and necessary as was the Thirteenth Amendment outlawing slavery. Is this not the constitutional way? Is this not the better way?

It was the nationalization of moral issues by the Supreme Court, and its no-appeal dictates—ordering God, the Bible, and the Ten Commandments out of every public school in America, creating a constitutional right to abortion, declaring pornography to be constitutionally protected, striking down every state law dealing with homosexual sodomy—that turned the culture war into America's second civil war.

There are two ways toward truce. One is to create a Supreme Court of justices who will leave these decisions with the states. The other is for the Congress to reassert its authority over these issues and append to all laws dealing with social and moral issues, like the Defense of Marriage Act, an amendment denying jurisdiction over that law to any federal court. Congress has the power to circumscribe the jurisdiction of all federal district and appellate courts that are its own creations. Congress also has the power in Article III, Section II of the Constitution to restrict the jurisdiction of the Supreme Court.

In Article III, Section II, the second paragraph reads,

> In all Cases affecting Ambassadors, other public Ministers and Consuls, and those in which a State shall be Party, the supreme Court shall have original Jurisdiction. In all the other Cases before mentioned, the supreme Court shall have appellate Jurisdiction, both as to Law and Fact, with such Exceptions, and under such Regulations as the Congress shall make.

Because this weapon has been used only sparingly in two centuries does not make it a dead letter—or a useless weapon for a determined and resolute Congress, if ever we could elect one.

The states were meant to be laboratories of democracy. And in the Constitution, the Founding Fathers left us a path to a cold peace in the culture wars.

Turning Back an Invasion

To understand what must be done to preserve our country, consider how a smaller country fights to preserve its national identity. How does Israel resist the centrifugal forces of multiculturalism? It is a nation 20 percent Arab and Druze, with the Jewish population tracing its roots to every continent and most especially the West and the old Ottoman world. How does Israel meet the threat of deconstruction? How does Israel prevent herself from being inundated by the mass migrations of modernity?

Israel fights ferociously to preserve her religious and ethnic identity. Immigration is restricted to those who are Jewish by birth or faith. While Jews from all over the world are urged to settle in Israel or on the West Bank, no Palestinian is permitted to return to the home of his father or grandfather. The rights of land ownership extended to Jews are not extended to non-Jews. Jewish history is taught in the schools. The Hebrew language has been revived. A Jewish currency, the shekel, has been created. There is talk of annexing all major Jewish settlements on the West Bank and, in exchange, giving up Israeli land contiguous to the West Bank where Arabs reside. Many Israelis say openly that while they wish to keep their Jewish population they would let the Arabs go. They seek an overwhelming Jewish majority in a Jewish state. Israelis understand it is not ideology that makes a nation. It is not democracy. Jews are a people. And Israel is unapologetic about preserving its ethnic and religious character.

Millions of Americans feel the same way. Yet were an American to propose an immigration policy to keep the United States predominantly Christian and European—the rationale behind the Immigration Act of 1924—he or she would be denounced as a racist, a xenophobe, and un-American.

The normal and natural instincts of our people have been demonized and the nation cowed by its ruling class—until the uprising of 2007 and the crushing defeat of an establishment that tried to ram a massive amnesty of illegal aliens and their corporate collaborators down America's throat.

To halt the Third World invasion we need moral fortitude and political will. And if we do not find these virtues soon in our leaders, we will lose the country. For what is happening on our Mexican border is a graver threat to our survival than anything happening in Iraq. If we do not wish to become that "tangle of squabbling nationalities" of which TR warned, not really a nation at all, ten tough but simple steps are necessary.

1. No amnesty for the 12 to 20 million illegal aliens.
2. A security fence from San Diego to Brownsville.
3. Rigorous enforcement of immigration laws against employers.
4. A federal requirement that all employers verify the identity and Social Security number of all workers, through a toll-free call.
5. A cutoff of all federal and state benefits, except emergency, to those who cannot prove they are in the country legally.
6. Justice Department support for states like California and Arizona and towns like Hazelton, Pennsylvania, and Farmers Branch, Texas, that seek to help enforce immigration laws by punishing landlords and businesses who flout federal laws by renting to or hiring illegal aliens.
7. A congressional declaration that children born to illegal aliens are not automatic citizens. The Fourteenth Amendment never intended that they be so.
8. An end to "chain migration" by telling legal immigrants that while they may bring wives and minor children with them, adult children, siblings, and parents must get in line like everyone else.
9. Declare English the official language of the United States, and strip the Supreme Court of any right of review of the law.
10. A time-out on legal immigration, such as the one from 1924 to 1965, and the annual admission of only the

number urged by John Kennedy when he endorsed reform, fifty years ago: 150,000 to 250,000. For it is
among the tens of millions of legal immigrants that the
illegals find sanctuary.

If these measures are enacted, the invasion can be halted, millions of illegals will go home quietly as they did in 1954, and the
nation can begin to assimilate and Americanize the scores of
millions who have come legally in the last thirty-five years.
Within ten years our national nightmare will be over.

Without a program like this, we lose America, for we are
reaching a point of no return. According to the Census Bureau,
if immigration continues at present rates, the U.S. population in
2060 will be nearing half a billion people. To today's 301 million
will have been added 167 million, to reach 468 million living in
the USA.[7] The *increase alone* will equal the entire population of
the United States when Kennedy took the oath. Of that 167
million, 105 million will be immigrants, almost all of them from
the Third World, which will be like having the entire population
of Mexico today move into the United States.[8]

How America's unique character and national identity can
survive this invasion, unprecedented in history, is impossible to
see. Americans never voted for this invasion, never wanted it.
Yet it is being done to us. Why?

Economic Patriotism

The United States is losing its trade wars with China, Japan,
Asia, the European Union, Canada, and Mexico not because of
any inefficiency of our workers but because of the ideology of
our intellectuals and the greed of our corporatists.

Three events occurred in recent decades to make nineteenth-century classical liberalism and its free-trade dogmas not only obsolete but suicidal for a nation that would remain the world's first power.

First is the mobility of capital. Capital is no longer tied to the nation. It travels around the world seeking the highest rate of return at the click of a computer mouse. Information and technology travel at the same speed.

Second, hundreds of millions of workers have been added to the world labor pool by the liberation of Eastern Europe, the collapse of the Soviet Union, China's embrace of autocratic capitalism, and India's abandonment of state socialism. All now welcome capital, and their workers are all willing to work as hard as Americans for a fraction of U.S. wages.

This gives China, Asia, and Eastern Europe an immense competitive advantage in the courtship of production.

Third, where the United States has a federal-state corporate income tax rate of 40 percent, the average corporate tax rate in the European Union has lately been cut from 38 to 24 percent.[9] The EU raises revenue through a value added tax, tacked on to the price of products at each stage of production. The average VAT in Europe is about 20 percent.

Under WTO rules, nations are allowed to rebate the VAT on exports and impose an equivalent tax on imports. This is what Europe does in trade with the United States.

The effect is a double disadvantage for U.S. goods. Assume a VAT of 20 percent of the cost of a new car. If Volkswagen ships 100,000 cars to the USA priced at $20,000 each, $2 billion worth of Volkswagens, the company can claim a rebate of the VAT of nearly $4,000 a car, or $400 million, a powerful incentive to export to America. But each $20,000 U.S. car arriving on the docks of Europe will have 20 percent, or $4,000, added to its sticker price.

This amounts to a subsidy for exports to the United States and a tax on imports from the USA. How big is this problem? Huge. Some 94 percent of all U.S. exports go to VAT countries, and the average VAT imposed by our trading partners is 15 percent. The tax disadvantage to U.S. producers has been estimated at $279 billion.

How do we level the playing field? Under the Border Tax Equity Act introduced in 2007 in the House, the United States would impose a tax on imported goods and services equal to the VAT imposed on our exports—and use the revenue for rebates to U.S. exporters to cover the taxes foreign nations impose. What would this accomplish?

An immediate and dramatic shrinkage of the trade deficit. A sudden strengthening of the dollar. A halt to the exodus of U.S. manufacturers. The start of a mass movement of plants and factories back to the United States. To evade the border tax, foreign manufacturers would expand production in the United States. Instead of going abroad, jobs would start coming home, and the first jobs created would be in fiercely competitive high-tech industries where a small price hike and small cost reduction can be decisive.

We need to rewrite U.S. tax law to prosper America first.

What is killing U.S. industry is the greed of the transnationals and the reflexive recoil from any proposal that does not conform to the dogmatic truths of the free-trade cult. If we do not jettison this ideology, the United States will be stripped of its manufacturing and technological supremacy.

Under the Border Tax Equity Act, in ten years, America will have restored her industrial dynamism. Ideally, the tax burden should be wholly lifted off of exports, the products of U.S. workers, and placed on imports, the products of foreign workers. This is the way Washington and Hamilton intended it. This is the way America became the most self-sufficient republic in history. This is the way to ensure American sovereignty and self-sufficiency forever.

An End to the Crusades

In 2003, with the authorization of both the House and the Senate, President Bush ordered the invasion of a nation that had not attacked us, did not threaten us, and did not want war with us— to strip it of weapons it did not have. It was an unnecessary war, a war of choice; and five years on, no one knows how it will end. But the invasion of Iraq is the greatest strategic blunder in U.S. history. Consider the costs.

Four thousand Americans dead, nearly 30,000 wounded, over half a trillion dollars lost. Scores and perhaps hundreds of thousands of Iraqi dead. A half decade of misery for their families. Four million refugees, 2 million of whom have fled the country. Expulsion or flight of most of Iraq's Christians. A Sunni-Shia war of mutual atrocity. A strategic victory for Iran. An Al Qaeda base camp and training site in Anbar for assassins and suicide bombers whose next targets will be friendly Arab nations and the United States itself.

As Lawrence Wright, author of an acclaimed history of the terror organization behind 9/11, wrote, "Al Qaeda was essentially dead" in 2002, after U.S. forces had run bin Laden out of Afghanistan. Bush's war brought Al Qaeda back to life. Wright quotes jihadist theoretician Abu Musab al-Suri: "the American occupation of Iraq inaugurated 'a historical new period' that almost single-handedly rescued the jihadi movement just when many of its critics thought it was finished."[10]

And there is other blowback of this misbegotten war.

Iraq may break up and the war spread across the Arab world. In the Middle East, the United States has never been more detested. The pool of Islamic young who hate us, from which Al Qaeda recruits, has never been broader or deeper. Our alliances have been shredded, our world leadership lost. Though Bush denounced as isolationists those who opposed his war, he has done more than any man in history to isolate the United States.

Our leaders did not think it through going into this war. But we must think it through before coming out. At the end, however, like the British and French before us, we must withdraw U.S. ground forces from that part of the world. For our imperial presence is the cause of our problems. Bin Laden sent his 9/11 killers over here, because we were over there.

The crusades are over. After Afghanistan and Iraq, Americans will not support another ground war to bring the blessings of democracy to the benighted. Iraq has taught us there are limits to U.S. power. The U.S. military may be unequaled at crushing armies and seizing capitals. It cannot rebuild nations or create democracies where none has ever existed. After five years in Iraq and six in Afghanistan, we have learned that we Americans lack the perseverance and patience of an imperial people. We are not Romans. We are not Victorians. Our dead in Iraq and Afghanistan are not 1 percent of the losses we suffered in the Civil War, or 10 percent of our dead in Vietnam. Yet, our generals are saying *"no más"* and the nation is saying it is time to come home.

Time to cease deceiving ourselves. If two of Kipling's "savage wars of peace" have so stretched American forces, how can we honor all the commitments made over sixty years to defend nations all over the world?

Answer: We cannot. U.S. foreign policy is bankrupt. We lack the strategic assets to cover our strategic liabilities. Either the United States doubles or trebles its armed forces, or we shed commitments and tell old allies their defense is now their responsibility.

The Bush Doctrine is dead.

Americans may cheer the rhetoric of "world democratic revolution" and "ending tyranny in our world." But they are not willing to send their sons to die to make Mesopotamia safe for democracy. Two-thirds of the nation wants out of Iraq. And if Americans are unwilling to make the sacrifices to rebuild and democratize Iraq, are they willing to make the far greater sacrifices required to conquer Iran?

Lest we forget, the United States in 1945 had 12 million men under arms. Ike's peacetime military boasted 3 million. Today's armed forces number 1.4 million. More than 200,000 are women. Should the president propose to draft America's young to fight a long war for global democracy, he would not get one-fourth of either house of Congress. As we cannot police the planet with armed forces of one-half of 1 percent of the nation, all of them volunteers, we must give up the empire, as all the other imperial nations had to do. It is over.

Events are imposing a new foreign policy on the United States, similar to the one the nation pursued for most of its history, when there was no conscription. It is not isolationism—America has never been isolationist—but noninterventionist. No nation benefited more from staying out of the European and Asian wars of the nineteenth century than did we. No nation benefited more from staying out of the alliances of the early twentieth century and the Great War than did we. No nation benefited more from having remained aloof from the alliances of the 1930s and World War II as long as we did, than did we. Whence comes this compulsion for America to involve herself in every quarrel and every war on every continent?

As it does not serve America's interest, whose interests does it serve? *Cui bono?* Who benefits from all these commitments, all these wars?

Of all the wars around this world of nearly two hundred nations, how many truly affect our security, our survival? If nations do not threaten us or attack us, or imperil interests vital to us, what business is it of ours whether they are ruled by autocrats or democrats, ayatollahs or Islamists, generals or presidents for life? The internal politics of foreign nations should be of no concern to us, unless their regimes, as in the Cold War, are possessed of an ideology premised upon war with us.

With the end of the Cold War the need for a National Endowment for Democracy came to an end. Its business in the late Cold War was to subvert Communist regimes by supporting democrats. Now that those regimes have fallen, NED should pass away. If we do not want Moscow engaging in clandestine political activity in our country, why would we finance and sustain clandestine political activity in Moscow or the former republics of the USSR? Has not the loss of Russia's friendship awakened our president to the damage these compulsive meddlers have done to our country?

No nation on earth can want war with the United States, given our preponderance of land, air, and sea and nuclear power. However, we have entered alliances and given war guarantees to nations that are in constant quarrels, and America could be drawn into countless wars in coming years to fulfill commitments made half a century ago, in another world.

The United States should review every alliance and terminate virtually all of them. For alliances are the transmission belts of war. If, after having severed an alliance, we decide America must come to the defense of some embattled nation, then this generation should make the decision itself, the constitutional way, after consideration by Congress. But no decision for war should ever be dictated for the United States to fulfill the terms of some treaty entered into when this writer was in parochial school.

Recall history. Britain went to war with Germany in 1914, the bloodiest war in all of history up to that time, because the king of Belgium called on the king of England to honor a commitment to Belgian neutrality the British had entered into—in 1839.

A Grand Bargain with Iran?

Since the Iranian revolution of 1979, relations between the ayatollahs and the United States have been as hostile as those between Mao's China and the United States between 1949 and 1972. With major differences.

Where Iran was responsible for holding fifty-two U.S. diplomats hostage for 444 days, and is said to have been behind the Khobar Towers bombing that killed nineteen American servicemen in Saudi Arabia, Mao's China was responsible for the Stalinist liquidation of 30 million people, and the deaths of most of the 37,000 U.S. soldiers who perished in the Korean War, and for the brutalization and brainwashing of American prisoners of war.

In the evil it has done or in its damage to the United States, the Iran of the ayatollahs cannot compare to the China of Mao. And if Nixon could go to Beijing and toast Chairman Mao, certainly the United States can consider ending the Cold War with Tehran. For the ideology of the Iranian revolution is no more anti-American than was that of Mao's China when Nixon landed there in February of 1972.

What is the critical shared interest of our two nations?

Neither would benefit from war. The United States can smash Iran, but it cannot occupy the country or convert it into an American-style democracy. And destruction of Iran could lead to breakup of the country—with Kurds, Azeris, Arabs, and Baluchis splitting from the dominant Persians, who are 50 percent of the population. Balkanization of Iran could bring hellish problems, far greater than any we confront today. America would have no allies in such a war. We would make millions more Islamic enemies. And there would be many Iranians hell-bent on building a nuclear bomb and detonating it in the United States. Moreover, our forces in Afghanistan and Iraq would pay the price of a U.S. attack on the Iranian Revolutionary Guard.

We would have three wars going in the Middle and Near East at a time when our military tells us the army is breaking from two.

What does Iran seek? Clearly, she seeks an end to sanctions, to be brought back into the community of nations, to be treated with respect. She seeks access to Western drilling equipment to exploit her depleting resources of oil and gas. She seeks a return of the billions the shah gave us for weapons that we did not deliver. She wants no Taliban in Kabul and no Sunni revanchists or Saddamists ruling Baghdad. She wants security guarantees from the United States. She seeks to become the dominant power in the Persian Gulf, and given her size and population, this is a certain eventuality, if Iran is not destroyed, as Iraq has been, by the United States. She wants her full rights under the Nuclear Non-Proliferation Treaty, which means Iran will not give up her right to process nuclear fuel and operate nuclear power plants. She wants an end to the U.S. policy of regime change and the use of U.S. and Israeli special forces and the Mujahedin-e-Khalq in Iraq, for acts of sabotage in Iran, or for stirring up minorities against the central government.

What does American want from Iran? An end to Iranian assistance to our enemies in Iraq and Afghanistan, an end to Iran's military assistance to Hamas and Hezbollah and other groups that use terror against the United States, Israel, and our Arab allies, and an end to Iran's nuclear program before it reaches the point where Tehran can build atomic weapons.

It is said that, in 2003, after the U.S. occupation of Iraq, Tehran made, through the Swiss embassy, an offer to negotiate with the United States just such a "grand bargain" as described above, but Dick Cheney and the neocons vetoed it. In 2006, Martin Walker, editor of UPI, outlined the terms of the "grand bargain."

The bargain, as spelled out by the Iranians, offered to accept a two-state solution for Israel and Palestine, to rein in Iranian support for what the United States considered terrorist groups, cooperation with the United States in Iraq and Afghanistan and against al-Qaida, and to join a comprehensive security agreement with the countries of the Persian Gulf. This would include an agreement to exclude nuclear weapons, which in effect suggested that Iran was prepared to suspend its nuclear program.

In return, Iran wanted full diplomatic recognition from the United States, along with a suspension of U.S. sanctions and an agreement to drop plans for regime change and support for groups opposed to the Iranian regime.[11]

Such a bargain looks good today, especially if it included an Iranian agreement to renounce nuclear weapons and allow inspection of all nuclear facilities. But, as Walker writes, history is full of might-have-beens, and the hubris of the administration in the spring of 2003 was too great to entertain any offer from the hated mullahs, whom they planned next to take down.

In the near future, the United States has three options in dealing with Iran. We can launch a war, the outcome of which could be disastrous for both nations. We can continue to sanction and contain Iran, but that will not halt her nuclear progress. We can try to negotiate, to determine what Tehran will require to curtail its nuclear program, short of reaching the capacity to build atomic weapons. History argues that America should have attempted that third option years ago.

As for the Middle East, our vital interest there is the free flow of oil out of the Gulf, an interest shared by Europe, Japan, China, and all the nations in the region, including Iran, whose economy depends on the export of oil and natural gas. The great threat to the oil interest is the rise of regimes interested less in maintaining the world economy and national income than in fomenting an Islamic revolution and a war of civilizations. The question for the United States is whether preventing Islamic revolution is best served by keeping U.S. troops in the region or by pulling them out and relying on U.S. naval and airpower to prevent any nation from achieving hegemony in the Gulf and and with it control of the life blood of the global economy.

Who Lost Russia?

In October 1986 this writer was with Ronald Reagan at Hofde House in Reykjavik at the climactic moment of the Cold War,

256

when Reagan angrily rejected a belated demand by Mikhail Gorbachev: The Soviet leader had said Reagan must give up a U.S. missile defense as a final concession for "the deal of the century," an agreement to rid the world of nuclear weapons.

Twenty years later, I wonder how we would have responded if Gorbachev had asked for one more day of meetings to make a new offer, and that next day, Gorbachev had said this to Ronald Reagan:

"President Reagan, my people and I realize we must end the Cold War. And so we offer the United States the following bargain:

"We will destroy all our intermediate-range SS-20s missiles in Europe, if you will remove and destroy your Pershing and cruise missiles. Following that, we will permit the Berlin Wall to be pulled down and Berlin united. We will accept unification of Germany under West German rule. We will allow what you call our 'satellite regimes' in Eastern Europe to fall peacefully, and be replaced by democracies. We will pull all Red Army troops out of Central and Eastern Europe. We will let Lithuania, Latvia, and Estonia go free, as they were before June 1940. We will let Ukraine become independent. We will remove all Soviet forces and bases from Cuba, for we realize this is in your backyard. We will dissolve the Soviet Union into fifteen free nations, end the monopoly on power of the Communist Party, embrace democracy, and call off the Cold War.

"All we ask is that you not take advantage of us by moving NATO into Eastern Europe, the Baltic republics, or any former republic of the Soviet Union, that we be allowed to have our Monroe Doctrine, as you are entitled to yours."

By the time Gorbachev left office in December 1991, this miraculous end to the Cold War had come to pass. What did we do? We seized upon our "unipolar moment" to seek geopolitical advantage at Russia's expense. We violated the understanding with Moscow, moved NATO into Eastern Europe and the Baltic republics, and, by the time of the NATO summit in Latvia in 2006, we had plans to move NATO into Ukraine and Georgia.

At the Munich Security Conference of 2007, President Putin lashed out, accusing the United States of reigniting the Cold War. "The process of NATO expansion has nothing to do with the modernization of the alliance," he thundered. "We have the right to ask, against whom is this expansion directed?"[12]

The answer is clear: NATO expansion is directed at Russia.

Among the historic failures of the Bush era has been the loss of Russia, the conversion of that immense land from a friendly country into a nation 58 percent of whose people look on the United States with hostility. Vladimir Putin is not without fault, but primary responsibility rests with President Bush and the Russsophobic neoconservatives he brought to power with him.

Moving NATO onto Russia's doorstep, planting U.S. bases in former Soviet republics, interfering in elections in Kiev, Tiblisi, and Minsk, bombing Serbia, hectoring Russia for backsliding on democracy, and planting antimissile missiles in Eastern Europe ruined the American-Russian entente of Ronald Reagan and George H. W. Bush.

There is no more important relationship on earth than that between the world's two greatest nuclear powers. And there is no more important work of the next president than to repair the damaged relationship.

America should get out of Russia's space and get out of Russia's face.

As Iran has neither an ICBM nor a nuclear weapon, let alone a nuclear warhead, there is no compelling need for an ABM system in Poland. By 2 to 1 the Polish people, who did not ask for it, do not even want it.[13]

We should cancel plans for that system and shut down U.S. bases in all former Soviet republics unrelated to the Afghan war. These are imperial irritants and inviting targets for terrorists. They aggravate China and Russia, just as Chinese or Russian bases in Mexico or Cuba would aggravate us.

If America has a Monroe Doctrine, regarding as a hostile act the establishment of foreign military bases in the Caribbean or Central America, so Russia is entitled to her own Monroe Doctrine. That means keeping U.S. bases outside her "near abroad" and out of former republics of the USSR.

Which brings us to NATO. The liberation of the captive nations of Eastern Europe and the Baltic republics was a triumph of the West and an epochal advance for freedom. But to convert these countries into NATO allies was monumental folly. The Baltic states add nothing to U.S. strength. But our commitment to go to war for Latvia, Lithuania, and Estonia, against a nuclear-armed Russia, whose army could be in Riga, Vilnius, or Tallinn in twenty-four hours, was an act of post–Cold War hubris. The arrogance of power. How does this commitment strengthen the United States? One need not be a Bismarck to question whether a military alliance with Estonia is worth losing the friendship of the largest nation on earth.

The time has come to review what we have done to lose our legacy from Reagan and to assess the need for a military alliance against a regime and an empire that disappeared twenty years ago. Six decades after World War II, why are we still responsible for the defense of Europe?

No other nation maintains forces all over the world. No other country has ever had so many treaty commitments to fight for other nations. Yet to suggest that we review these commitments and dismantle these alliances is to invite attack as an isolationist. During the Cold War, when the world was the arena of conflict, there were reasons for these commitments. What is the case today, other than the drive to empire or nostalgia for the moral clarity and mighty role we played throughout the forty years of the Cold War?

Rather than closing bases in the United States, we need to shut down bases in foreign lands. We need to bring American troops home and restore our traditional role as the great arsenal of democracy and strategic reserve of Western civilization. Let us then use the savings to repair, refit, and reequip our armed forces, ravaged by the wars in Iraq and Afghanistan, to defend America and her vital interests. Let Europeans, a third of whom say we are the primary threat to peace, undertake primary responsibility for their own continent.

Since the Cold War, two-thirds of all U.S. forces have been withdrawn from Europe. The rest should come home and the United States should cede the alliance to Europe and give notice that Article V of NATO—an attack on one is an attack on all—is being allowed to lapse. In the remote chance of a war in Europe, the United States will decide, through its constitutional process, whether to become involved.

If the United States wishes to retain air or naval bases in Europe, we can negotiate the terms with the nations involved. Europeans have long demanded they be given a greater role in the defense of their continent. Let us give them the lead role. After John F. Kennedy's election in 1960, President Eisenhower urged him to pull U.S. forces out of Europe, lest the Europeans become too dependent on America. Kennedy did not. Forty-eight years later, the next president should take Eisenhower's advice.

China and Korea

China is contained in every direction.

To the north are Mongolians, Kazakhs, and Russians. To the west Muslim Uighurs with no love for the Han Chinese. To the south a nuclear-armed Pakistan, a nuclear-armed India, and a Vietnam capable of defending itself. To the east Taiwan, South Korea, Japan. Only Taiwan is a potential cause of conflict between us, and every president since Nixon has declared Taiwan a part of China. Though any Chinese military move against Taiwan would rupture our economic and diplomatic ties, we cannot be committed forever to go to war to prevent Taiwan from assuming the status of Hong Kong.

Half a century after the first Korean War, there is no reason U.S. troops should be the first to die in a second. North Korea is no longer a frontier province of Stalin's empire. Any new conflict would be a Korean civil war in which no vital U.S. interest would be imperiled. Today, thanks to U.S. sacrifices from 1950–1953 and our assistance since, South Korea has forty times the economy of the North and twice the population. It is time Seoul undertook full responsibility for its own defense and U.S. troops were brought home. In 1778 America needed the assistance of the French to win our Revolutionary War. Fifty years later, we could take care of ourselves. So, too, can South Korea.

Putting America First

In the presidential campaign of 1992, this writer urged withdrawal of two-thirds of all U.S. troops in Europe. In time it happened. And how has America suffered?

How have we been diminished by the termination of our

alliance and the closing of our bases on Taiwan? What have we lost from the closing of our bases in Saudi Arabia or the expulsion of the U.S. Air Force and Navy from Clark Air Force Base and Subic Bay? Now that we are gone, Manila seems more appreciative of us, indeed, anxious to have us come and help run down the allies of Al Qaeda in the southern islands. Does it make sense that 30,000 U.S. troops are defending a border in Korea, when a Third World invasion is pouring across our own border with Mexico? What will it profit us if we win in Iraq and lose the Southwest?

This is not a call to isolationism. No nation with 30 percent of the world's economy and one-fourth of its GDP tied up in trade, which is keeper of the world's reserve currency and leader of all its international institutions, and which has diplomatic and ancestral ties to every country on earth, is ever going to be an isolationist nation. But it is a call to recognize the wisdom in what Gerald Ford told one journalist after the invasion of Iraq, which he had opposed: "I just don't think we should go hellfire damnation around the globe freeing people, unless it is directly related to our own national security."[14]

As Franklin Roosevelt said in 1936, "We are not isolationists, except insofar as we seek to isolate ourselves from war." This we must do, for, of all the nations of the earth, our nation, the most prosperous and successful, has the most to lose and the least to gain from constant war.

John F. Kennedy was both an idealist and a realist. In November 1961, in his address "A Long Twilight Struggle," he had it right:

[W]e must face the fact that the United States is neither omnipotent nor omniscient—that we are only six percent

262

of the world's population—that we cannot impose our will upon the other ninety-four percent of mankind—that we cannot right every wrong or reverse each adversity—and that therefore there cannot be an American solution to every world problem.

If we are to make the twenty-first century the Second American Century, the first imperative is to recognize that not only is the Cold War over, the post–Cold War era is now over. Pax Americana is finished. We must stop trying to conquer or convert the world to our way of thinking or our way of life. Only empires have the kind of commitments we have today. And the age of empires is over, and we Americans never really were an imperial people. Even Teddy Roosevelt wanted to be rid of the Philippines a few years after we took them.

As George Kennan wrote, "Surely the essential and important thing in the life of our own state is not what we do with regard to other nations, but what happens right here among us, on this American territory, for which we are responsible. Our foreign policy is only a means to an end."

Our day of reckoning is at hand. Time to mind our own business. Time to lay down the burden and come home. Time to put America first.

Acknowledgments

In the Mac for most of 2007, with repeated title and subtitle changes, *Day of Reckoning* is the fourth book on which I have worked with Tom Dunne of St. Martin's Press, our first being *Death of the West*. He has my gratitude for his counsel, his constant challenges to my ideas and wording, and his confidence that these views not only needed but would be accorded a hearing in the run-up to the presidential campaign of 2008.

My thanks, again, to Fredi Friedman, who first came to visit me in the White House in 1985 to urge me to write my memoirs, which still, the Lord willing, lie ahead, and who has been friend, editor, and agent for seven books going back to *Right from the Beginning*.

My gratitude also to my researcher and footnoter, Dr. Frank Mintz, for his monthly trips down from Martinsburg with the latest edited draft of *Day of Reckoning*, with the comments and corrections he has provided since we worked together on *A Republic, Not an Empire*.

Finally, thanks to Charles McMillion, trade authority and economic patriot, for letting me use two of his graphs. And special thanks to my wife, Shelley, for putting up with having the author arise in the midnight hours and descend to the cellar to produce this book.

As for my friend the late Dr. Russell Kirk, the great conservative scholar and author and chairman of the Buchanan Brigades in Michigan in 1992, to whom this book is dedicated, he seems ever to grow wiser as I grow older.

—Pat Buchanan, McLean, October 2008

Notes

Introduction: How Nations Perish

1. Strobe Talbott, "The Birth of the Global Nation," *Time*, July 20, 1992, p. 70.
2. Ibid.
3. Dan Quayle, Address to the Commonwealth Club of California, May 19, 1992. commonwealthclub.org
4. Patrick J. Buchanan, *State of Emergency* (New York: St. Martin's Press, 2006), pp. 176–77.
5. Abraham Lincoln, "The Perpetuation of Our Political Institutions," Address Before the Young Men's Lyceum of Springfield, Ill., Jan. 27, 1838; Patrick J. Buchanan, "Path to National Suicide," May 22, 2007. humanevents.com
6. Buchanan, "Path to National Suicide," op. cit.
7. Theodore Roosevelt, Address, Knights of Columbus, New York City, Oct. 12, 1915.
8. Angela Stephens, "Americans, Mexicans Reject Border Fence," June 23, 2007. WorldPublicOpinion.org
9. "American Views of Mexico and Mexican Views of the U.S," Zogby Poll, June 6, 2002. *NumbersUSA*
10. "U.S. Soccer Team Faces Chants of 'Osama': Mexican Fans Also Boo National Anthem During Olympic Qualifier," Associated Press, Feb. 11, 2004. MSNBC.com; Alan Wall, "Mexicans Chant: Americans (Mostly) Cower," Feb. 28, 2004. VDARE.com

Notes

1: The End of Pax Americana

1. Daniel Dombey, "Imperial Sunset: America the All-powerful Finds Its Hands Tied by New Rivals," *Financial Times*, Feb. 13, 2007, p. 11.

2. Quoted in Paul Starobin, "Beyond Hegemony," *National Journal*, Dec. 1, 2006.

3. Charles Krauthammer, "Democratic Realism: An American Foreign Policy for a Unipolar World," Address to the American Enterprise Institute, Feb. 10, 2004 (Washington, D.C.: AEI Press, 2004), p. 2.

4. Fareed Zakaria, "After America's Eclipse," *Washington Post*, Jan. 29, 2007, p. A15.

5. Ibid.

6. David Ignatius, "Going Nowhere Fast," *Washington Post*, Feb. 21, 2007, p. A15. washingtonpost.com

7. Lee Keith, "Abdullah: U.S. Occupation 'Illegitimate,' " Associated Press, March 29, 2007.

8. Ignatius, op. cit.

9. Richard Haas, "A Troubling Middle East Era Dawns," Oct. 16, 2006. FT.com

10. Robert Samuelson, "Farewell to Pax Americana?" *Washington Post*, Dec. 14, 2006, p. A31. washingtonpost.com

11. Ibid.; Niall Ferguson, "A World Without Power," *Foreign Affairs*, July/August 2004, transcript, p. 2.

12. Ferguson, p. 8.

13. "Colin Powell: US Losing Iraq War," BBC News, Dec. 18, 2006. http://bbc.co.uk; Karen de Young, "Powell Says U.S. Losing in Iraq, Calls for Drawdown by Mid-2007," Dec. 18, 2006, p. A20. washington post.com

14. "Iraq Study Group: Change Iraq Strategy Now," CNN.com http://www.cnn.com/2006/POLITICS/12/06/Iraq.study.group/index.html

15. Ann Scott Tyson, "General Says Army Will Need to Grow," *Washington Post*, Dec. 16, 2006, p. A01. washingtonpost.com

16. Dombey, op. cit.

17. Glenn Beck, "Interview with Netanyahu," Nov. 26, 2006. transcripts .cnn.com

18. "Al Qaeda Resurgent," editorial, *New York Times*, Feb. 25, 2007. nytimes .com

19. James Morrison, Embassy Row column, "Brazil's Anti-U.S. Bent," *Washington Times*, Feb. 6, 2007. washingtontimes.com

20. Dombey, op. cit.

21. Morrison, "Orange Blues," "Brazil's Anti-U.S. Bent"; Peter Finn,

"Unswayed by West, Russia Continues Georgia Blockade," *Washington Post,* Oct. 4, 2006, p. A21.

22. William Hawkins, "Financing U.S. Pre-eminence," *Washington Times,* Jan. 29, 2007, p. A15; Patrick J. Buchanan, " 'On-to-Baghdad!' or 'Stop at Kabul!' " Syndicated Column, Oct. 23, 2001. Creators.com

23. "U.S. a 'Pariah' from Bush Policies, Kerry Says," *Washington Times,* Jan. 25, 2007, p. A5.

24. Patrick J. Buchanan, "Panic in Davos World," Creators Syndicate, March 14, 2006. WorldNetDaily.com

25. Ibid.

26. Ibid.

27. Joe McDonald, "U.S. Treasury Secretary Visits China," Associated Press, March 7, 2007. washingtonpost.com

28. Todd Lassa, "Ford: $12.7 Billion in Red Ink for '06," *Motor Trend,* Jan. 25, 2007.

29. Martin Crutsinger, "Trade Deficit Sets Record for 5th Year," Associated Press, March 14, 2006. Yahoo Finance; "Revised GDP Shows U.S. Economy Grew 2.5 Percent in Fourth Quarter," *Beacon Journal,* March 30, 2007. Ohio.com/beaconjournal; Matt Moore, "Euro Rises to Record High Versus Dollar," Associated Press, Feb. 27, 2007. Yahoo Finance.

30. Jim Lobe, "A Bad Year for Empire," Dec. 23, 2006. Antiwar.com; Starobin, op. cit.

31. "BBC Survey: Iran, Israel, US Have Most Negative Image in World," *Hindu,* March 6, 2007. hindu.com

32. Mark Murray, Deputy Political Director, NBC News, "Republicans Abandoning Bush: NBC/WSJ poll: President's, Congress' Ratings Drop to Lowest Levels Ever," June 13, 2007. MSNBC.com; Jeffrey M. Jones, "Just 18% Approve of Job Congress Is Doing," Gallup News Service, Aug. 21, 2007. The Gallup Poll.

33. Quoted in Jeremy Grant, "Learn from Fall of Ancient Rome, Official Warns US," *Financial Times,* Aug. 14, 2007, p. 2.

34. Ibid.

35. Ibid.

36. Quoted in Andrew Roberts, *A History of the English-Speaking Peoples Since 1900* (New York: HarperCollins, 2007), p. 457.

2: End of a Unipolar World

1. Henry Luce, "The American Century," *Life,* Feb. 7, 1941.

2. Dwight David Eisenhower, "Preventive War," *U.S. Military Dictionary,* Oxford University Press, Press Conference, 1953. Answers.com

Notes

3. Barton Gellman, "Keeping the U.S. First; Pentagon Would Preclude a Rival Superpower," *Washington Post,* March 11, 1992, p. A-1; Patrick J. Buchanan, *A Republic, Not an Empire* (Washington, D.C.: Regnery Publishing, 1999), p. 8.

4. Barton Gellman, "Pentagon War Scenario Spotlights Russia . . . ," *Washington Post,* Feb. 20, 1992, p. A1; Buchanan, *Republic,* p. 8.

5. Ibid.

6. Ibid.

7. Gelman, "Keeping the U.S. First," p. A-1; Buchanan, p. 8.

8. Gelman, ibid.; Buchanan, pp. 8–9.

9. Gellman, ibid.; Buchanan, p. 9.

10. Ibid.

11. Ibid.

12. Gelman, "Pentagon War Scenario," p. A-1; Buchanan, p. 9.

13. Patrick J. Buchanan, *Where the Right Went Wrong* (New York: St. Martin's Press, 2004), p. 15.

14. Buchanan, *Republic,* p. 46.

15. Buchanan, *Right Went Wrong,* p. 15.

16. George W. Bush, "Address to a Joint Session of Congress and the American People," Sept. 20, 2001, transcript, pp. 2, 3. whitehouse.gov

17. Patrick J. Buchanan, "Whose War Is This?" *USA Today,* Sept. 26, 2001, op-ed page.

18. Governor George W. Bush, "A Distinctly American Internationalism," Ronald Reagan Presidential Library, Simi Valley, California, Nov. 19, 1999.

19. "The Second Gore-Bush Debate," Debate Transcript, Oct. 11, 2000, Commission on Presidential Debates.

20. "Bush Shares Meal with Troops," eMediaMillWorks, Nov. 21, 2001, transcript, p. 5; "President Shares Thanksgiving Meal with Troops," Office of the Press Secretary, Nov. 21, 2001. whitehouse.gov

21. "President Delivers State of the Union Address," Jan. 29, 2002, transcript, p. 3. whitehouse.gov

22. "President Delivers Graduation Speech at West Point," Office of the Press Secretary, June 1, 2002, transcript, p. 2. whitehouse.gov

23. Ibid.

24. Ibid., p. 3.

25. Buchanan, *Right Went Wrong,* p. 25.

26. Ibid.

27. Ibid.

28. Ibid., p. 27.

29. Patrick J. Buchanan, "After the War," *American Conservative,* Oct. 7, 2002; Buchanan, *Right Went Wrong,* p. 29.

30. Patrick J. Buchanan, "Have We Hit the Tar Baby?" Syndicated Column, April 15, 2003, p. 1.

3: The Gospel of George Bush

1. Marcus Tullius Cicero, BrainyQuote.

2. Antoun Issa, "Roots of Injustice Push Lebanon Toward Civil War," Feb. 19, 2007. Antiwar.com

3. Scott P. Richert, "Imagining the Permanent Things," *Chronicles,* March 2007, p. 29.

4. George A. Panichas, ed., *The Essential Russell Kirk: Selected Essays* (Wilmington, Del.: ISI Books, 2006), p. 345.

5. Russell Kirk, "The Neoconservatives: An Endangered Species," Heritage Lecture No. 178 (Washington, D.C.: Heritage Foundation, 1988), pp. 7–8.

6. Panichas, ed., p. 346.

7. Richert, op. cit.

8. Kirk, "The Neoconservatives," pp. 6–7.

9. Panichas, ed., p. 348.

10. Walter Pincus, "British Intelligence Warned of Iraq War," *The Washington Post,* May 13, 2005, p. A18.

11. Panichas, ed., p. 359.

12. Roy P. Basler, ed., *The Collected Works of Abraham Lincoln,* vol. 7 (New Brunswick, N.J: Rutgers University Press, 1953), p. 23.

13. Allan Nevins, *The War for the Union,* vol. 1: *The Improvised War* (New York: Charles Scribner's Sons, 1959), pp. 337–38.

14. Ibid., p. 388.

15. John Willson, "The Gospel That Nobody Knows," *Chronicles,* April 2007, p. 32.

16. Ibid., p. 33.

17. Arthur S. Link, ed., *The Papers of Woodrow Wilson,* vol. 37: May 9– August 7, 1916 (Princeton, N.J.: Princeton University Press, 1981), p. 113.

18. Robert H. Ferrell, *American Diplomacy,* rev. and expanded ed. (New York: W. W. Norton, 1969), p. 501.

19. Dwight MacDonald, *Memoirs of a Revolutionist: Essays in Political Criticism* (New York: Farrar, Straus and Cudahy, 1957), p. 93.

20. Robinson Jeffers, "The Eye," *The Double Axe & Other Poems* (New York: Random House, 1948), p. 126.

21. Kirk, "Neoconservatives," p. 7.

22. Patrick J. Buchanan, "America First—and Second and Third," *National Interest,* Spring 1991, p. 77.

23. Ibid., p. 81.

24. Patrick J. Buchanan, *Where the Right Went Wrong* (New York: St. Martin's Press, 2004), p. 17.

25. John Milton, "Sonnet XII: I Did but Prompt the Age to Quit their Clogs," Representative Poetry Online. http://rpo.library.utoronto.ca/poem/1452 .html

26. "President Discusses the Future of Iraq," Feb. 26, 2003, transcript, p. 3. whitehouse.gov

27. Governor George W. Bush, "A Distinctly American Internationalism," Ronald Reagan Presidential Library, Simi Valley, California, Nov. 19, 1999. mtholyoke.edu; "Bush Outlines Foreign Policy," BBC News, Nov. 20, 1999. http://news.bbc.co.uk; "Governor Bush Discusses Foreign Policy in Speech at Ronald Reagan Library," Nov. 19, 1999. GlobalSecurity .org

28. "The Second Gore-Bush Debate," Debate Transcript, Oct. 11, 2000, Commission on Presidential Debates.

29. "President Bush Discusses Freedom in Iraq and Middle East," Remarks by the President at the Twentieth Anniversary of the National Endowment for Democracy, Nov. 6, 2003, transcript, p. 5. whitehouse.gov

30. Marvin Olasky, "Woodrow Wilson's Folly: The Private and Public Life of a President," *Philanthropy, Culture and Society,* Capital Research Center, March 1998, p. 7.

31. Ibid.

32. Ibid.

33. Terry Jeffrey, "Ayatollah 1, First Amendment 0," *Human Events,* Dec. 10, 2003. humanevents.com

34. Ibid.

35. Ibid.

36. Ibid.

37. Patrick J. Buchanan, "The Martyr of Mosul," June 22, 2007. humanevents .com

38. Kirk, "Neoconservatives," p. 9.

39. "President Bush Discusses Iraq Policy at Whitehall Palace in London," Office of the Press Secretary, Nov. 19, 2003, transcript, p. 2. whitehouse.com

40. Ibid.

41. Terrence P. Jeffrey, "McCain vs. Rumsfeld," *Washington Times,* Feb. 25, 2007, p. B-4.

42. Bush at Whitehall, transcript, p. 4.
43. Jeffrey, "McCain vs. Rumsfeld."
44. Bush Second Inaugural, Jan. 20, 2005, transcript, p. 1.
45. Ibid., p. 2.
46. Ibid., pp. 2–3.
47. Patrick J. Buchanan, "An Inaugural Formula for Endless War," Jan. 26, 2005. theamericancause.com
48. "Support for Regime Change Falls to 15% in U.S.," *Angus Reid Global Monitor,* March 15, 2007, p. 1.
49. David S. Broder, "The Fading Freedom Mission," *Washington Post,* March 11, 2007, p. B7.
50. "President Discusses Freedom and Democracy in Latvia," Washington, D.C.: Office of the Press Secretary, May 2005. whitehouse.gov
51. Joshua Kurlantzick, "Across Asia, the Generals Strike Back," *Washington Post,* June 15, 2007, p. B3.
52. Ibid.
53. "President Bush Addresses American Legion National Convention," Salt Lake City, Aug. 31, 2006, transcript. whitehouse.gov
54. "President Delivers State of the Union Address," Washington, D.C.: Office of the Press Secretary, Jan. 23, 2007. whitehouse.gov
55. Peter Bergen and Michael Lind, "A Matter of Pride," *Democracy,* Winter 2007, p. 10.
56. Thomas Wagner, "Doctors Drawn to Top Terror Posts," *Washington Times,* July 4, 2007, p. A10.
57. Ibid.
58. Stephen Fidler, "From Alienation to Annihilation," *Financial Times,* July 8, 2007, p. 3.
59. Ibid.
60. Bergen and Lind, p. 13.
61. Robert Beum, "The Divinization of Democracy," *Modern Age,* Spring 2007, p. 120.
62. Ibid., p. 128.
63. A. J. P. Taylor, *From Sarajevo to Potsdam* (New York: Harcourt, Brace & World, 1967), pp. 135–36.
64. Patrick J. Buchanan, *Right from the Beginning* (New York: Little, Brown, 1988), p. 336.
65. Edmund A. Opitz, "Architects of Leviathan," Paper Delivered to Hillsdale College, October 1973; Edmund A. Opitz, "Introduction," *The 1995 Lord Acton Essay Competition,* Acton Institute for the Study of Religion and Liberty.

66. Edmund Burke,"Letter to a Member of the National Assembly," 1791, *The Works of the Right Honorable Edmund Burke*, vol. 4 (1899), pp. 51–52; *Respectfully Quoted: A Dictionary of Quotations*. Bartleby.com; "Edmund Burke, 1729–1797," *Quotations*. conservativeforum.org

4: Imperial Overstretch

1. Steven E. Meyer, "Carcass of Dead Policies: The Irrelevance of NATO," *Parameters*, Winter 2003–04, p. 83; James Chace, "A Strategy to Unite Rather Than Divide Europe," *NATO Enlargement: Illusions and Reality*, ed. Ted Galen Carpenter and Barbara Conry, eds. (Washington, D.C.: Cato Institute, 1998), p. 177.

2. Walter Lippmann, *U.S. Foreign Policy: Shield of the Republic* (Boston: Little, Brown, 1943), p. 9.

3. Ibid., pp. 42–43.

4. George Washington, "Farewell Address," *The Annals of America*, vol. 3, publisher William Benton (Chicago: Encyclopedia Britannica, 1968), p. 61; Patrick J. Buchanan, *A Republic, Not an Empire* (Washington, D.C.: Regnery Publishing, 1999), p. 66.

5. Charles A. Beard, *A Foreign Policy for America* (New York: Alfred A. Knopf, 1940), pp. 17–18; Buchanan, pp. 66–67.

6. J. A. S. Grenville and Bernard Wasserstein, *The Major International Treaties Since 1945: A History and Guide with Texts* (London and New York: Methuen, 1987), p. 119; Buchanan, p. 31.

7. Grenville and Wasserstein, p. 124.

8. Taiwan Relations Act, Public Law 96–8, 96th Congress. USINFO.State.gov.

9. *Treaties and Alliances of the World: An International Survey Covering Treaties in Force and Communities of States* (New York: Scribner's, 1968), p. 190; Buchanan, p. 32.

10. *Treaties and Alliances*, p. 188.

11. Buchanan, p. 33.

12. *Treaties and Alliances*, p. 144; Buchanan, p. 33.

13. Ibid.

14. Gordon M. Hahn, "The West Lost Russia," *Moscow Times*, Aug. 29, 2007, p. 7.

15. "Ratcheting Up Rhetoric" in "Special Report: Rapprochement with Russia?" *Washington Times*, June 10, 2007, p. A5.

16. James Sterngold, "After 9/11, U.S. Policy Built on World Bases," *San Francisco Chronicle*, March 21, 2004. SFGate.com

17. Ibid.

18. Ibid.

19. Chalmers Johnson, "The Arithmetic of America's Military Bases Abroad: What Does It All Add Up To?" Jan. 10, 2004. tomdispatch.com

20. Christopher Treble, "Breaking Ranks," *American Conservative,* March 12, 2007, p. 23.

21. Doug Bandow, "War Without Consequences? Absurd," May 22, 2007. mises.org

22. Patrick J. Buchanan, "America First—and Second, and Third," *National Interest,* Spring 1990, pp. 78–79.

23. Jeane J. Kirkpatrick, "A Normal Country in a Normal Time," *National Interest,* Fall 1990, p. 40.

24. Ibid.

25. Ibid., p. 41.

26. Charles Krauthammer, "Universal Dominion: Toward a Unipolar World," *National Interest,* Winter 1989–90, p. 49.

27. Ibid., pp. 48–49.

28. Kirkpatrick, pp. 40–41.

29. Ibid., pp. 43–44.

5: Who Shall Inherit the Earth?

1. Guy de Jonquières, "My Seat at the Ringside of History in the Making," *Financial Times,* March 29, 2007, p. 13.

2. Ibid.

3. Craig Whitlock, "On Its 50th, EU Faces an Identity Crisis," *Washington Post,* March 25, 2007, p. A12.

4. Lucia Kubosova, "EU Weakens Our Identity by Ignoring Christianity, Warns Pope," March 26, 2007. euobserver.com; Mark Landler, "European Union, at 50, Seeks Footing as the World Shifts," *New York Times,* March 26, 2007, p. A3. nytimes.com

5. Frances D'Emilio, "Pope: Europe Losing Faith in Its Future," Associated Press, March 24, 2007. Breitbart.com

6. David R. Sands, "At 50, EU Defies Doubters," *Washington Times,* March 25, 2007, pp. A1, A5; George Parker, "FT/Harris Poll Results," Dec. 16, 2005. FT.com; Patrick J. Buchanan, "The Mid-Life Crisis of the EU," March 30, 2007. humanevents.com

7. Martin Wolf, "Why Liberalism Is the Right Future for a Declining Europe," *Financial Times,* March 14, 2007, p. 13.

8. Hilaire Belloc, *The Great Heresies* (Salem, N.H.: Ayer Company, Publishers, 1985), pp. 126–27.

9. "Population 2005," World Development Indicators Database, World Bank, 1 July 2006.

10. "Total GDP 2005," World Development Indicators Database, World Bank, 1 July 2006.

11. Ibid.

12. Cheryl Wetzstein, "Americans See Media Aiding Moral Decline," *Washington Times,* March 8, 2007, p. A12.

13. Alvin Rabushka, "U.S. And China: Which Way?" *Washington Times,* Aug. 23, 2007, p. A14.

14. Ibid.

15. Ibid.

16. "China Rising: The Next Global Superpower," Jan. 26, 2007. Antiwar .com; Edward Cody, "China Boosts Military Spending," March 5, 2007. washingtonpost.com

17. "Rumsfeld: China Buildup a Threat to Asia," Associated Press, June 4, 2005. MSNBC.com

18. Jo Johnson and Richard McGregor, "China Raises Tension in India Border Dispute," *Financial Times,* June 11, 2007, p. 6.

19. Immanuel Kant, "Perpetual Peace: A Philosophical Sketch," 1795. www .mtholyoke.edu

20. Alfred Lord Tennyson, "Locksley Hall," *English Poetry III: From Tennyson to Whitman,* Harvard Classics: 1901–1914. Bartleby.com

21. David R. Sands, "Khalizad: Lack of Reform 'Mortal Threat' to U.N.," *Washington Times,* March 16, 2007, p. A14.

22. Jerome R. Corsi, "Bush Administration Advances on Path of Creating North American Union," Online Human Events, Sept. 21, 2006.

23. Kelly Taylor, "Coming Through: The NAFTA Super Highway," *New American,* Aug. 7, 2006, pp. 12–17.

24. Paul Starobin, "Beyond Hegemony," *National Journal,* Dec. 1, 2006. nationaljournal.com

25. Ibid.

26. William Langewiesche, "City of Fear," *Vanity Fair,* April 2007, p. 158.

27. Ibid., p. 165.

28. Ibid., p. 177.

29. Steven Weber and Ely Ratner, "Who Screwed Up Globalization?" *Los Angeles Times,* Jan. 21, 2007. latines.com

30. Starobin, op. cit.

6: Deconstructing America

1. Daniel Patrick Moynihan, *Pandaemonium: Ethnicity in International Politics* (New York: Oxford University Press, 1994), p. 24.

2. Stanley Monteith, "The Diabolic Plan," Reprise of Richard Lamm's Address, "A Plan to Destroy America," May 2006. RaidersNewsNetwork.com

3. "Queen Elizabeth Sees Virginia Anew," May 3, 2007, Associated Press, MSNBC.com.

4. Ibid.

5. Patrick J. Buchanan, "Queen's Fancy PC Footwork in Jamestown," May 7, 2007. VDARE.com

6. Ibid.

7. "From Jamestown's Swamp: Pocahontas Was the Least of It," editorial, *Washington Post*, May 12, 2007, p. A14.

8. Ibid.

9. "Multimedia Tour: Monument Ave," *Discover Richmond*. discoverrichmond.com

10. Ronald Reagan, "Our Revolution: Farewell Address," Jan. 11, 1989, *National Review Online*, June 5, 2004. nationalreview.com

11. Elaine Sciolino, "The Sarkozy of the Future Jousts with the Chirac of the Past," *New York Times International*, May 11, 2007.

12. Harold O. Brown, "Powers, Principalities, Spiritual Forces: Charging Toward the Dies Irae," *Chronicles*, August 2005, p. 17.

13. James Madison, Alexander Hamilton, John Jay, *The Federalist Papers*, with an introduction by Willmore Kendall and George W. Carey (New Rochelle, N.Y.: Arlington House), p. 38.

14. Ibid.

15. Jeff Jacoby, "The Role of Religion in Government: Invoking Jesus at the Inauguration," *Boston Globe*, Feb. 2, 2001, p. A15; Patrick J. Buchanan, *The Death of the West* (New York: St. Martin's Press, 2002), p. 144.

16. Scott Bauer, "VA Allows Wiccan Symbols on Headstones," April 23, 2007, Associated Press. Yahoo.News.

17. John Lloyd, "Study Paints Bleak Picture of Ethnic Diversity," Oct. 8, 2006. FT.com

18. John Leo, "Bowling with Our Own," *City Journal*, Summer 2007, vol. 17, no. 3.

19. John Leo, "Let the Segregation Commence . . . Separatist Graduations Proliferate at UCLA," June 13, 2007, *City Journal*, Spring 2007, vol. 17, no. 2.

20. Ibid.

21. Cal Thomas, "Vanishing England," *Washington Times*, Aug. 29, 2007, p. A17.

22. Ibid.

23. Abraham Lincoln, First Inaugural Address, Washington, D.C., March 4, 1861.

24. Walter Lippmann, *U.S. Foreign Policy: Shield of the Republic* (Boston: Little, Brown, 1943), p. 137.

7: Colony of the World

1. Gabor S. Boritt, *Lincoln and the Economics of the American Dream* (Chicago: University of Illinois Press, 1994), p. 130.

2. Alfred E. Eckes, Jr., *Opening America's Market: U.S. Foreign Trade Policy Since 1776* (Chapel Hill: University of North Carolina Press, 1995), p. 30.

3. Elting E. Morrison, ed., *The Letters of Theodore Roosevelt*, vol. 1 (Cambridge: Harvard University Press, 1951), p. 504.

4. "Bush on the Record," *Wall Street Journal*, Feb. 1, 2007, p. A16.

5. Chesterton quoted in Joseph Pearce, *Small Is Still Beautiful* (Wilmington, Del.: ISI Books, 2006), p. 42.

6. Ibid., pp. 50, 51.

7. Ibid., p. 49.

8. Milton Friedman to Pat Buchanan, Dec. 30, 1997. Author's files.

9. James Neuchterlein, "Counterrevolutionary: Milton Friedman: A Biography by Lanny Ebenstein," *Commentary*, May 2007, p. 65.

10. Friedman to Buchanan.

11. Ian Simpson Ross, *The Life of Adam Smith* (Oxford: Clarendon Press, 1995), pp. 327–28, 320.

12. Milton Friedman and Rose Friedman, *Free to Choose* (New York and London: Harcourt, Brace, Jovanovich, 1979), pp. 38, 50.

13. Ibid., p. 51.

14. Ibid., p. 52.

15. Ibid., p. 51.

16. John Bright and James E. Thorold Rogers, eds., *Speeches on Questions of Public Policy by Richard Cobden, M.P.*, vol. 1 (London: Macmillan, 1870), pp. 362–63.

17. William R. Hawkins, "The Anti-History of Free-Trade Ideology," *America Asleep: The Free Trade Syndrome and the Global Economic Challenge* (Washington, D.C.: U.S. Industrial Council Education Foundation, 1991), p. 57.

18. Ibid.

19. Ibid., pp. 55, 43.

20. Friedrich List, *The National System of Political Economy* (New York: Augustus M. Kelley, Publishers, 1966), pp. 174–75.

21. Ibid., p. 144.

22. Hawkins, p. 54; List, p. 133.

23. List, p. 144.

24. Elizabeth John, ed., *The Collected Writings of John Maynard Keynes,* vol. 17: *Activities 1920–1922 Treaty Revision and Reconstruction* (London: Macmillan, 1977), p. 451.

25. Patrick J. Buchanan, *The Great Betrayal* (New York: Little, Brown, 1998), p. 58.

26. Alan Tonelson, "Woe Betide Those Who Spurn Manufacturing," *Financial Times,* April 4, 2007, p. 10.

27. Friedman and Friedman, p. 45.

28. "Gomory: Transferring Production Offshore Is Not Free Trade," *Manufacturing & Technology News,* Sept. 17, 2007, p. 4.

29. Ibid.

30. Ibid., p. 5.

31. "U.S. Global Trade in Autos/Trucks/Parts," U.S. Dept. of Commerce presented by MBG Information Services; Charles W. McMillion, "Federal Reserve Report Shows Industry Output Declined in Q4 and Again in January," mgbinfosvcs.com; "Trade Deficit Realities," *Washington Times,* Feb. 18, 2007, p. B2.

32. Patrick J. Buchanan, "Free Trade and Funny Math," Feb. 27, 2007. Townhall.com

33. U.S. Dept. of Commerce, BEA and MBG Information Services; Buchanan, "Funny Math."

34. Martin Crutsinger, "Factory Jobs: 3 Million Lost Since 2000," Associated Press, April 20, 2007. Breitbart.com; Barbara Hagenbaugh, "U.S. Manufacturing Jobs Fading Away Fast," *USA Today,* Dec. 12, 2002. USATODAY.com

35. "Stagflation?" editorial, *Washington Times,* June 19, 2007. washingtontimes.com

36. Greg Ip and John D. McKinnon, "Bush Reorients Rhetoric, Acknowledges Income Gap," *Wall Street Journal,* March 26, 2007, p. 2.

37. David Cay Johnston, " '05 Income, on Average, Still Below 2000 Peak," *New York Times,* Aug. 21, 2007, pp. C1, C8.

38. "Stagflation?" op. cit.

39. Ibid.

40. John G. West, *Darwin Day in America: How Our Politics and Culture Have Been Dehumanized in the Name of Science* (Wilmington, Del.: ISI Books, 2007), p. 105.

41. Joseph D. Becker, "How to Limit Executive-Pay Scandals: Executive Pleonexia," *New Republic,* May 5, 2007. tnr.com
42. "2007 Executive Pay Watch," AFL-CIO, Washington, D.C.
43. Johnston, op. cit.
44. Matthew Miller and Tatiana Serafin, eds., "America's 400 Richest," *Forbes,* Sept. 21, 2006. forbes.com
45. "More Than $1 Billion Needed to Make Forbes List," Associated Press, Sept. 21, 2007. http://finance.myway.com
46. David Cay Johnston, "Pay at Investment Banks Eclipses All Private Jobs by a Factor of 10," *New York Times,* Sept. 1, 2007, pp. B1, B6.
47. Ibid.
48. John Holusha, "Huge Profit at Goldman Brings Big Bonuses," *New York Times,* Dec. 12, 2006. nytimes.com
49. Buchanan, *Great Betrayal,* p. 223.
50. Alan Tonelson and Peter Kim, "U.S. Manufacturing Lag," *Washington Times,* Jan. 31, 2007, A-16.
51. Ibid.
52. Benjamin Pimentel, "High-Tech Industry's Loss of Jobs Slowed in 2004: Only 25,300 Positions Were Lost, Compared with 333,000 in 2003," *San Francisco Chronicle,* April 26, 2005. sfgate.com
53. Catherine Holahan, "The Myth of High-Tech Outsourcing," *Business Week,* April 24, 2007. businessweek.com
54. Doug Cameron, "Spotlight Boeing 787 Dreamliner—'Green' Plastic Airliner Takes Off," *Financial Times,* July 1, 2007. FT.com
55. Ibid.
56. "Indebted," *Washington Times,* March 18, 2007, p. B-2; C. W. McMillion, "Awash in Debt. . . .", memo, Feb. 13, 2007.
57. "Indebted," *Washington Times.*
58. Daniel Gross, "Lost Highway: The Foolish Plan to Sell American Toll Roads to Foreign Companies," *Slate,* March 29, 2006. slate.com; Amy Goldstein, "Strapped States Try New Route, Lease Toll Roads to Foreign Firms," *Washington Post,* June 14, 2006, p. A1. washingtonpost.com
59. Gross, op. cit.
60. Ibid.
61. Goldstein, op. cit.
62. Sebastian Mallaby, "The Next Globalization Backlash," *Washington Post,* June 25, 2007, p. A19.
63. Ibid.
64. Steven R. Weisman, "A Fear of Foreign Investment," *New York Times,* Aug. 21, 2007, pp. C1, C5.

65. Lawrence Summers, "Funds That Shake Capitalist Logic," *Financial Times,* July 29, 2007. FT.com

66. W. Dennis Wrynn, *Detroit Goes to War: The American Automobile Industry in World War II* (Osceola, Wisc.: Motorbooks International, 1993); Buchanan, *Great Betrayal,* p. 76.

67. Ibid.

68. "Automakers and Autoworkers," *Washington Times,* May 18, 2007, p. A-18.

69. Martin Fackler, "Toyota Set to Lift Crown from GM," *International Herald Tribune,* Business, Dec. 22, 2006; Yuri Kageyama, "Toyota Tops GM in 1Q Global Sales," Associated Press, April 24, 2007. Yahoo Finance.

70. Chris Isidore, "Imports About to Overtake Big Three," CNN, Feb. 6, 2007. Money.com; Mari Sako, "Automobile Industry," IEBM Handbook of Economics, printout, p. 2. imvp.mit.edu.papers

71. "Gomory: Transferring Production Offshore Is Not Free Trade," op. cit., p. 1.

72. William Greider, "The Establishment Rethinks Globalization," *Nation,* April 30, 2007. http:www.thenation.com/doc/20070430/greider

73. List, p. 133.

74. Richard McGregor, Kevin Done, and Doug Cameron, "China Plans to Challenge Boeing and Airbus," *Financial Times,* March 19, 2007. FT.com

75. "Politics and the Yuan," editorial, *New York Times,* July 7, 2007, p. A12.

76. Karl Marx and Frederick Engels, *Collected Works,* vol. 6 (New York: International Publishers, 1976), p. 465.

77. Jerome R. Corsi, "Truck Drivers from India to Take U.S. Jobs?" *WorldNetDaily,* July 21, 2006. WorldNetDaily.com

78. Alan S. Blinder, "Free Trade's Great but Offshoring Rattles Me," *Washington Post,* May 6, 2007, p. B4.

79. Ibid.

80. Patricia Cohen, "In Economics Departments, a Growing Will to Debate Fundamental Assumptions," *New York Times,* July 11, 2007, p. A37.

8: Day of Reckoning

1. Merle Haggard, "Are the Good Times Really Over for Good?" http://www.sing365.com

2. Peter Brimelow, "Alien Nation: Round 2," *National Review,* April 22, 1996, pp. 43–45.

3. Strobe Talbott, "The Birth of the Global Nation," *Time,* July 20, 1992.

4. Patrick J. Buchanan, *The Death of the West* (New York: St. Martin's Press, 2002), p. 5.

Notes

5. Robert J. Samuelson, "Making the Think Tanks Think," *Washington Post,* Aug. 1, 2007, p. A17. washingtonpost.com

6. Ibid.

7. Srdja Trifkovic, "Half a Billion 'Americans'?" Fall 2007, chronicles-magazine.org; "Immigration to Add 100+ Million to U.S. Population by 2060," PRNewswire, Aug. 30, 2007. Yahoo News

8. Trifkovic, op. cit.

9. Daniel J. Mitchell, "Corporate Taxes: America Is Falling Behind," *Tax & Budget,* no. 48, Cato Institute, July 2007.

10. Mort Kondracke, "Democrats, Bush Should Agree to Fight Al Qaeda," *Laurel Leader-Call,* July 30, 2007.

11. Martin Walker, "Iran's Grand Bargain," United Press International, May 9, 2006.

12. Thom Shanker and Mark Landler, "U.S. Undermines Global Security, Putin Declares," *International Herald Tribune,* Feb. 10, 2007.

13. "Most Poles Remain Opposed to Missile-Defense Base," *Wall Street Journal,* Aug. 27, 2007, p. A5.

14. Bob Woodward, "Ford Disagreed with Bush about Invading Iraq," *Washington Post,* Dec. 28, 2006, p. A1. washingtonpost.com

Index

Abdenur, Roberto, 18–19
Abdullah, King, 15
Acheson, Dean, 25, 29, 131, 158
Adams, John, 103, 104, 111, 112
Afghanistan, 2
  and Christianity, 76–77
  Taliban in, 18, 35
  U.S. war in, 35, 122, 130, 138, 250
African Americans
  civil rights movement, 175–176
  Dred Scott decision, 171–172,
    183, 242
  Emancipation Proclamation, 63
  Thomas Jefferson and, 61–62,
    171
  Abraham Lincoln and, 62–64
  racism, 183–184
  segregation, 171
  slavery and, 61–62, 169, 171–173,
    175, 183
  in U.S., 7, 186
"After America's Eclipse"
  (Zakaria), 14
Ahmadinejad, Mahmoud, 17, 77,
  103, 149, 159
Al Qaeda, 34–35, 41, 149, 165, 249
Allais, Maurice, 192
"America First—and Second and
  Third" (Buchanan), 131–132

"American Century, The" (Luce), 27
American Civil Liberties Union,
  180
American Conservative magazine,
  51–52
American Dilemma (Myrdal), 183
Amin, Idi, 37
Animal Farm (Orwell), 59
ANZUS Pact of 1951, 118–119
Arendt, Hannah, 178
Armenia, 2, 121
Aron, Raymond, 56
Arthur Andersen, 209
Ashe, Arthur, 172
Asian Economic Community,
  155–156
Assad, Hafez al-, 34, 78, 145
Associated Press, 169
Atta, Muhammad, 97
Attali, Jacques, 192
Australia
  U.S. treaties with, 118–119
Austrian-Hungarian Empire, 1
automobile industry, 218–222
Axis of Evil, 37–39
Azerbaijan, 2

Baader-Meinhoff Gang, 98
Bacevich, Andrew, 46, 74

Baker, James, 28
Bartley, Robert, 237
Basque secessionist movement, 4
Bastiat, Frédéric, 196
BBC, 22
Belgium, 4
Belloc, Hilaire, 141, 144
Benedict XVI, Pope, 142
Benton, Thomas Hart, 63
Berezovsky, Boris, 124
Bernanke, Ben , 223
"Beyond Hegemony" (Starobin),
    162–163
Biden, Joe, 32
bin Laden, Osama, 19, 94, 97,
    127–128, 250
"Birth of the Global Nation, The"
    (Talbott), 3–4, 5–6
Blair, Tony, 17, 61, 170
Blinder, Alan S., 231–232
Bolivia, 5
Bolton, John, 159
Boorstin, Daniel, 89
Border Tax Equity Act, 248–249
Bosnia, 3
Bowling Alone (Putnam), 6
Brawley, Tawana, 183
Bremer, Paul, 85
Brezhnev Doctrine, 48
Broder, David, 91
Brooks, David, 20
Brown, Gordon, 170
Brown, Harold O. J., 32, 178
Browning, Robert, 13
Brzezinski, Zbigniew, 167
Buchanan, Patrick J.
    on America's imperial overreach,
        33–34
    on American nationality, 7
    on Bush's crusade, 91
    on the Cold War, 131–132
    on the "democratist temptation,"
        73–74
    on U.S. invasion of Iraq,
        51–52
Burger, Peter, 96, 97
Burke, Edmund, 25, 104–105

Bush, George H. W., 19, 106, 258
    Gulf War (Desert Storm), 24,
        28–30, 40
    New World Order, 28–30
Bush, George W.
    and the environment, 159
    and free trade, 161–162, 191,
        223–224, 246–249
    incompetence of, 24–25
    and illegal immigrants, 10–11,
        139, 162, 237, 244–246
    and neoconservatism, 72–73,
        74–78, 78–79, 80–81, 81–86,
        123, 255
    and 9/11, 34–35, 35–37, 45,
        99–100, 102
    polls and approval ratings, 15, 22,
        91, 130
    religion of, 74–75, 79, 83
    Wolfowitz Memorandum, 30–34
    the world democratic revolution,
        12
Bush, George W. (quotations and
    speeches), 13, 49–50, 70
    American Enterprise Institute
        (2003), 75, 78–79
    American Legion (2006), 93–95
    on Communism, 105–106
    on containment, 41
    Czermin Palace (Prague, 2007),
        100–101, 105–106
    Democracy and Security
        International Conference
        (Prague, 2007), 75
    on free trade, 191
    on freedom and democracy,
        78–79
    inaugural address (2005), 75,
        89–91
    on the Iraqi war, 93–94
    on Iraqi democracy, 88–89
    National Endowment for
        Democracy (2003), 70, 75,
        81–86, 252
    in Riga (Latvia), 92–93
    on successful societies, 81–86
    on terrorism, 36–37, 88–89

on Taiwan, 118
State of the Union (2007), 75, 95–100
West Point Manifesto (2002), 39–40, 41–44, 75–77, 80
Whitehall Palace (2003), 75, 87–89
Bush (George W.) administration
antimissile defense, 122, 258
Axis of Evil, 37–39
Bush Doctrine, 46–48, 49–51, 129, 251
and China, 118, 129, 152–153, 261
Iraq, invasion and occupation of (Operation Iraqi Freedom), 16–23, 51–53, 102, 111, 129–130
National Security Strategy of the United Sates, 45–46, 50–51, 125–128
preemptive attacks/preventive wars, 48–51, 125–128
and Russia, 121–125
and the trade deficit, 202–203, 220–221, 246–249
treaty obligations, 128–130
and the U.S. economy, 206–207
war in Afghanistan, 35, 122, 130, 138, 250
Byron, George Gordon, Lord, 99

California, Hispanics in, 8–9
Canada
secessionist movement in, 4
U.S. trade deficit and, 222, 235
Carnegie, Andrew, 209
Carter Doctrine, 47
Case for Goliath, The (Mandelbaum), 165–166
Castro, Fidel, 18, 59, 176
Catalan secessionist movement, 4
CENTO (Central Treaty Organization), 116
Chavez, Hugo, 18, 98, 159, 166
Chechnya, 4, 5
Cheney, Dick, 255

Chesterton, G. K., 55, 192
China, 45, 140
Chinese-Russian relations, 19
and Communism, 154
economic growth, 80, 150–152, 153
and military technology, 132–153
and minorities, 154
population, 150
and Taiwan, 129, 152, 155, 261
U.S.-Chinese relations, 118, 129, 152–153, 261
U.S.-Chinese trade deficit, 20–21, 150–151, 203, 221, 222, 224–227
as a world power, 149–155
See also Taiwan
Christianity
in Europe, 141–142
Islam and, 76–77, 85, 249
U.S. cultural revolution and, 176–179, 180–181, 187–88, 242
Chronicles, 64–65
Chrysler, 219, 220
Churchill, Winston, 1, 69–70, 101, 103, 170
Cicero, 55
Citigroup, 207
"City of Fear" (Langewiesche), 163
Civil Rights Act of 1964, 176
Civil War, 7, 40, 49, 62–65, 102, 106, 188
Clay, Henry, 197
Clemenceau, Georges, 84
Clinton, Bill, 121, 130, 182, 206
CNN, 18
Cobden, Richard, 196
Cold War, 2, 40–41, 115, 176, 230, 256–258
Commonwealth Club of California, 6
Communism, 59, 70, 87, 98, 102–103, 105–106, 121, 154
See also Marxism
Coolidge, Calvin, 202
corporate greed, 207–210, 237–238
Correa, Rafael, 98

Index

Crash (film), 182–183
Croatia, 3
Cuba, 7, 40, 113
Cuban missile crisis, 48–49
cultural revolution, 148, 173–175, 176–179, 180–181, 187–88, 240–243
  gay marriage, 241–242
Czechoslovakia, 3, 100–101

d'Estaing, Valéry Giscard, 142
D'Souza, Dinesh, 148
Dagestan, 4
Dangerous Nation (Kagan), 58
Daniels, Mitch, 215
Davis, Jefferson, 172
Davos Conference, 20
  2007, 14, 15
de Gaulle, Charles, 118
Declaration of Independence, 60–61, 64
Defense of Marriage Act, 242
democracy, 104–105
Desert Storm. *See* Gulf War
Diderot, Denis, 60
Doha Round (2006), 20
Doolittle, Jimmy, 218
Douglas, William, 64
Dred Scott decision, 171–172, 183, 242
"Drug of Ideology, The" (Kirk), 56–57
Dubai port deal, 20
Duke rape case hoax, 183
Dulles, John Foster, 29, 116, 131

East Pakistan (Bangladesh), 5
Ecuador, 5
Edison, Thomas, 209–210
Egypt, 17
Eisenhower, Dwight D., 27, 30, 115–116, 131, 260
Eisenhower Doctrine, 47
Eliot, T. S., 104
Elizabeth II, 169–173, 174
End of History, The (Fukuyama), 80, 151

Enemy at Home: The Cultural Left and Its Responsibility for 9/11, The (D'Souza), 148
Enron, 209
Erhard, Ludwig, 151
Estonia, 123
Euripides, 238
Europe
  Christianity and, 141–142
  illegal immigrants and crime, 165
  Muslims as immigrants in, 139
European Economic Community, 133
European Union (EU), 121, 137–138, 140–143, 236–237, 238, 247

Fatah, 15
Federalist No. 2 (Jay), 179
Ferguson, Niall, 16
Fidler, Stephen, 96
Financial Times, 96, 141–142, 143, 182, 199, 212, 227
"First Universal Nation, The" (Wattenberg), 174
Fitzgerald, Scott, 210
Forbes 400, 208
Ford, Gerald, 262
Ford, Henry, 209
Ford, "Tennessee Ernie," 213
Ford Motor Company, 21, 219, 220
Fourteen Points, 66–67, 69, 113–114, 157
Fox, Vicente, 161
France, 1, 4, 18
Frankfurter, Felix, 83–84
Franklin, Ben, 186, 213
Franks, Tommy, 88
Free to Choose (Friedman), 194
free trade, 161–162, 191–196, 196–206, 223–224, 246–249
  Border Tax Equity Act, 248–249
  and corporate greed, 207–210, 237–238
  globalization, 191–196, 224–227
  and jobs, 228–229
  liberals and libertarians and, 227–229

and manufacturing, 199–203
outsourcing, 229–234, 248–249
trade deficit, 202–203, 220–221,
    246–249
Freedom House, 123
Frémont, Jessie Benton, 63
Frémont, John, 63
Frick, Henry Clay, 209
Friedman, Milton, 192, 193–195,
    200–201, 224
Friedman, Thomas, 20, 164
French Revolution, 60
Fukuyama, Francis, 27, 80

Galbraith, J. K., 192–193
Gangs of New York, The, 6
Gates, Bill, 210
Gellman, Barton, 30–31
George III, 61
Georgia, 2, 121, 121–123
    Rose Revolution, 19
Germany
    in Afghanistan, 18
    Communism, 98, 102–103
    Hitler-Stalin pact, 71
    Nazism, 59, 70, 87, 98, 102–103,
        104
    Weimar Republic, 98, 102
    and World War II, 49
Gettysburg Address, 62, 64–66
Gettysburg Gospel, The (Boritt),
    64–65
Gibran, Khalil, 55
Global Crossing, 209
*Global Trade and National
    Conflicting Interests*
    (Gomory/Baumol), 201
globalization, 191–196, 224–227
    and corporate greed, 237–238
    and crime, 164
    free trade, 161–162, 191–196,
        196–206, 223–224, 227–229
    and manufacturing, 199–203
    outsourcing, 229–234
GM (General Motors), 21, 219, 220
Goldman Sachs, 209
Gomory, Ralph, 201, 224

Google, 225
Gorbachev, Mikhail, 31, 120–121,
    257
Gore, Al, 36, 80
Grant, Ulysses S., 124
Grasso, Richard, 208
Great Britain, 4, 14, 24
    crime rates, 170, 185
    emigration from, 185
    illegal immigrants and, 185
    Iraq, troop withdrawal from, 17
    Ireland and, 2
    Muslims in, 170, 185
    race riots in, 170
    Scotland and, 4
    Wales and, 4
    War of 1812, 40, 113
    World War II and, 1
Greeley, Horace, 63
Greenspan, Alan, 21
Greider, William, 225
Gross, Daniel, 214–215
Gulf War (Desert Storm), 24, 28–30,
    40, 111

Haas, Richard, 15
Haggard, Merle, 235
Hahn, Gordon, 123
Haig, Al, 98
Halsey, William J. "Bull," 68
Hamas, 15, 17, 20, 43, 98
Hamilton, Alexander, 193, 195, 202,
    230
Harries, Owen, 131
Harriman, E. H., 209
Havel, Vaclav, 142
Hemingway, Ernest, 210
Hezbollah, 17, 43, 98
high-tech deficit, 211–212, 225
Hill, James J., 209
Hitler, Adolf, 40, 59, 68, 69, 98,
    104, 114, 158
Ho Chi Minh, 94, 176
Hobbes, Thomas, 166
Hugo, Victor, 16
Humala, Ollanta, 166
Humala, Rafael, 98

Huntington, Samuel P., 162–163
Hussein, Saddam, 27–28, 41, 188

ideology, 55–57
  and America's wars, 60–70
  Communism, 59, 87, 98, 102–103,
    105–106, 154
  democratism, 57, 73–74
  fascism, 70, 98
  Jacobinism, 60, 70
  Leninism, 59
  Maoism, 59, 151, 154
  Marxism, 58–59, 70–73
  Nazism, 59, 70, 87, 98, 102–103,
    104
  neoconservatism, 57, 72–73,
    73–74, 123, 255
  Stalinism, 59, 71
Ignatius, David, 14, 15
immigrants, 6–12
  and crime, 165, 170
  hostility toward, 10–11
  illegal aliens, 9, 10–11, 139, 162,
    237, 244–246
Imus, Don, 183
India, 5, 122
Indonesia, 5
Intel, 225
International Bank for
  Reconstruction and
  Development, 158
International Court of Justice, 158,
  159
International Monetary Fund, 158
International Trade Organization,
  158
Internet, 230
Iran, 122, 249
  Bush and, 38–39
  ethnic problems in, 5
  as a nuclear power, 17, 129,
    254–255
  and terrorist acts, 45
  U.S. and 253–256
Iraq
  Bush and, 38–39
  Christians in, 5, 85, 249

elections in, 17–18
  ethnic problems in, 5
  troop withdrawals from, 17
  U.S. invasion and occupation
    (Operation Iraqi Freedom),
    16–23, 51–53, 87–89, 102, 111,
    129–130, 236, 249
  U.S. invasion and occupation,
    opposition to, 51–53
Ireland, 2
Irish in America, 6
Islam, 95
  and Christianity, 76–77, 85
  and democracy, 76–77, 84–86
  intolerance of, 145–146
  and secularism, 76
  and violence, 5, 145, 170, 185
  U.S., hostility toward, 148–149
  the West, hostility toward, 170,
    185
  as a world power, 143–149
  and Zionism, 145
  See also Muslims
Islamic Jihad, 43
Islamists
  and elections, 98
  and the U.S., 138
Israel, 147
  and Iran, 18
  Lebanon, attack on, 15, 17, 102
  and multiculturalism, 243–244
  and the Six-Day War, 49
  U.S. relations with, 120
Italy, 4, 18

Jackson, Andrew, 113, 197
Jackson, Thomas J. "Stonewall,"
  172
Jacobinism, 60, 70
Jamestown settlement, 169–173, 174
Japan, 158
  automobile industry in, 219–220
  and Pearl Harbor, 40, 45, 49,
    67–68
  U.S. trade deficit and, 222
  U.S. treaties with, 117
  as world power, 155–156

Index

Jay, John, 179
Jeffers, Robinson, 68
Jefferson, Thomas, 60–62, 112, 195, 241
   Declaration of Independence, 60–61, 64, 65–66
   and slavery, 61–62, 171
Jeffrey, Terry, 84
Johnson, Chalmers, 126–127
Johnson, Lyndon B., 38, 88
Johnson, Samuel, 61
Jonquières, Guy de, 141–142

Kagan, Frederick, 58
Kahn, Herman, 68
Kant, Immanuel, 156–157
Kashmir, 5
Kazakhstan, 2, 122
Kennan, George, 86, 263
Kennedy, Edward, 32
Kennedy, John F., 48–49, 115–116, 181, 246, 260, 262–263
Kennedy, Paul, 13–14
Kerry, John, 20, 242
Keynes, John Maynard, 192–193, 198–199
Khalizad, Zalmay, 159–160
Khomeini, Ayatollah, 41
Khorokovsky, Mikhail, 124
Khrushchev, Nikita, 78
Kim, Pete, 211
Kim Jong-Il, 17, 41
Kim Il-Sung, 45
King, Martin Luther, Jr., 9, 175
King, Martin Luther, Sr., 175
King, Rodney, 183
Kipling, Rudyard, 104, 250
Kirk, Russell, 55, 55–57, 62, 86
Kirkpatrick, Jeane, 132–133, 134
Kissinger, Henry, 118
Korean War, 40, 116, 117
Kosovo, 3, 122–123
Krauthammer, Charles, 133–134
Kurdistan, 102
Kuwait, 28
Kyoto Protocol, 159
Kyrgyzstan, 2, 122

Langewiesche, William, 163
Latin America
   illegal immigrants and crime, 165
   U.S. treaties with, 119
Le Monde, 35
League of Nations, 83–84, 87, 98, 113–114, 157–158
Lebanon
   elections in, 17
   Israel's attack on, 15, 17, 102
Lee, Robert E., 172
Lega Nord, 4
LeMay, Curtis, 67–68
Lenin, Vladimir, 60, 71
Leninism, 59
Leo, John, 183, 184
Libby, I. Lewis "Scooter," 30
Libya, 45
Lincoln, Abraham, 8, 40, 49, 102, 130–131, 188, 191, 195, 202
   Emancipation Proclamation, 63
   Gettysburg Address, 62, 64–66
   and slavery, 62–64
Lind, Michael, 96, 97
Lippmann, Walter, 109–111, 189
Lipset, Seymour Martin, 169
List, Friedrich, 197–198, 224
Lithuania, 30–31
Lloyd George, David, 84, 170
"Locksley Hall" (Tennyson, 157
"Lost Leader, The" (Browning), 13
Louis XVI, 60, 100
Luce, Henry, 27, 167

McCain, John, 88–89
Macedonia, 3
Machiavelli, Niccolò, 23
McKinley, William, 98, 191
McKinnell, Henry, 208
Madison, James, 171, 197, 202
Mallaby, Stephen, 216
Mandelbaum, Michael, 165–166
Manila Pact of 1954, 116, 118
manufacturing, 199–203
Manufacturing & Technology Report, 201

Mao Zedong, 38, 41, 45, 94, 155,
  253–254
Maoism, 59, 151, 154
Martin, Paul, 161
Marx, Karl, 58–59, 71–72, 229
Marxism, 58–59, 70–73
Masaryk, Tomas, 100–101
MEChA militants, 166
Medicare, 235, 239–240
Mein Kampf (Hitler), 59
Mengistu, 37
Merkel, Angela, 142
Message, The (film), 77
Mexico
  illegal immigrants, 10–11, 139,
    162, 165, 237
  race and ethnicity in, 5
  U.S. trade deficit, 203, 222
Microsoft, 225
Middle East, elections in, 17
Milton, John, 5, 76
Monroe, James, 47, 171
Monroe Doctrine, 47
Montenegro, 3
Morales, Evo, 18, 98, 166
Morgan, J. P., 209
Moro, Aldo, 98
Moynihan, Patrick, 5
Muhammad, 76
multiculturalism, 148, 173–175,
    176–179, 180–181, 187–88,
    240–243
  gay marriage, 241–242
Murdoch, Rupert, 218
Musharraf, Pervez, 35
Muslims
  and guerrilla warfare, 146–148
  as immigrants in Europe, 139,
    170, 185
  population of, 145
  See also Islam
Muslim Brotherhood, 17, 98, 145
Mussolini, Benito, 67, 69, 98, 158
Myrdal, Gunnar, 183

Napoleon, 59, 100, 112
Napoleon II, 124

Nardelli, Robert, 208
Nation, 225
National Association of
  Manufacturers, 230
National Endowment for
  Democracy, 70, 75, 123
National Interest, 73, 131, 162
National Journal, 22, 162–163
*National Security Strategy of the
  United Sates,* 45–46
Native Americans, 7, 175
  colonists and, 170–171, 173
NATO (North Atlantic Treaty
  Organization), 35, 43, 115–116,
  116, 121, 123, 130, 165, 258
Nazism, 59, 70, 87, 98, 102–103,
  104
neoconservatism, 255
  Bush and, 72–73, 74–78, 78–79,
    80–81, 81–86, 123
  and democratism, 57, 73–74
Netanyahu, Benjamin, 18
New Mexico; Hispanics in, 9
New Republic, 180, 207
New York Times, 18, 20, 30, 84, 167,
    208–209, 227
New Zealand
  U.S. treaties with, 118–119
Newsweek magazine, 14
Niemeyer, Gerhardt, 72
Nigeria, 5
9/11, 33–34, 45
  Bush and, 34–35, 35–37, 102, 147,
    188, 250
Nixon, Richard, 22, 120, 122,
    253–254
Nixon Doctrine, 47
"Normal Country in a Normal
  Time, A" (Kirkpatrick),
  132–133
North American Free Trade
  Agreement (NAFTA),
  160–162, 203
North American Union (NUA),
  160–163, 238
North Korea, 261
  Bush and, 38–39

as a nuclear power, 17, 129
See also Korean War
Novak, Michael, 56

Obrador, Manuel López, 18, 98, 166
Olasky, Marvin, 84
Olmert, Ehud, 15
Ortega, Daniel, 18, 98
Orwell, George, 57, 59

Pahlavi, Mohammad Reza, Shah of Iran, 78
Pakistan, 5, 122, 138, 149
  tribal areas, 18
  U.S. treaties with, 118
Palestine
  elections in, 17
  Islamic violence in, 5
Palestine Liberation Organization (PLO), 145
Pandaemonium (Moynihan), 5
Pape, Robert, 127
Paradise Lost (Milton), 5
Paulson, Henry M., 20–21, 223
Pax Americana, 13–25, 29, 137–138, 263
Pearce, Joseph, 192
Permanent Court of International Justice, 158
"Perpetual Peace" (Kant), 156–157
Peru, 5
Philippines
  Islamic violence in, 5
  Spanish-American War, 7, 40, 113
  U.S. treaties with, 118
Pinochet, Augusto, 78
Pitt, William, 200
Plato, 156
Pocahontas, 171
Polk, James K., 49
Powell, Colin, 16
Powhatan, Chief, 171
Present at the Creation (Acheson), 158
privatization, 216–218

Puerto Rico, 113
Putin, Vladimir, 19, 35, 124, 124–125, 130, 258
Putnam, Robert, 6, 182

Quayle, Dan, 6
Québécois, 4
Quinn, Anthony, 77

Rabushka, Alvin, 150,153
Randolph, A. Philip, 175
Ranstorp, Magnus, 96
Ratner, Ely, 164
Reagan, Ronald, 19, 22, 27, 38, 51, 106, 120–121, 159, 174–175, 193, 206, 221, 237, 238–239, 256–257, 258
Reagan Doctrine, 47–48
Red Brigades, 98
Rees-Mogg, William, 169
Republic, Not an Empire, A (Buchanan), 33–34
Republican Party
  and the U.S. economy, 206–207, 229–234
Revolutionary War, 40, 60–62, 106
Rice, Condeleezza, 15
Rise and Fall of the Great Powers, The (Kennedy), 13–14
Robespierre, Maximilien, 60
Rockefeller, John D., 209
Roe v. Wade, 8, 181, 242
Romney, Mitt, 241–242
Roosevelt, Franklin D., 15, 65, 98, 158, 202, 262
  and the Four Freedoms, 69–70
Roosevelt, Theodore, 191, 195, 202, 209, 237, 263
Rousseau, Jean-Jacques, 60, 178
Rumsfeld, Donald, 34–35, 152
Rushdie, Salman, 77, 146
Russia, 140
  Chinese-Russian relations, 19
  and Lithuania, 30–31
  secessionist movement in, 4
  U.S.-Russian relations, 19, 120–125, 256–260

Russian Empire
World War I and, 1
See also Soviet Union
Russian Revolution, 1, 71
Ruth, Babe, 207

Saakashvili, Mikhail, 19
Sadr, Moqtada al-, 17–18, 20, 98
Sageman, Mark, 96
Salisbury, Lord, 109, 170
Samuelson, Robert, 16, 239–240
San Francisco, 126–127
São Paulo (Brazil), prison riots in,
163–164
Sarkozy, Nicolas, 175
Satanic Verses (Rushdie), 146
Saud, King Abdul Aziz ibn, 15
Saudi Arabia, 37, 127–128
Say, Jean-Baptiste, 197
Schoomaker, Peter, 17
Schwartzkopf, Norman, 28
Scotland, 4
Scottish National Party, 4
SEATO (Southeast Asia Treaty
Organization), 116, 118
Second American Century
(Brzezinski), 167
"Second Coming, The" (Yeats), 1
Serbia, 3, 122–123
Seward, William , 124
Sharon, Ariel, 15
Simpson, O. J., 183
Sistani, Ali al-, 84
"Sixteen Tons" (song), 213
Slate, 214–215
slavery, 61–62, 169, 171–173, 175,
183
Emancipation Proclamation, 63
Thomas Jefferson and, 61–62
Abraham Lincoln and, 62–64
Slovenia, 3
Small Is Still Beautiful (Pearce), 192
Smith, Adam, 193, 193–194
Smith, John, 171
Social Security, 235, 239–240
Social Contract, The (Rousseau), 60
Solzhenitzyn, Alexander, 123

Sorrows of Empire, The (Johnson),
126
South Korea, 261
U.S. treaties with, 116–117
See also Korean War
sovereign wealth funds (SWFs),
215–218
Soviet Union
collapse of, 1–2, 140, 237
Communism, 59, 70, 87
Hitler-Stalin pact, 71
See also Russia
Spain, 4
Spanish-American War, 7, 40, 113
Spengler, Oswald, 138
Stalin, Joseph, 2, 38, 41, 45, 67,
69–70, 78, 114, 115, 125
Stalinism, 59, 71
Starobin, Paul, 22, 162–163
State of Emergency (Buchanan), 7
Sterngold, James, 126–127
Stuart, J. E., 172
successful societies, 81–86
religious freedom, 82
rights of women, 82
and the will of the people, 81–82
Sudan, 5
Summers, Lawrence, 217–218
Suri, Abu Musab al-, 249–250

Taft, Robert A., 129
Taiwan
China and, 129, 152, 155, 261
U.S. and, 117–118, 261–262
Tajikistan, 2, 122
Talbott, Strobe, 3–4, 5–6, 11, 237
Taliban, 18, 35, 130, 138
Talleyrand, 100
Taney, Roger B., 171
Tannehaus, Sam, 128
Taylor, A. J. P., 104
Tennyson, Alfred, 157
terrorism, 88–89, 95, 97–100
Axis of Evil, 37–39
Muslims and, 146–148, 185
9/11, 33–34, 34–35, 35–37, 45,
102, 188

and the U.S., 45–46
terrorists
  class and education of, 96–98, 99
Texas, Hispanics in, 9
Thailand
  Islamic violence in, 5
  U.S. treaties with, 118
Thomas, Cal, 185
Time magazine, 3–4, 98, 237
Tonelson, Alan, 199, 211
Trotsky, Leon, 78
Truman, Harry S., 38, 47, 69, 103, 125
  See also NATO
Truman Doctrine, 47
Turkey, 102, 140
Turkmenistan, 2
Tyco, 209

U.S. Foreign Policy: Shield of the Republic (Lippmann), 109–111
Ukraine, 2, 121
  Orange Revolution, 19
United Kingdom, 1, 2, 4, 14
United Nations, 159–160
United States
  African Americans and, 7, 61–64, 171–173, 175–176
  alliances and treaties, 111–116, 116–120, 128–130, 252–253
  automobile industry, 218–222
  birth rate, 8
  civil rights movement, 175–176
  cultural revolution, 148, 173–175, 176–179, 180–181, 187–88, 240–243
  as debtor nation, 212–213, 215–218
  de-Christianizing of, 176–179, 180–181
  disuniting, 179–184
  free trade, 161–162, 191–196, 196–206, 223–224, 227–229
  greed and corruption, 207–210, 237–238
  high-tech deficit, 211–212, 225

highway system, leasing out, 214–215
Hispanics in, 8–11, 181
history of, 169–189
illegal aliens in, 9, 10–11, 139, 162, 237, 244–246
immigration, 6–12, 139, 186–187
infrastructure, 236
manufacturing, 199–203
Medicare, 235, 239–240
national security and foreign investment, 217–218
Native Americans and, 7, 170–171, 173, 175
population, 8, 181–184
racial composition, 181–184
second American century, 166–167
Social Security, 235, 239–240
trade deficit, 202–203, 220–221, 222–224, 246–249
trade deficit (U.S.-Chinese), 20–21, 150–151, 203, 221, 222, 224–227
U.S.-Russian relations, 19, 120–125, 256–260
United States (military actions), 29–30
  Civil War, 7, 40, 49, 62–65, 102, 106, 188
  Cold War, 2, 40–41, 115, 176, 230, 256–258
  defense spending and preparedness, 110–111, 115–116, 125–128
  Gulf War (Desert Storm), 24, 28–30, 40, 111
  Iraq, invasion and occupation of (Operation Iraqi Freedom), 16–23, 51–53, 102, 111, 129–130, 236, 249
  Korean War, 40, 116, 117
  military forces, 19, 51, 115–116, 120, 126–127, 236, 251, 260, 261–262
  preemptive attacks/preventive wars, 48–51, 125–128

United States (military actions),
   (cont.)
Revolutionary War, 40, 60–62, 106
Spanish-American War, 7, 40, 113
Vietnamese War, 40, 176
war in Afghanistan, 35, 122, 250
war with Mexico, 40, 49
War of 1812, 40, 113
World War I (Great War), 1, 3, 7,
   40, 66–67, 71, 113–114, 187
World War II, 1–2, 7, 40, 45, 49,
   67–70, 114, 158
See also Pax Americana
Updike, John, 12
Uzbekistan, 2, 122

Vanderbilt, Cornelius, 209
"Vanishing England" (Thomas), 185
Vanity Fair, 128
Venezuela, 5
Victoria, 170
Vietnamese War, 40, 176
Virginia, 171–173
Voting Rights Act of 1965, 176

Wal-Mart, 225
Wales, 4
Walker, David, 23
Walker, Martin, 255–256
Wall Street (film), 207
Wall Street Journal, 237
War of 1812, 40, 113
Washington, George, 111–112, 115,
   130, 195, 202, 213
Washington Post, 16, 30, 88, 92, 216,
   239–240
Washington Times, 206
Wattenberg, Ben, 73, 174
Weathermen, 99
Weber, Steven, 164
Wellington, Arthur Wellesley, Duke
   of, 113

west, decline of, 138–140
West Point Manifesto, 39–40,
   41–44, 75–77, 80
Wilkins, Roy, 175
Wilson, John, 64–65
Wilson, Woodrow, 18, 46, 65, 72,
   106, 187, 202
Fourteen Points, 66–67, 69,
   113–114, 157
League of Nations, 83–84, 87, 98,
   113–114, 157–158
Wolf, Martin, 143
Wolfowitz, Paul, 30–34, 128
World Bank, 158
world government, 137–138,
   156–160
World Trade Organization (WTO),
   158, 247
World War I (Great War), 1, 3, 7,
   66–67, 71, 187
and the Fourteen Points, 66–67,
   69, 113
treaties, 114
World War II, 1–2, 7, 67–70, 114,
   158
Atlantic Charter, 69–70
films about, 68
Four Freedoms, 69–70
Pearl Harbor, 40, 45, 49, 67–68
"World Without Power, A"
   (Ferguson), 16
WorldCom, 209
Wright, Lawrence, 249

Yeats, W. B., 1, 2
Yeltsin, Boris, 28–29, 31, 130
Yugoslavia, 3
Yushchenko, Victor, 19

Zakaria, Fareed, 14
Zimbabwe, 37
Zimmermann, Arthur, 187